Ray W. Pierson
9-5-'63

Lincoln
Christian
Seminary
Payson, Ill

Varieties of English Preaching 1900–1960

'Woodbine Willie'
(G. A. Studdert Kennedy):
a 1923 cartoon by Ronald Sinclair

Varieties of English Preaching 1900-1960

HORTON DAVIES
Putnam Professor of Religion in Princeton University

SCM PRESS LTD
BLOOMSBURY STREET LONDON
PRENTICE-HALL, INC.
Englewood Cliffs, N.J.

Published in the U.S.A. by
PRENTICE-HALL, INC.
Englewood Cliffs, N.J.

Library of Congress Catalog Card Number:
63–11791

C

Printed in Great Britain

To my father
DAVID DORIAN MARLAIS DAVIES
Minister of Christ's Gospel
for over fifty years in the
fellowship of the Congregational Churches
in Wales, England, Scotland, the Channel Islands;
faithful expositor, compassionate counsellor,
promoter of Christian unity & social prophet,
in gratitude

Contents

Illustrations

Preface and Acknowledgments

MY chief debt is inadequately acknowledged in the Dedication. As a son of the Manse it was a great privilege to hear the lively Word of God preached and applied with insight and compassion to a variety of families and callings in three countries. Sunday was always the peak of the week and its climax was reached when the congregation settled back into their pews to hear one who might be a son of thunder (Boanerges) or a son of consolation (Barnabas), and was often both in the same sermon. For this exalted and expectant moment the rest of the week was the preparation, the explanation and the justification. It was for this that my two brothers and sister and I had endured a week of tiptoeing past the study, of running to fetch books from the library or the bookshop or to hunt out or verify quotations from literary sources, of hearing the illustrations and anecdotes and observations tried out on the family, and of receiving the visits of the disturbed and bereaved and the desperately poor, and, on special occasions, of sharing in the pastoral visitation.

In such a context (confirmed by my own ministry for four years in war-time London) how could one doubt that the ministry was a high calling and preaching a pre-eminent privilege? Had I not seen Welsh miners and steel-workers (near Port Talbot), Scottish shipbuilders and shopkeepers (in Greenock), English textile operators and executives (in Manchester), naval officers and ratings, professors, doctors and businessmen (in war-scarred Southampton), as well as market-gardeners, hoteliers and holiday-makers (in the island of Jersey) arrive worried in the church and leave with clearer conviction and the courage of faith? My father's long and vivid memory and mellow judgment and experience carried me back to the hopeful beginning of this century. Between us we have heard most and, I suppose, discussed the strengths and weaknesses of all the preachers who appear in these pages. This book may therefore be understood as a rather formal account of a lengthy series of imaginary telephone conversations between the author in New Jersey and his father now enjoying an active and serene retirement in the Old Jersey off the coast of France. It is as much his book as mine.

Each of the preachers has lived, like the flocks entrusted to him, in desperate times—through crises of war, secularism, scepticism and social turbulence. Twice the lights have gone out in Europe and left a spiritual black-out which did not vanish when the electric lights were switched on again. In nihilistic days when the winds of change swept like hurricanes through the land, the brave, though often flickering, torches of the preachers blazed more brightly by contrast. The company of Christ's followers was smaller, but it was more united and committed. The sense of loyalty was tempered and trained in a resistance movement of the Spirit. Supremely, the deeper demands of God and his challenges in a changing society were found to be answerable only in grace.

A numerical assessment of British Christianity in the six decades from Jowett to Stewart would disclose a weaker Church. A qualitative evaluation in terms of allegiance would probably reveal a stronger Church, because there were few temptations to merely nominal membership. This, in turn, reflects the increasingly profound and relevant qualities of the messages from the pulpits. The later theological signs of the times are three. A more realistic Biblical theology, a greater sensitivity to the economic and interracial implications of the Gospel, and a significant renewal of the ecumenical resources of worship, are increasingly reflected in the pages and preachers which follow.

While I alone accept responsibility for selecting the preachers as representatives of different types of pulpit proclamation, I am happy to acknowledge the advice that I have received from several friends. This includes conversations with the Rev. Dean Elmer G. Homrighausen and the Rev. Professor Donald Macleod of Princeton Theological Seminary; the reading and improving of my manuscript by the Rev. Dr John Bishop, Visiting Lecturer at the same Seminary; and, not least, the suggestions contained in the stimulating letters of the Rev. David Edwards of the SCM Press in London. Also I wish to thank the Rev. Dr Emory Stevens Bucke, Editor of *Religion and Life*, for permission to reproduce in Chapter 3 an enlarged version of an article on Dean Inge which first appeared in the Spring 1962 issue of his quarterly. To all these gentlemen, as to my wife, I am deeply grateful.

1

Trends and Varieties of English Preaching: 1900–1960

THE English preacher of today can hardly be accused of standing six feet above criticism in a coward's castle. The censure could be more fitly directed at his Victorian predecessor, the pulpit orator. The Victorian preacher surveyed his vast congregation from his quarterdeck of a platform, like a ship's commander, threatening the mutinous beneath him with an eagle and authoritarian eye. The status of the modern preacher, as befits his reduced congregations, is humbler. As E. H. Jeffs has written: 'Instead of mounting his pulpit as a throne, the modern preacher is rather in the position of being summoned into the witness-box.'[1] Even this sober estimate might be questioned, since 80 per cent of the British people condemn the preacher unheard.

1 · *Then and Now*

Certainly the Victorian preaching 'stars' ascended their pulpits or platforms, as Moses had descended from Sinai, to thunder forth the Divine will to expectant

[1] *Princes of the Modern Pulpit* (London: Sampson, Low; undated), p. 3.

crowds. It was then the heyday of the popular preacher. No Anglican considered his visit to London complete if he had not heard Dean Church in St Paul's Cathedral or Dean Stanley in Westminster Abbey. In the same way the visiting Free Churchman would have considered a Sunday wasted if he had not heard the mesmerizing Spurgeon in his three-tiered 'Tabernacle' or seen the lion-maned Parker in the marble pulpit of City Temple.

Famous preachers were personages of great public influence in those days. So many were the American visitors to City Temple that Parker declared that the pews at the back stretched to the Rocky Mountains. So influential was Spurgeon that his Sunday morning sermons appeared in Monday's papers in the United States and Australia.[1]

Even the lesser known preachers had their devoted enthusiasts. Thomas Burke the novelist recounts in his *London in My Time* (1934):

> I remember clearly how they discussed and weighed and compared, and how Aunts would come with news of a wonderful preacher heard at some outlying church, in the manner of an impresario reporting to the opera-directors on a new Wotan. Parties would be made to visit this discovery, and on return they would sit about criticising his matter, his delivery, his gestures and how far he surpassed or fell short of their particular standards of unction and delivery.[2]

The modern pulpit does not lack personalities, but they are far less flamboyant and authoritarian than their

[1] See the present author's *Worship and Theology in England*, vol. 4: *From Newman to Martineau, 1850–1900* (1962), Chap. X, 'The Power of the Victorian Pulpit,' for analyses of Newman, Robertson, Dale and Spurgeon.

[2] p. 146.

Victorian predecessors. Moreover, the modern preacher does not need to be, as they did, an incidental purveyor of education and amusement. The era of spell-binders (as of pulpit oratory) was abruptly terminated by World War I. Glittering generalities, purple-patched and windy rhetoric, the authoritarian tone and temper of personages—all were swept away by scepticism.

In the ensuing decay of morals and disillusion with dogma, few personalities made any wide impact in the pulpit. Pre-eminent among the exceptions were the greatly beloved 'Woodbine Willie' (Geoffrey Studdert Kennedy), 'Dick' Sheppard, and—to a lesser degree—Canon W. H. Elliott. It was no accident that their manner and colloquial, conversational diction were as different from oratory as an urgent telephone summons. These gracious 'charismatic' preachers dropped all dignified reserve in favour of a personal confrontation on a 'man to man' basis. Their *charisma*[1] denied authoritarianism in the pulpit, and even ecclesiasticism. They saw that the most urgent need of the time was to present Christ as the friend of the poor and the oppressed *in action*. A man of similar ideals, experiences and conviction was 'Tubby' Clayton, the co-founder of Toc H.

While newspaper editors and reporters may deplore the absence of individualists in the modern pulpit (forgetting that Dean Inge, Bishops Barnes and Henson,

[1] *Charisma* is a term used by modern sociologists to indicate a dynamic personality, who is often a domineering one. In the Greek of the New Testament the various derivatives of *Charis* refer to the 'Grace' of God in Christ and, in a secondary sense, to those persons who are 'gracious.' If the former meaning might occasionally apply to the personalities of some Victorian preachers, the latter meaning alone is applicable to Studdert Kennedy and Sheppard. They were grace-endued and therefore gracious personalities.

Archbishop William Temple and Monsignor Knox, as well as Dr Donald Soper and others, continued to provide them with lively 'copy'), there is another side to the question. As Dr Donald Macleod so rightly insists, the princes of the Victorian pulpit 'had large and impressive followings, but few had congregations in the sense that a strong, cohesive Christian community continued with well-organized zeal and undiminished vitality after their death.'[1] The Victorian preacher, like the magnet that he was, attracted the individuals to himself and to the Christ he proclaimed, but these 'iron-filings' (apt metaphor for passive sermon-tasters) were rarely related to each other organically as members of the same adopted family of God. Thus, if the magnet was removed by death or distance, the filings fell apart and away. Small wonder, then, that the incisive theologian, P. T. Forsyth, warned the preacher that Christ's Church 'is not the arena for his individualism,'[2] much less his vanity. The warning was desperately needed, especially by those for whom the cult of personality was more important than the pursuit of truth.

The modern English minister is happier in the truer conception of the ministry and of the Church which views him as a first violinist in the orchestra of faith, rather than as the soloist. Moreover, he is less likely to forget that God alone is the Conductor!

There were, however, two personalities in the twentieth-century pulpit for whom the love of truth was a passion. They were close friends—Bishop Hensley

[1] *Word and Sacrament: A Preface to Preaching and Worship* (1960), p. 3.

[2] *Positive Preaching and the Modern Mind* (5th imp., 1957), p. 72. This prophetic work first appeared in 1907.

Henson and Dean Inge. They were examples of preaching that was courageously honest and thoroughly practical. For this reason this has been described as 'Reasonable Preaching' (Chapter 3). Henson's preaching, in particular, is marked by independence of judgment and balanced sagacity. For him Christianity was essentially 'Light' and 'Leaven.'[1] That is, it was both the revelation of Divine truth in the Incarnation and the Cross, and the agent for the transformation of character. A writer and preacher of admirable exegetical sermons,[2] and a most penetrating interpreter and unsparing critic of his times, his comments on the nature of preaching deserve the most serious consideration.[3] Yet even he lamented that the day of individualism in the pulpit was over.

2 · *Changes in Sermon Tone, Style and Length*

In the last sixty years there has been a revolution in the mode of English preaching. With the splendid exception of Sir Winston Churchill's noble war-time speeches, oratory has been under a cloud. It has been dirtied by political dictators, sullied with the taint of glib hypocrisy, and linked with herd-psychology.[4] It recalls attempts to assault the personality by softening the resistance of meditative reason.

[1] See *Light and Leaven, Historical and Social Sermons to General Congregations* (1897).

[2] See a recent selection of Bishop Henson's sermons, edited with an introduction by C. J. Stranks, *Theology and Life* (1957).

[3] Henson's frank and judicious autobiography is *Retrospect of an Unimportant Life* in 3 vols. (1942, 1943, 1950). For some unusual comments on preaching, see III, pp. 15, 114, 312, 327 f., 331.

[4] A most suggestive study of coercive conversion and brainwashing is that of William Sargant, *Battle for the Mind* (1957).

Moreover, the Christian faith and ethical way have been subjected to relentless attacks. The accumulating criticisms from Darwin's day to Freud's have involved a radical reshaping of the defence and exposition of the Christian faith and life. In addition, the rapid changes in the political and social maps of Europe and Africa, not to mention the seismic shock caused to the conscience by Hiroshima and Nagasaki, all counsel caution and moderation. Interim judgments and shortened horizons are the order of the day. Inevitably, the trumpet speaks with an uncertain sound. Often it is deliberately muted.

To be sure, in the last two decades there have been signs of experimentation and of renewal in the Churches. The gradual recovery of a Biblical theology, the primary importance now accorded to Divine worship, and the stimulus and hope of the Ecumenical Movement working towards the reunion of a divided Christendom, have all contributed to the restoration of a quiet, but uncomplacent, confidence within the ranks of the committed. This calm assurance is, however, expressed in the appropriate mode of a confidential tone, not with oratorical certitude.

The modern sermon is also much briefer than its Victorian counterpart. The latter was a marathon effort, which required the stamina of a Hector and the voice of a Stentor. (Modern acoustic aids have superannuated Stentor, and Hector is relegated to the soap-box.) The difference may be seen by comparing nineteenth-century Spurgeon with twentieth-century Campbell Morgan, and no one could call Morgan short-winded. Ashley Sampson's anthology, *Famous English Sermons* (1940), shows that Spurgeon's concentrated sermon on 'The Immutability of God' takes up 24 pages, while Morgan's

'The Psalm of the Two Ways' requires only 12 pages. A fair surmise would be that the Victorian sermon lasted 45 minutes and over, while the typical present-day sermon averages from 20 to 25 minutes.

The brevity of the modern sermon may be explained partly by the restriction of the functions of the modern preacher, and partly by the concision of speech encouraged by radio and television. The modern preacher is neither adult education lecturer nor entertainer in the pulpit. Today there are ample sources of information and entertainment available, and, as the Rev. Kenneth Slack indicates, 'at a more serious level, men seem to turn more readily for religious enlightenment to the paperback than to the pulpit.'[1] Moreover, the sobriety of our times discourages jocularity in the pulpit, though a spontaneous expression of humour is often a welcome relief. Even so, Dean Inge, Bishop Henson, and Monsignor Ronald Knox (as, to a lesser extent, Bernard Manning) prove that wit in and out of the pulpit did not die with Sydney Smith.

Broadcasting helped to change the style and tone of public discourse from the oratorical to the intimate. It also prepared the public for succinct and pointed statement. Perhaps it has over-prepared the public for brevity, for it is doubtful if the modern congregation, in most cases, can concentrate on serious issues for more than 20 minutes. (The exceptions are Drs Martyn Lloyd-Jones of Westminster and James S. Stewart of Edinburgh, and the Rev. John R. W. Stott of All Souls', Langham Place, London, who can hold congregations for 40 minutes or more.)

[1] *The British Churches Today* (1961), p. 73.

3 · *Changes in Theological Emphasis*

The change in theological emphasis has been less noticeable among the ardent Evangelicals of the Anglican and Free Churches (whose important expository preaching is considered in Chapter 8) than among the majority of preachers. At the risk of over-simplification (omitting the impact on preaching of the more rarefied views of existentialism, demythologizing, and language philosophy), three major theological trends may be discerned between 1900 and 1960. These can be labelled successively: 'The New Theology'; 'Neo-Orthodoxy'; and, tentatively, 'The Gospel of the Church for Society.'

The so-called 'New Theology' was the English equivalent of the American 'Social Gospel.' It dominated the pulpits for the first fourteen years of the century, was gradually weakened by the impact of the First World War and its aftermath, and almost faded out in the apocalyptic age of the brown-shirts and black-shirts of the thirties. In more chastened form, it has recently re-emerged on a stronger theological basis.

It had many leaders. The Rev. C. Ensor Walters, the distinguished Methodist social crusader, had sat as a fellow vestryman in the St Pancras ward of London with George Bernard Shaw. The Rev. C. Silvester Horne, an eminent Congregationalist, left the pulpit of Whitefield's Tabernacle in London to promote his social crusade as a member of the House of Commons, and taught that 'the ballot-box is the sacrament of brotherhood.' Dr John Clifford was the veteran Baptist champion of educational and social justice. The most impressive (if afterwards the most disillusioned) leader was

Dr R. J. Campbell, the young minister of London's City Temple, whose book on *The New Theology* appeared in 1907.[1]

The New Theology was a socialistic version of the historic Christian faith, replacing Christ the Saviour with Christ the Philanthropist and Social Reformer. The more guarded Anglican exponents of the social implications of the Christian faith, among whom were Bishop Charles Gore and Canon Scott Holland, were suspicious of the theology though sympathetic to its social compassion.

The 'New Theologians' protested against the complacent piety, the restrictive creedal or confessional forms, and the top-heavy institutionalism of the Churches, and the bourgeois attitude which they believed was responsible for alienating artisans from commitment to Christianity. Typical of the spirit of the time was Gore's castigation of unrestrictedly competitive Capitalism in the wry epigram: 'Each for himself and God for us all, as the elephant said when he danced among the chickens.'

The social compassion and courage of these preachers was magnificent, and the sounding-boards of their pulpits rang like bells—the clang of prophetic denunciation alternating with the chime of compassion. In retrospect, however, most were too impatient in rejecting or minimizing the universality of personal sinfulness (the correlate is the universal need of redemption), as in reducing the status of the eternal Son of God to that of an inspired carpenter, prophet and reformer, and the work of the

[1] See Albert Clare, *The City Temple, 1640–1940* (1940), pp. 138–172.

Church to that of a social settlement. The nemesis of the movement was found in Neo-Orthodoxy, for it stressed precisely those elements of the historic Christian faith which the New Theology had jettisoned.

However, the contemporary preacher in England is not blind to the social implications of the Gospel, so that the legacy of the 'Social Gospel' remains, if in a more widely diffused form. Nowadays the 'Gospel' is primary, and the 'Social' strictly subordinate. Britain today is a social welfare state, brought into being by a combination of the political radicals and the Christian social conscience. While this is not a classless society, it is a more open-ended society, and certainly a far less class-conscious community. The emphasis in preaching has therefore shifted to a condemnation of the racialistic prejudices that thwart the love of the neighbour, whether in the new West-Indian or African ghettoes arising in the English industrial cities, or in the economically and educationally impoverished homelands from which the emigrants came.

The theological emphasis presently prevailing has been named 'The Gospel of the Church for Society.' This indicates that its authority and drive is Divine revelation, received anew in the worship of the Divine-human Society, which exists to worship God and serve him in the world. It is a synthesis of Neo-Orthodoxy, the Ecumenical and Liturgical Movements, and the social implications of the 'New Theology' more widely applied.

Neo-Orthodoxy itself took varied forms. In the Roman Catholic Church it was largely a rediscovery of the massive theology of St Thomas Aquinas applied to the contemporary situation. Its relevance had been shown by Étienne Gilson and Jacques Maritain, quite apart from the Dominicans of whose order St Thomas was the greatest ornament. Among Anglicans there were also several Thomists, and not a few scholars who sought for renewal in the Fathers of the first five centuries. Many other Anglican thinkers were impressed by Eastern Orthodoxy, among them Archbishop William Temple who found the thought of the lay theologian and philosopher Berdyaev extremely congenial.

Among the Methodists there were many who returned to a study of Wesley, and several erudite men who rediscovered Luther as the road to a new Reformation. On the part of the sons of Geneva (the Presbyterians and the Congregationalists), there was a concern to return to the systematic Biblical theology of John Calvin and to consider the rich theology of the Word of God which Karl Barth continues to expound in successive volumes of the weighty *Church Dogmatics*.

Among all shades of the Neo-Orthodox there was a return to the distinctively Biblical dimensions of grace, sin, and eschatology. There was also a renewed concern for exegetical preaching, aided by many stimulating New Testament studies. Among these, the work of Professor C. H. Dodd and the Rev. Sir Edwyn Hoskyns was particularly fruitful. In the former's *Apostolic Preaching*, as in the latter's *Cambridge Sermons* (to take perhaps the most widely known of their writings), there was a new conception of the Kingdom of God. No longer was the Kingdom conceived (as with the 'New Theology') as the sum total of decent co-operative human ventures to establish a more humane society, nor was it thought of as a future event or utopia which the generations must strive to establish. Rather was it conceived to have begun in the Apostolic proclamation of the life, death, resurrection, and ascension of Christ and the donation of the Holy Spirit. It was the rule of God actualized in every age by the power of the judging and saving Word of God proclaimed by the saved and saving Church, which is the Body of Christ. It was a Kingdom inaugurated and sustained by God in crisis and perfected in eternity. It was neither planned by men nor gradually achieved by them.

In consequence, the preacher became again the herald of God's Good News, the announcer of the mighty acts of God in Christ. He was also the representative of the Church confronting the world. His private opinions were strictly irrelevant, when they were not impertinent. His understanding of human nature and of the nature of the Christian Society was deeply corporate. It is reflected in Berdyaev's definition of the Christian religion as 'Communion and therefore Community' rather than in Whitehead's one-sided judgment that 'Religion is what a man does with his solitariness.' Thus, today's preacher is bound to be less of an individualist (and far less likely to be eccentric) than his Victorian predecessor because of the new ecumenical and liturgical emphases.

It is increasingly recognized that the highest and most characteristic activity of the Christian Church is worship—the response of the people of God to the revelation of God. This has three consequences. First, worship is rarely thought of as a mere preliminary to the preaching. Secondly, the Sacraments are seen to be—equally with the Word preached—iron-rations of the wayfarer, rather than the truffles of the unusually pious. Thus there is a better balance of Worship, Sermon, and Sacrament. As Dr John Bishop has expressed it: 'The Word spoken and the Word acted are both Sacramental, and it is the Word which turns both the speech and action into Sacraments.'[1] Finally, worship is increasingly seen as the stimulus to sacrificial social service. This is because it re-enacts the Sacrifice of the eternal Son of God for all the sons of men and requires the members of Christ's Body to offer themselves as 'a living sacrifice, which is your reasonable service.'

4 · *Functions and Varieties of Preaching*

While fashions of style, tone, length and theological emphasis change, the underlying functions of the preacher (as of the Gospel he proclaims) do not alter. The tasks of the preacher of God's Word are four.

1. His first task is *to remove objections to his message and to establish its relevance.* This first encounter with the doubtful, indifferent, or hostile is styled 'Apologetical Preaching.' Its task is to vindicate the Christian faith. This is done by exposing and, if possible, overcoming the intellectual, psychological and moral barriers to belief and by demonstrating that the Gospel of God as transforming truth fulfils the nature and destiny of man.

Most of the preachers included in this study have preached sermons of this type, defending the Christian faith with special reference to modern criticisms. Two of them, Archbishop William Temple and Professor Herbert Farmer (see Chapter 9), have consistently

[1] *Study Notes on Preaching and Worship* (1949), p. 52.

commended the Christian faith to men and women of intellect and sensitivity with unusual distinction. They have sympathetically considered and attempted to answer the most diverse criticisms from the quarters of modern philosophy, the physical and biological sciences, as well as from sociology and psychology, in sermons, addresses, and books. Although their later writing and preaching is more definitely theological than apologetical, they more than any other English preachers warrant inclusion as representatives of 'Apologetical and Theological Preaching.'

Dr Leslie D. Weatherhead, the most widely-known English preacher of our day, has made his own apologetical contribution by proving that the potentially most dangerous foe of Christianity, namely psychology, can be turned into an effective ally. Though he is not by any means limited to 'Psychological Preaching' (Chapter 6), this is his distinctive contribution to the modern pulpit.

In their own way, Dean Inge and Bishop Hensley Henson were also apologists, for they insisted upon intellectual honesty in the pulpit and warned that if orthodoxy was obscurantist then heresy would seem the highest illumination.

2. A second permanent function of preaching is *to deepen the congregation's understanding of God*, and, assisted by the interior power of the Holy Spirit in preacher and congregation alike, *to awaken and confirm faith*. It requires of the preacher a disciplined subjection to the authority of the Revelation of God recorded in Holy Scripture and renewed in the experience of the Church of the centuries, as well as a deep love of people as persons. The declaration of the mighty acts of God

for the liberation of the human race from its slavery to egotism, anxiety, suffering and the fear of death, through the Incarnation, Passion, Sacrificial Death, Resurrection and Ascension of Christ and his promised Return, makes the ordained minister Christ's ambassador and herald.

This, the historic type of expository preaching, has been recovered with power in our own day, as may be seen in Chapter 8. Three distinguished exemplars of it are: Dr Campbell Morgan, famous on both sides of the Atlantic; Dr W. E. Sangster, whose masterly illustrations make this type of preaching cogent without being dull; and Dr James Stewart of the Church of Scotland, here studied because his influence is international and his renown particularly strong in England. These, with such Anglicans as the Rev. John R. W. Stott and the Rev. D. W. Cleverley Ford (Director of the College of Preachers), stand firmly in the tradition of evangelical orthodoxy.

3. The third function of preaching (strictly an extension of the second) is *to teach the holy love of God so as to elicit the response of adoration*. Many different varieties of preaching can be included in this wide category.

Some preachers like Dr J. H. Jowett are exponents of Christ-mysticism. Their aim was to attach individual souls to Christ by the chain of adoration. Such preaching is called 'Devotional Preaching' (Chapter 2). Dean Inge was another mystic and authority on Christian mysticism. In the case of Monsignor Ronald Knox, the mysticism is essentially corporate and ecclesiastical, rather than individual. It found its natural flowering in the rich loam of the Roman Liturgy. It is therefore called

'Liturgical Preaching' (Chapter 5). Although he excelled in this type of preaching, he was also a subtle Biblical expositor and witty apologist. Nor should the mystical quality of Archbishop Temple's later sermons, addresses and books (particularly his *Readings in St John's Gospel*) be forgotten.

The two exemplars of 'The Preaching of Truth Through Personality' (Chapter 4), Sheppard and Studdert Kennedy, were also mystics. Their personalities were living epistles bearing the scarlet signature of their Master. Their graciousness was a response to the prodigality of the Divine grace in Christ, an unconventional, uncalculating and spendthrift outpouring of Christian love for social outcasts and victims of the industrial struggle.

4. The fourth function of preaching is *to help men to rediscover that their near or remote neighbours of every race and class are brothers in Christ*. The motivation is compassion (literally a *suffering with* others), not sentimentality.

All preachers must engage in this type of Moral or Ethical preaching. Two forms of ethical preaching have prevailed in the last sixty years. The one kind stresses individual responsibility for the near neighbour as a permanent obligation. The other form, new in our own time on the widest scale, insists that Christians have an obligation for the remote neighbour, which can only be expressed through the instrumentality of political and social change.

Bishop Henson and Dean Inge (see Chapter 3), as well as Professor C. S. Lewis, argue for the first type of ethical responsibility, and are, in fact, suspicious of the claims of social justice. The outstanding Christian exponent of the claims of social justice was Archbishop William Temple, especially in his famous and widely discussed *Christianity and the Social Order*. He taught the Church of England and many beyond its borders to think of the love of the neighbour in terms of the solidarity of justice, instead of in the older terms of individual patronage.

Many preaching prophets follow in his train. These include Dr George MacLeod, the founder of the Iona Community; Dr Donald Soper, the improbable combination of sacramentalist, socialist, pacifist and superb apologist; Dr Mervyn Stockwood (Bishop of Southwark); and the foes of *apartheid*, Bishop Trevor Huddleston of Tanganyika and Father Michael Scott. Happily their influence is in the ascendant and most are too busy proclaiming the Gospel to find time to edit volumes of their collected sermons.

It will be noted that Chapter 7 is entitled 'Distinguished Lay Preaching.' It was included to draw attention to the fact that certain laymen have been among the most acute defenders and expounders of the Christian faith. In addition, two of them were most effective preachers. They were Bernard Lord Manning and Clive Staples Lewis. Professor C. S. Lewis is, of course, an Anglican of wide fame. B. L. Manning[1] was a Free Churchman who stood proudly in the tradition of Orthodox Dissent. That is, he was orthodox in his doctrine, but dissented from the idea of an established

[1] Manning is also very highly thought of by the General Secretary of the British Council of Churches, the Rev. Kenneth Slack. See *The British Churches Today*, p. 66, for a perceptive tribute to Manning's writings, 'so small in volume, so rich in content.'

Church, while admiring the liturgy of the Church of England. His historical writings deserve to be better known, especially his *Essays in Orthodox Dissent*. His two volumes of published sermons might well be the envy of most ministers for their Biblical insights, candour, wit, and relevance. It is in such gifted laymen, as apologists and witnesses, that a great Church reservoir of untapped talent lies.

The studies of the fourteen preachers which follow are designed to represent the leading varieties of preaching in England during sixty glorious and inglorious years. Many excellent preachers have been excluded because their variety of preaching was not distinctively modern, or because their versatility precluded distinction in any one variety of preaching. It seemed better to offer portraits of fourteen preachers than thumb-nail sketches of double that number. Many readers will inevitably find that their favourite preacher is missing from this gallery, but they may find consolation in striking up new acquaintances beyond their denominational walls. Certainly they will meet or rediscover fourteen very different, interesting, and unusually gifted preachers, representative of the varieties of English preaching in six decades. Even if an occasional preacher in this short volume fails to speak to their condition, they may wish to be reminded of George Herbert's salutary advice:

> The worst speaks something good; if all want sense God takes a text, and preacheth patience.[1]

[1] *The Temple: The Church Porch*, lxxii.

2

Devotional Preaching

J. H. JOWETT

IT may be the fate of the prophet to be thought behind the times, when he is in advance of them. As G. K. Chesterton said, it is not that Christianity has been tried and found wanting, it is rather that it has been found hard and not tried. This was also J. H. Jowett's conviction: he was content to be thought old-fashioned because he knew that the future would prove him right.

1 · *Against the Stream*

At a time when all the notable pulpits of America and England were rife with argument, Jowett led his people into the quietude of the Upper Room. While other ministers noisily debated the reconstruction of doctrine and the so-called 'New Theology,' or the reconstruction of society according to the imperatives of the 'Social Gospel,' Jowett stressed the culture and discipline of the devotional life. While the majority of ministers and members concentrated on the activism that estimates by statistics, Jowett concentrated on the individual cure of souls by the means of meditation.

His remarkable volume of sermons, *The Transfigured*

Church, which appeared in 1910, was fifty years ahead of its time. It had already diagnosed the sickness of the Church as due to two weaknesses. The first was a lack of awe in its conception of God; the second, a severe limitation in its understanding of the nature of brotherhood, which excluded the artisans. Its claim that the Church needed a theological, liturgical and social reformation showed astonishing foresight. Like P. T. Forsyth, another prophet of the Congregational churches, Jowett saw that God's Fatherhood must be linked with his Holiness; otherwise the Christian idea of God degenerated into a belief in 'Our Grandfather Who art in heaven.' In his vivid and arresting way Jowett said: 'We have toyed with the light, but forgotten the lightning. We have rejoiced in the Fatherhood of our God, but too frequently the Fatherhood we have proclaimed has been throneless and effeminate.'[1] He concluded: 'If we banish the conceptions which inspire awe, we of necessity devitalise the very doctrines of grace, and if grace is emasculated then faith becomes anaemic, and we take away the very tang and pang of sin.'[2] In our century he anticipated Otto with his analysis of the category of the 'numinous' or the 'holy' as the very essence of religion, and in his concern for corporate worship was a forerunner of the Liturgical Movement.

Jowett is the apostle of reverence and of awe, and therefore of the primacy of adoration in private and public worship and in life. In this concern it has taken the Churches fifty years to catch up with Jowett, for there is no emphasis of the Christianity of our day more

[1] *The Transfigured Church* (1910), p. 20.
[2] *Ibid.*, p. 21.

central than the conviction that worship is the power-house of the Christian life and that all service to men is motivated and nerved by the sacrifice of the Son of God renewed in what is variously termed the Mass, the Eucharist, the Holy Communion, or the Lord's Supper. If Jowett's own understanding of the Holy Communion was too retrospective, technically termed 'Memorialism,' he was emphatic in his prayers and his sermons that the deepest note in the Christian symphony was the fellowship with Christ in his sufferings.[1]

His determination to concentrate on devotional preaching was neither dully conservative nor deliberately antiquarian. He abhorred the triviality of the merely topical sermon which owed more to the newspapers than to the Word of God. He considered that the discussion of the hypothetical and variable conclusions of Biblical and historical criticism in the pulpit were turning ministers and people into critics rather than into convinced and covenanted disciples. 'When life is a picnic,' he stated acidly, 'we play with theology: when life is a campaign we grope for a religion.'[2] His own deepest concern may be discerned in his private prayers:

> My Father God, I pray that my eyes may be open to discern the footprints of my Lord. Let me not shrink from the difficult track if it bear the blood-tracks of the Crucified. Help me to follow whithersoever He doth lead. Thy will be done!

[1] His entire volume of devotional sermons, *The School of Calvary* (1910), the title of which comes from the statement of St Francis of Assisi that 'Calvary is the Academy of Love,' is devoted to this theme, as are several sermons in other volumes.

[2] *Ibid.*, p. 59.

. . . My Risen Lord, I pray that I may know the fellowship of Thy sufferings. Let me not be contented to taste of Thy grace; let me share in Thy travail.

. . . My Father in heaven, I pray that Thou wilt keep the fire of my devotion burning.[1]

Similarly, for most of his years in the ministry, he refused the blandishments of the 'Social Gospel,' because he believed that while it was the Church's duty to proclaim the principles of social redemption and reconstruction, yet the practical application of the laws of Christ for common life demanded an expert technical knowledge of politics and economics. But this no minister of the Gospel possessed. Thus the exponents of the 'Social Gospel' from the pulpit were both abrogating their primary responsibility and pretending to a competence which they did not have. Moreover, he denied that a change of environment necessarily improved the citadel of personality; it was simply untrue to say that the more opulent therefore the godlier. His single aim, in preaching the apostolic themes, was so to present the incarnate Christ, crucified and risen, that admiration would lead to worship, and worship to the expulsion of the unholy and the strengthening of the will for the service of God and men.[2] Yet this unexciting task (as others might conceive it) was performed with such

[1] Taken from his book *The Daily Altar* (1907), prayers for 18th January, 21st April and 5th February respectively.

[2] Yet Jowett recognized that worship had its dangers. Chief among them was a luxuriating in emotion for its own sake, or what R. W. Dale called a 'valetudinarian spirituality.' He cautioned that 'the waters of unfulfilled emotion congeal into frost, and the very ministers of intended service become the friends of a severer alienation. . . . We cease to be able to enter into the sufferings of Christ, and the Savior suffers alone.' (*Ibid.*, pp. 76–77.)

depth, practicality and brilliance that Jowett was reputed to be the 'greatest living preacher.'[1]

Dr Jowett despised those who courted popularity in the pulpit, but people crowded to his services in the four churches in which he preached: three English Congregational churches (in Newcastle, Birmingham and London) and one American (Fifth Avenue Presbyterian Church, New York City). He never stooped to the meretricious and he gained, not the fleeting popularity of the 'muscular' parson or the sensationalist, but the admiration of the multitude in America and England who discerned in him the utterly dedicated disciple.

2 · *The Calling and Making of a Minister*

Since it is one of his distinguishing marks that, as Dean Homrighausen suggests, 'he had a high conception of his holy calling as a minister,' it is essential to learn how he came to this understanding and who his mentors were and what they taught him.

He was born into the humble but devout home of a tailor in Halifax, Yorkshire, on 23rd August 1863. He attended the evangelical but liberal ministry of Dr Enoch Mellor, renowned minister of the Square Congregational Church in the industrial city. After attending the Hipperholme Grammar School he became a pupil teacher in one of the state schools in Halifax and the composition which he wrote as part of the final examinations for his teaching certificate was adjudged to be the

[1] See E. H. Jeffs, *Princes of the Modern Pulpit* (n.d.), p. 51; Alexander Gammie, *Preachers I have Heard* (n.d.), p. 60; and *J. H. Jowett* (1950), ed. and intro. by Elmer G. Homrighausen, p. 10.

best in the nation for that year. Clearly the master stylist was already in the making.

His ambition had been focused on the law, with the eventual hope that he might become a member of Parliament. It speaks volumes for the dedication of his Sunday-school teacher and for Jowett's admiration of him, that it was this Mr Dewhirst who deflected Jowett's ambition. On learning by accident that Jowett was to enter a Halifax firm of lawyers and sign the articles of indenture on the following day, Dewhirst looked disappointed and said, 'I had always hoped that you would go into the ministry.' Jowett reconsidered the matter of his vocation and it became clear to him that the preacher's calling was diviner than the politician's. 'It was the result,' he said, 'of no urgent argument, nor the issue of any calculation of profit and loss: it was a gracious constraint, an inclination born of love, a decision shaped by the worship of Jesus Christ.'[1] Immediately, he entered on a rigorous course of ministerial training.

As a student in Edinburgh, Jowett now learned from Henry Drummond that there is no necessary dichotomy or division between Christianity and culture, and that the most persuasive evangelist attempts an individual approach to every human soul. The example of many ministers had instructed him that congregations will only follow a preacher as he follows Christ and that private devotions are the indispensable preparation for public worship and witness. With the help of his theological teachers and great assiduity on his part in studying the Scriptures in the original languages, he

[1] A. Porritt, *John Henry Jowett* (1924), p. 21.

learned that God's true servant is the minister *of the Word*. He recognized, in other words, that the preacher is either under the authority of the Divine revelation or he is overreaching himself. By the Edinburgh pulpit-masters he was taught that preaching is the art of persuasion and that if he was to bring the imagination of his congregations into the captivity of Christ, he would have to be a poet-preacher. From Masson of Edinburgh University he learned of the subtle apparatus of metaphor and simile, alliteration and assonance, the structure and pace of sentences, the use of epigram and antithesis, the cogent simplicity of Anglo-Saxon diction, and many other lessons, which together provide an understanding of the anatomy of English style. He concentrated on style, for by it poets and preachers insinuate their way into the human heart and stir the impulses of admiration and awe. In sum, experience—if only he were observant—would provide him with a deeper knowledge of human callings and motivations; his studies had already given him the knowledge of God's message and transforming power and of the way to write and deliver sermons that would speak to the human condition with piercing relevance.

There is one curious absence in his years of training: although these were years of theological turbulence Jowett never seems to have gone through a crisis of intellectual doubt. This must be attributed to the liberal evangelicalism of the ministries he attended; but it left him ill equipped for, and even apparently uninterested in, the task of reaching the intelligent outsider. His task, therefore, would always be to edify the convinced rather than to convince the doubting.

3 · *Four Flocks*

Since Jowett's was a retiring personality which fled the limelight, the chief interest in his ministries is to be found in the differing nature of the congregations, both English and American, and his response to their needs.

Newcastle: 1889–1895

Late in 1889 Jowett was ordained to the ministry of the Congregational churches and inducted to the pastorate of St James's Congregational Church, Newcastle-upon-Tyne. In the course of his statement of faith before ordination, the congregation heard Jowett make a very revealing confession, which accounts for his concentration thereafter almost exclusively on devotional preaching. 'May I confess,' said Jowett, 'that my greatest difficulty in College has been to combine the study of theology with the maintenance of a spiritual life?'[1] He had already made his decision not to add his hammer to the iconoclasts who were bringing down the ancient cathedral of doctrine, for in the same address he said: 'My prayer is that the teaching of this pulpit may be constructive and not merely destructive.'[2] His was an old head on young shoulders.

Jowett's task, therefore, was to find a new way to preach tried and trusty ancient truth. He applied to himself the aim that Alexander Pope chose for his poetry: 'What oft was thought, but ne'er so well expressed.' He preached, however, a Gospel of delicate sympathy rather than of sturdy strength. But his practical compassion was working at least as hard as his craft for

[1] *Op. cit.*, p. 55. [2] *Ibid.*, p. 56.

sermon construction. He addressed tramps in the common lodging-houses of the city and arranged for them to receive magazines and newspapers. Though he and his wife had no children of their own, and waited ten years before adopting a daughter, he set himself out to capture the children and young people. He held special children's services and could transform irritations into triumphs. On one occasion his children's address was interrupted by four boys shrilly blowing penny whistles at the back of the congregation. Immediately a deacon led them out of the church into the vestry behind and four disconsolate small boys were waiting for Jowett's admonition when the service was over. His first words to them were: 'Can't you fellows play on tin whistles better than that? If you can't, I shall have to get Mrs Jowett to give you some lessons.' A few weeks later the same quartet played a hymn on their tin whistles at the children's service and thereafter they were Jowett's slaves.[1]

In the six years at Newcastle Jowett made the transition from Emerson to Evangelicalism, from preaching a Gospel of 'God helps those who help themselves' to a Gospel which answers the cry, 'Help of the helpless, O abide with me.' When delivering his farewell message to his Newcastle congregation as he prepared to leave for Carrs Lane, Birmingham, he summed up the lessons of his ministry:

> I have learned this lesson—that sin is mighty but God is mightier; I have learned that man is impotent to redeem himself; I have learned that no man need be regarded as beyond redemption; I have learned that for the ruined life there is a power and a peace and a joy unspeakable; I have

[1] *Ibid.*, pp. 62–63.

learned that the care and misery of this Church are in the homes where Christ is absent; I have learned that the happiest and most beautiful homes connected with this congregation are the homes of the redeemed.[1]

Birmingham: 1895–1911

As successor to Dr R. W. Dale of Birmingham, Jowett accepted the burden of a theological Atlas. Carrs Lane was probably the most influential of all the Free Churches outside London and Dale had left an unforgettable impress on both it and the city of Birmingham, as a doctrinal preacher and the exponent of civic righteousness. Here gathered the captains of industry and commerce, professional men and artisans and their families who were used to the strong meat of the Gospel. Jowett knew that he could not possibly become a second Dale, since his temperament, approach and experience were different; but he was wise enough to read everything Dale had written. He had, however, one gift that Dale had only begun to covet at the end of his ministry—the capacity to reach the emotions of men, while Dale had only appealed to their intellects and wills. What Jowett did was to offer the troubled and bereaved a Gospel of comfort, while at the same time his own presentation of the faith to the successful and apparently self-confident became more rigorous in its demands. Dale's writings taught Jowett the central importance of God's grace; but no one needed to teach Jowett how to present it graciously. Indeed, Jowett once confessed to a friend that until he succeeded Dale he had been in some danger of mere prettiness in preaching. Dale's congregation being a great stronghold of Evangelicalism

[1] *Ibid.*, p. 68.

demanded the expository preaching of the central texts and themes of the Old and New Testaments. Jowett responded to the challenge and, like the honey that Samson found in the carcase of the lion, sweetness persisted in the context of a new strength.

Sir William Robertson Nicoll, the distinguished editor and theological essayist, wrote of a visit that he paid to Carrs Lane. His account illuminates Jowett's appeal when in his prime. He first commented on the worship: 'The great simplicity, reality, sympathy and tenderness of the prayers moved one strangely.' He was also impressed by the style of the preacher: 'Of the startling wealth and beauty of Dr Jowett's diction, the incisiveness of his contrasts, the overwhelming power of his appeals it is impossible for me to write adequately.' His third observation touched on the intensity of Jowett's personality in his preaching: 'In Dr Jowett everything preaches. The voice preaches, and it is a voice of great range and compass, sweet and clear through every variety of intonation. The eyes preach, for though Dr Jowett apparently writes every word of his sermons, he is extraordinarily independent of his manuscript. The body preaches, for Dr Jowett has many gestures, and not one ungraceful. But, above all, the heart preaches.' Nicoll's critique concludes with the statement that Dr Jowett's appeal to the heart held the great congregation spellbound from beginning to end of the sermon, so that 'the tension of listening, the silence, and the eagerness of the crowd, were almost oppressive,' yet it was also 'very wonderful and very uplifting.'[1] Jowett's preaching

[1] *Ibid.*, pp. 76–77, where Porritt cites an article in *The British Weekly*, 22nd December 1910.

was not only the perfect product of superlative artistry in style and structure; it was also the effect of the incandescent flame of integrity that shone through all he said. As in the case of John Henry Newman, men felt they were overhearing a saint in his orisons.

New York City: 1911–1918

The most exhilarating as well as the most exacting transition Jowett ever made was from Birmingham, England, to the Fifth Avenue Presbyterian Church in New York City, then reputed to be the 'church of millionaires.' It marked a change from a comfortable to an opulent congregation, but even more a change from English traditionalism to American experimentalism in outlook. The New York newspapermen immediately assumed that Jowett would be a 'character' with decided views of the world. They found him a frail, immaculately dressed, sober and apparently taciturn man with no flare for racy or witty speech or for the sensational. It may even be guessed that the officials of the Fifth Avenue Church were surprised at the simplicity of Jowett's way of life. The *Mauretania*, on which the Jowetts crossed the Atlantic, was delayed and, in consequence, had to dock at midnight. The leaders of the Fifth Avenue Church had engaged a suite of rooms at the Gotham Hotel and the chef had been instructed to remain on duty to prepare the Jowetts a special meal. The order to the chef, telephoned from the ship to the hotel, was: 'Dr and Mrs Jowett would like two bowls of bread and milk.' This was, as Porritt remarks, a parable of the unassuming spirit in which he began his American ministry.[1] It is

[1] *Ibid.*, p. 142.

equally significant that Jowett asked to receive the same salary as he had been getting in England, with due allowance for the increased cost of living. Jowett could not be bought, and thus he retained his freedom to speak of the values of the Kingdom of God that upset all secular and monetary evaluations.

In the early days Jowett wrote: 'I am learning to resist almost every hour of the day the tremendous forces that would push me here and there. I do not know what time ministers here spend in their studies. They are evidently engaged in a hundred outside works which must leave them very little time to prepare their message.'[1] He was determined to spend every morning in his study, otherwise he did not see how he could ever prepare worthwhile messages. It was his firm conclusion, despite the risk of being misunderstood by standing on it, that 'I feel the preaching of the Word of God is incomparably my first work in New York.'[2] He felt it to be all the more important because, as the Bishop of New York told him, 'the people are starving on merely social topics and essays on remote themes.'[3] One can only admire Jowett's unwillingness to be cajoled by the social blandishments of the wealthy or to yield to the expected sensationalism of the journalists. He would not be deflected from the task of a meditative and devotional ministry, even by quite legitimate demands for his services as a preacher on special occasions in the United States or in Canada. He wrote to a friend in downright fashion: 'I should think my typewriter would almost acquire the habit of declining these things of its own

[1] *Ibid.*, p. 145.
[2] *Ibid.*, p. 146.
[3] *Ibid.*, p. 145.

accord. I am perfectly sure that what is needed here is concentration on one's own particular work.'[1]

Jowett concentrated every part of his mind and heart to the ministry of the sanctuary, and the result was that those who came to pry stayed to pray. The congregations grew in numbers and in spiritual vitality. Jowett attributed it all to his constant proclamation of the Gospel of Grace—a Gospel of comfort to the despondent and a Gospel of power to the weak of will—and he proclaimed it with the contagious glow of glorious certainty.

It was a remarkably cosmopolitan and influential congregation which Jowett led. 'This is a marvellous place,' wrote Jowett. 'I sat in the vestry on Wednesday to see people who wished to join the Church. Among those who came were two Swiss, a German, a Scotchwoman, and several Americans. . . . This afternoon after the service the last four men I spoke to were an American, a Spaniard, a Greek and an Italian.'[2] That was the attraction of New York; but for the magnetic attraction of Jowett's services we must turn to the testimony of his assistant minister, the Rev. James Palmer. The latter wrote:

> And what a congregation he had! I have counted four Bishops of the Episcopal Church at one service. It was not so uncommon to see as many as three hundred ministers present on a Sunday afternoon. Priests of the Roman Catholic Church and Rabbis of the Hebrew people were in constant attendance. The President, members of his Cabinet

[1] *Ibid.*, p. 148. Jowett shirked the glare of publicity, and he thanked God that it held no lure for him: 'He has made me graciously numb to it all. . . . And that is an answer to prayer.' (E. H. Jeffs, *Princes of the Modern Pulpit*, p. 66.)

[2] Porritt, *op. cit.*, p. 162.

> and prominent statesmen attended the services from time to time, and frequently desired his views on national affairs. The representative men of wealth and the leaders of industry were there. Men of letters and professional men and women were among his admirers. And then a wonderful company of missionaries and travelers sought the opportunity to hear him.

The significant addition is then made: 'The humble, too, were equally esteemed by him. No discrimination was made at his Church door.'[1]

Jowett made Fifth Avenue Presbyterian Church a great centre of spiritual leadership in America. It was all the more necessary as from 1914 onwards the clouds of war darkened the skyscape of the soul. In 1917 America had committed her forces behind the Allies and Jowett's English patriotism was no longer in conflict with American neutralism. A characteristic production of the New York ministry was the book, *The Whole Armour of God* (1916), a vigorous series of studies of the Christian Life, each based on a military analogy and prefaced by a prayer, the soul's greatest armament. Jowett was, however, no propagandist for chauvinism. Of the 49 illustrations and references, it is significant that 12 are to famous evangelists, 12 to poets and men of letters, 8 to magnanimous statesmen, 6 to missionaries, 3 to scientists and 8 to explorers and military men, and 2 of the latter recall the military mystic, General Gordon. If Jowett was leaving his impact on America, America was leaving her impress on Jowett. This can be most readily seen in his references to the journal of John Woolman, to the life of Frances Willard, and to the example of D. L.

[1] *Ibid.*, pp. 164–165.

Moody in these sermons. Some measure of his own leadership can be seen that when it was known that Westminster Congregational Church, London, was inviting him to become its minister, he was strongly urged to accept it by Lloyd George, the British Prime Minister, while President Woodrow Wilson urged him in equally strong terms to continue his ministry in New York.[1]

London: 1918–1922

His final ministry in the English metropolis was to last only four years and it must have seemed an anticlimax after Fifth Avenue, partly because Jowett's health was failing and partly because after the relief of the Armistice a mood of cynicism and hard materialism settled on the war-jaded English people. His own congregations at Westminster were always crowded, but he found the vast ovoid sanctuary with its two-tiered galleries less conducive to worship than Fifth Avenue Presbyterian Church. Despite these disadvantages, Londoners were delighted to discover in Jowett's preaching new dimensions of the Gospel which he had not stressed in either Birmingham or New York. Three new implications of the Christian faith now absorbed his attention: the social, the international and the ecumenical (or church-unity) aspects of Christianity. Had not pernicious anaemia struck Jowett down at sixty, it is clear that a towering spiritual force would have led the English Free Churches through the difficult after-war years.

Some glimmerings of the prophetic Jowett had been seen in *The Transfigured Church* (1910), but he had thereafter concentrated on evangelical and devotional sermons.

[1] *Ibid.*, p. 190.

The sleeping prophet in him was roused to full vigour in the sermons he preached at Westminster Chapel and published as *God—Our Contemporary, Sermons for the Times* (1922). He was as alive as 'Dick' Sheppard and Studdert Kennedy to the necessity for a more democratic England, for the Churches to take the lead in active reconciliation among the peoples, and in this process for them to overcome the scandal of their disunity.

When it is argued that Religion and Politics are best kept apart, Jowett has his answer: 'God's decree runs through all things, and His Holy will is best in everything. What is good in religion can never be bad in business. What is rotten religion can never be sound economics. What is morally right can never be politically wrong.[1] "Thy will be done on earth!"' The new Jowett turns to the Incarnation of the Son of God as the axis of his preaching, where before it was the Cross, as he proclaims the democratic Christ:

> When He came among us to reveal the life and character of God, He housed His holy body in the narrow circle of a working man. In His boyhood He donned the workman's apron, and for thirty years, in a little market town, He served His fellows as the village carpenter. He was the bread-winner for a widowed mother, the eldest son of a large family. He knew the workman's lot, and if He be now alive how can labour be to Him anything but noble and venerable, and how can He regard the apron of the worker as anything but one of the robes of righteousness and one of the garments of salvation?[2]

[1] This sentence is an exact echo of the great tenet of Hugh Price Hughes, who pleaded with Gladstone for the removal of Parnell from his government on this basis. The London *Times* called this phenomenon 'the Nonconformist Conscience.'

[2] Porritt, *op. cit.*, p. 248.

Christ was the greatest of leaders, because he exemplified the sanctity of service for others, because he worked for the most inclusive of human communities—the Kingdom of God. Yet Jowett never sinks the 'Gospel' in the 'Social,' for his great sermon on 'The Christ of Today' ends with the recognition that he saves men from their sins:

> I present the Christ to you as the Christ of today. He is the greatest of all democrats, far ahead of the boldest of all. He is the Pioneer of all human enlargement, with a programme bigger than all. And He is the incomparable Emancipator, descending into the depths of secret bondage where no one else can follow. I present Him to you, the Christ, as the Saviour of today—Christ Jesus, the same yesterday, today, and for ever.

Moreover, what Jowett preached he also practised. In these four years he attended conclaves of the Anglican and Free Church leaders in attempts to shape plans that would unite the separated Christian Communions. He proposed the calling together of European Church leaders in Copenhagen to consider ways of making their Churches channels of reconciliation, and took a decisive part in their meeting. He and the Archbishop of York (Dr Lang, later Archbishop of Canterbury) swept through the nation addressing great peace meetings of the Churches to mobilize the dedication of all Christian people to international peace. There was the great Service of Thanksgiving which Jowett organized at the Royal Albert Hall in Kensington, with the Royal Family and the Prime Minister and his Cabinet in attendance. The hitherto cloistered devotional preacher had become not only a prophet of social righteousness but a man of action and organization.[1] His death was felt all the more poignantly in the nation because he was stricken at a time when all his mental and spiritual powers were at their zenith.

4 · '*The Charms of Christian Rhetoric*'[2]

Jowett's sermons are remarkable not for their daring originality or their speculative flights, but for their exploration of God's grace and their eliciting of man's response in worship. Even in this central purpose he would not have attained the influence he did but for a mastery of what a seventeenth-century English bishop quaintly calls 'the charms of Christian rhetoric.' Undoubtedly he was a born mystic: for him eternity in time and heaven on earth and God in man were translucent realities, while opaque to the majority of men and women in a secular century. He had a genius for spirituality, but the consummate artistry of the planning, development and phrasing of his sermons was the result of unremitting discipline and toil. He advised his Yale University auditory to 'pay heed to the ministry of style. When you have discovered a jewel, give it the appropriate setting. When you have discovered a truth give it the noblest expression you can find.'[3] No jeweller ever polished his diamonds more lovingly than Jowett his phrases; for he

[1] See Porritt's *Jowett*, pp. 188–212, for an account of these public activities, also Jeffs, *op. cit.*, pp. 3 f.

[2] This delightful phrase is taken from Bishop Fell's Life of Dr Henry Hammond (in Christopher Wordsworth's *Ecclesiastical Biography* (1818), vol. v, p. 352).

[3] The Lyman Beecher Lectures on Preaching at Yale University, *The Preacher, His Life and Work* (1912), pp. 139–140.

was convinced that diction and metaphors must be worthy of the Artist of the universe.

The first secret of his success was the selection of what he termed 'apostolic themes.' These he listed as: 'the holiness of God; the love of God; the grace of the Lord Jesus; the solemn wonders of the Cross; the ministry of the Divine forgiveness; the fellowship of His sufferings; the power of the Resurrection; the blessedness of divine communion; the heavenly places in Christ Jesus; the mystical indwelling of the Holy Ghost; the abolition of the deadliness of death; the ageless life; our Father's house; the liberty of the glory of the children of God.'[1] The unifying factor was grace. This he once defined as 'holy love on the move' and also as 'God unmerited, undeserved, going out towards the children of men, so that He might win them into the glory and brightness of His own likeness.'[2] This proclamation of the grace of God brought encouragement for the strugglers, invigoration for the exhausted, forgiveness for the penitent, serenity for the troubled, and assurance for the bereaved. It was essentially an attempt to convey the 'compelling tenderness of Jesus and the loving concern of God.'[3] Jowett made no apologies for preaching a Gospel of consolation and power. He recalled that Joseph Parker had said, 'Preach to broken hearts!' and that R. W. Dale had declared, 'People want to be comforted.'[4]

In the second place, the sermon was always for Jowett *part of the act of Christian worship*. No one was a better

[1] *Ibid.*, pp. 100–101.
[2] Cited Gammie, *op. cit.*, p. 63.
[3] *The Best of John Henry Jowett*, ed. Gerald Kennedy (New York, 1948), p. xvii.
[4] Porritt, *op. cit.*, p. 214.

expositor than Jowett of the view expressed by P. T. Forsyth: 'The Protestant idea is that preaching is part of the cultus.'[1] Robertson Nicoll and all perceptive observers recognized the intensity, immediacy and reality of his prayers. He produced a new hymnal for Carrs Lane Church in 1908: it was characterized by the avoidance of the unreal, whether in the exaggeratedly lugubrious and gloomy introspection or in the individual egotism of the Victorian hymns it eliminated. He divided the pastoral prayer into sections, announcing each subject as he was about to pray for it, and asked the congregation to respond at the close of each petition with 'Amen.' He also wrote a preface approving a selection of intercessory prayers and responses prepared by a young Congregational minister. He was a member of the Committee that produced the official Congregational manual of worship, *The Book of Congregational Worship* (1920). Himself a convinced Protestant, he openly confessed that in their worship and symbolism the Roman Catholics elicited a deeper awe and reverence than most Protestants. Of him it could truly be said that he spent as much time preparing the worship as the sermon.[2]

Assuming the preliminaries of an apostolic theme for his sermon, and the aspirational atmosphere of worship in which he preached, his sermons always impressed by their felicitous diction and illustration. Jowett had a vivid imagination and an inexhaustible fertility for inventing or finding the apt metaphor or simile.

The ingenuity of some of the metaphors and similes is

[1] *Positive Preaching and the Modern Mind* (1907), p. 97.

[2] See the chapter entitled 'The Service of the Sanctuary' in *The Preacher, His Life and Work* (1912), and Homrighausen's *J. H. Jowett*, pp. 201, 249.

amusingly apt. The fussiness that is assumed by some activist Christians to constitute going about their Father's business is symbolized by a hobby-horse, an exact image of motion without progress![1] Ineffective Christian witness is likened to a shell-case, now empty of explosive charge, which is used merely for a dinner-gong[2] or to dropping white snowflakes on an open sewer![3] His images are equally vivid when his mood is serious. He speaks of the Divine reassurance in afflictions as 'like birdsong in a thunderstorm.'[4] Sometimes the simile is none the less effective for being commonplace, as when human wills are described as the electric batteries of portable night-lights, 'good for so many flashes and good for nothing more; we have volitional spasms succeeded by forceless lethargy.'[5]

Most strikingly contemporaneous are the images Jowett draws from modern science. For example the grain of faith's energy that is like the mustard seed growing into a great tree is paralleled with the fact that 'there is energy stored in one grain of radium sufficient to raise five hundred tons a mile high.'[6] When Jowett is expounding the text 'For me to live is Christ,' he comments: 'The middle term *live* is defined in the union of two extremes. The two carbon electrodes of the arc-lamp are brought into relationship and the result is a light of brilliant intensity.'[7] Again, when he looks for an illustration of how hope keeps patience diligent he turns to the persistence of the brothers Wright in redesigning their aeroplane and to the inventor of the English Electric

[1] Homrighausen, *op. cit.*, p. 124. [2] *Ibid.*, p. 55.
[3] *Ibid.*, p. 98. [4] *The School of Calvary* (1910), p. 48.
[5] *The Transfigured Church* (1910), p. 156.
[6] *Ibid.*, p. 210. [7] *The School of Calvary*, p. 11.

railway who was thirty years at work upon it.[1] When describing the shield of faith, he claims that for Paul it 'was a screen to intercept the deadly rays.'[2]

Jowett's ability to captivate his auditory is also due partly to the expansion of their horizons by the illustrations, citations, anecdotes, and references to historical figures, in which his sermons abound. It is significant that the Homrighausen selection of sermons has 106 references and citations, in addition to the 189 metaphors and similes. Of the 40 references to or citations of English literature, Bunyan provides 5 and Shakespeare and Browning 2 each. In addition there are 29 historical references, 17 to personal experience, 13 to foreign lands (4 of them to the Swiss Alps), 3 to art and 2 anecdotes. Together this rich apparatus of images and illustrative references combine in a remarkable way to give concretion to abstract truth and to hold entranced the attention of hearer or reader.

In Jowett's mind, however, the references fulfilled a deeper purpose: they introduced his congregations to the communion of saints. That is, by the frequent references to the great mystics, the famous evangelists, the most sacrificial missionaries, the most elevated poets and the most altruistic statesmen, Jowett linked the Church militant on earth with the Church triumphant in heaven, and enabled his regiment to march with outthrust shoulders and firmer step. This is why Bunyan, the imprisoned, persecuted but never despairing prose-poet of the Christian pilgrimage, is so often on his lips. This is why in the first two meditations of *The School of Calvary* he finds occasion to introduce St Francis, Pascal,

[1] *The Whole Armour of God* (1916), p. 97. [2] *Ibid.*, p. 86.

Dr Samuel Johnson, John Tauler, John Wesley, General Gordon, Bengel, Thomas Boston, St Thomas Aquinas and his favourite Bunyan. He was also most anxious to deny that all the great Christians lived in the remote past. For this reason he included moving excerpts from the diaries of modern missionaries, so that by the remembrance of their sacrifices he might stir up his own people to emulate them. For example, of the 49 references he provides in *The Whole Armour of God*, there are 6 to missionaries, including Moffat, Livingstone, Chalmers and Francis J. Hall of Pekin. There are also references to 12 evangelists and 8 statesmen. He wanted to introduce men to the great saints and benefactors.

Another element in Jowett's style was his diction, the inevitable word in the right place. For example, he repeats ironically, 'Like a mighty army moves the Church of God' and then comments: 'Yes, but does she? Are not her regiments sometimes almost Falstaffian in their bedraggled impotence?'[1] How vividly he describes the determination of the early apostles in the two phrases, 'men of masculine handgrip, of magnificent tenacity'![2] Sometimes his diction is freighted like a Spanish galleon with the gold of Shakespearian echoes, as when he describes the hardness in the soil (and the soul) which militates against acceptance of the Gospel in 'the masses of the poor, hardened by the winter of their discontent or partially petrified by a still more perilous indifference.' The unheeding rich, in the antithetical and balancing phrase, are 'the classes hardened by the bright and lengthy summer of their opulence.'[3]

[1] *The Transfigured Church*, p. 29.
[2] *Ibid.*, p. 193.
[3] *Ibid.*, p. 13.

Allied to his gift for the right word was Jowett's gift for the clarifying epigram. How concisely he explained that faith is not a safe orthodoxy but hazardous adventure in the saying: 'Merely to hug a creed and take no risk is no more faith than to hug a time-table is to take a journey.'[1] One of his greatest sermons, 'Through Gethsemane to Olivet,' has this astringent conclusion: 'And so the gist of it all is this: thrones are for those who are fit to sit on them.'[2] How well he knew that 'the water of Calvinism was hard, hard enough, but it made bone, fine bone, bone that would never bend, bone that could only be broken.'[3]

5 · *Knots in the Grain*

For most of his ministry there were two classes of people for whom he had no appeal whatsoever: the honest doubter and the social reformer. To read his sermons one would never suspect that the twentieth century was, like the latter part of the nineteenth century, an age of grave intellectual doubt, or that men of integrity existed like Darwin, Huxley or Thomas Hardy who all lived by the Christian ethic but had to repudiate the 'theological trappings,' as they considered them, in which the teachings were enclosed. Except in the restricted sense that the best defence is attack, Jowett had no strategy to assist the agnostic to leap across the chasm of unbelief to the far shore of faith. Though in his later years at Westminster (and occasionally in an earlier

[1] *God—Our Contemporary*, p. 93.
[2] *The School of Calvary*, p. 96.
[3] Homrighausen, p. 209.

sermon, as in 'Blinding the Mind'[1]) he preached the social implications of the Gospel, he had deliberately turned away from this approach for most of his ministry. At the time his reasoning seemed convincing—at least to himself. He judged that preaching the 'Social Gospel' was 'to substitute the Old Testament message of reform for the New Testament message of redemption,' 'to become so absorbed in social wrongs as to miss the deeper malady of personal sin.'[2] Yet Jowett could also have argued that if he did not express this concern in the pulpit, he certainly gave practical expression to it. The Digbeth Institute, for the building of which he personally raised the necessary £25,000, was an admirable vehicle of the Social Gospel in a bleak part of Birmingham which was staffed and supported by Carrs Lane Church. By his concentration on the devotional approach, which cannot coexist with the critical, Jowett forfeited the hazards and the rewards of apologetical preaching.

A second criticism urged against him was that sometimes the strength of truth seemed overlaid with the decorations of style, or, to use the Biblical metaphor, that the lily-work was more important than the stout pillars on which it was engraved.[3] Certainly amid the hundreds of apt images there are a few that draw attention to themselves and therefore distract from the

[1] This is the 23rd sermon in *Things that Matter Most* (1913). Remembering this and suggestions in *The Transfigured Church*, not to mention the strong social emphasis in *God—Our Contemporary* (1922), Gerald Kennedy is certainly wrong in saying 'you will read in vain for any prophetic pronouncements on the sins of society' (*The Best of John Henry Jowett*, 1948, p. xv).

[2] *The Preacher, His Life and Work*, pp. 80–81.

[3] E. H. Jeffs certainly held this view. See *Princes of the Modern Pulpit*, pp. 67–68.

preacher's message.[1] Sometimes Jowett allowed his imagery to become so tropical that it almost drugged the senses, apart from smothering the sense. He knew this was a real danger, admitting that 'I have seen illustrations that are like pretty drawing-room lamps, drawing attention to themselves.' The best illustrations, he added, should be like honest street lamps, 'scarcely noticed but throwing floods of light upon the road.'[2] Presumably it was on account of the danger of distracting by decorativeness that he pruned his style in the years in New York and Westminster, for it is noticeable that his illustrations were fewer and more concise in the sermons of these years. A preacher's preacher as Jowett was, because of the finish of his technique, yet there were laymen who found the artifice cloying and, in expounding such themes as the Cross, an aesthetic intrusion. While all persuasion is, it might be argued, an art, yet some kinds of art are inappropriate for certain themes. The stark black-edged outlines and subdued hues of a Rouault or the nightmarish evocations of a Bosch seem more suitable for the Crucifixion than the pastel shades, the flowing lines and the artificial Arcadian delicacy of a Watteau or the jewelled decoration and stylism of the Pre-Raphaelites. There was clearly more of Rossetti than Rouault in Jowett's preaching style.

A related criticism was the charge of Gammie, who had heard all the famous preachers of the day, that Jowett's control of his voice was too perfect, too admirably

[1] For a badly mixed metaphor see *The Transfigured Church*, p. 224: '. . . some flower of the woods, growing there in a bed as rich as a bride's cake.'

[2] *The Preacher, His Life and Work* (1912), p. 141.

modulated, in a word, *contrived.*[1] He did not break out from his careful cadences and balanced antitheses, from his exquisite similes, and from his measured pace, into the blazing anger of righteous indignation which fractures rhetorical rules. He never slipped into unpremeditated asides or side-stepped, led by momentary inspirations. He seemed at times a rhetorical robot, the perfect imitation of a man—as if interior clockwork had set a Madame Tussaud's waxwork figure in motion. If this criticism is valid, it can only be partly so, otherwise the admiration of a Sir William Robertson Nicoll is inexplicable, not to mention the appreciation of thousands for whom he was *the* preacher of their lives.

Our final evaluation is that John Henry Jowett is an exceptionally able exponent of the devotional type of preaching in an excessively utilitarian age, who realized better than most of his fellows that no sacrificial service for God or men is ever accomplished apart from adoration in Christian worship which is the frankincense of obedience. This immaculate man, who might have been mistaken for a banker or a Harley Street medical specialist, was the Brother Lawrence of the pulpit, the practical mystic for whom every common bush was afire with God. We may close with an anecdote which reveals his modesty, humanity, humour, and devotion to the living God. Jowett recounts that when he was in Northfield he went out early one morning to conduct a devotional meeting in the woods for two or three hundred men

[1] *Preachers I have Heard*, p. 61: 'It was, perhaps, his control of himself in the pulpit which prevented him from exercising over his hearers that overmastering, overwhelming effect of some other preachers.'

from the Water Street Mission of New York City. The rest must be told in Jowett's own words:

> At the beginning of the service prayer was offered for me and the prayer opened with this inspired supplication: 'O Lord, we thank you for our brother. Now blot him out!' And the prayer continued: 'Reveal Thy glory to us in such blazing splendour that he shall be forgotten.' It was absolutely right and I trust the prayer was answered.[1]

[1] *The Preacher, His Life and Work*, pp. 150–151.

3

Reasonable Preaching

BISHOP HENSON & DEAN INGE

THE Church of England has claimed, since the time of Hooker, to honour Scripture, the tradition of the Early Church, and the use of reason. The Evangelicals have given first place to Scripture and the High Churchmen a primacy to tradition. It has been the distinction of Liberal Churchmen greatly to honour reason and in this succession have been the Cambridge Platonists of the seventeenth, the Latitudinarians of the eighteenth, the Broad Churchmen of the nineteenth, and the moderate Modernists of the twentieth century. Bishop Hensley Henson and his friend Dean Inge are notable exponents of this tradition in the pulpit. Indeed, in several respects they are alike. Their audacity and originality of utterance, their constant insistence that conduct is the true test of creed, their requirement that religion be reasonable, and their gift for lucid and even incisive expression, made them brothers in the cloth. Each was a stormy petrel finding his wings in leaden, controversial skies.

1 · *The Career and Character of Henson*

Henson was successively Fellow of All Souls College, Oxford, Head of Oxford House settlement in Bethnal

Green, Vicar of the great industrial parish of Barking in Essex, Canon of Westminster Abbey and Rector of St Margaret's (the parish church of the House of Commons), Dean of Durham, Bishop of Hereford, and, finally, from 1920 to 1939, Bishop of Durham. Possessing a mind of singular independence and maturity, trained in the long perspectives of history, which he expressed with cogent clarity in consummate English prose, he gave himself during a long and distinguished career to the perfecting of his preaching. His sermons, both for lucidity and originality as well as wisdom, are probably less faded for the modern reader than those of any of his eminent contemporaries, including even Archbishop William Temple and Bishop Charles Gore. The three volumes of his *Retrospect of an Unimportant Life* belie their modest title and constitute a brilliant interpretation of the life of the National Church during this troubled century in which he was himself a central figure, when he was not a penetrating spectator. The same work abounds in wise comments on the changing status and tasks of the clergyman and preacher.

To call this type of preaching 'reasonable' is no depreciation. No man was more critical of emotional appeals, windy rhetoric, or cheap demagoguery in the pulpit than Henson. He liked sermons to be lucid expositions of central themes in the Bible illuminating the will of God for human duty to which any person of spiritual insight and common sense would respond. His is sound, solid, clear, practical preaching at its best: its originality consists, not in daring images or flights of fancy, but in penetrating judgments expressed in pithy and pellucid prose.

Henson's was a manly and candid temper, the foe of pretentiousness alike in Church and State, whether expounded by overweening prelate or by arrogant politician. His devotion to the Christian faith and life expressed itself in undeviating insistence that the proof of the Christian creed was the decisive deeds done in Christ's name. He valued the Protestant, Catholic and National characteristics of the Church of England and ceased to be an apologist for the Establishment of it only when he believed that the rejection of the revised Prayer Book by Parliament demonstrated that Establishment was too high a price to pay for the loss of spiritual independence.

Although his frankness and integrity of life made foes, it is significant that the clergy of his diocese at his farewell summed up his two decades of rule as Bishop of Durham as 'a great and generous episcopate.' Dr C. A. Alington, a successor of Henson's in the Deanery of Durham, expressed his affectionate admiration in a poem which includes these lines that sketch him to life:

Here, with the warrior bishops of the past
We lay in peace of that long line the last;
Unresting soul, predestined from his youth
To ceaseless combat for the cause of truth. . . .
He waged, as led by some peculiar star,
With power and prejudice a truceless war:
While craven souls the big battalions seek,
He pledged his sword to service of the weak,
And self-consistent to a life's long end
Forgave no folly and forsook no friend. . . .
Still ready to unsheathe against his foes
The stainless steel of perfect English prose,
Or launch barbed shafts of epigram and wit

Which stung to laughter even those they hit:
Never by earth's injustices unmoved,
Lover of children and by children loved,
One whom though fools might fear, his flock could trust,
Gallant and generous, and wise and just
A fearless critic, who yet never swerved
From loyalty to that great Faith he served. . . .[1]

Honoured by a succession of high offices within the Church of England, he was greatly respected far beyond its borders. Yale University invited him to deliver the Lyman Beecher Lectures on Preaching in 1909, and a challenging volume, *The Liberty of Prophesying*, embodied the results. Twenty-six years later he delivered the Gifford Lectures at St Andrews University on the theme of Christian Morality.

2 · *The Development of a Candid Mind*

Henson, the chief shepherd of two dioceses, sometimes had the mien of a lone wolf. He came of an undisciplined mercantile family and was very largely a self-educated man. At Oxford he was an unattached student, unassociated with any college, and read for a History degree because that was the shortest course of study he could take. It was only when he had gained a first class honours degree and had been successfully examined for a Fellowship of All Souls College that he found himself in a brilliant and congenial society that gave him a sense of security. He deliberated some time before deciding to take holy orders (like that other great prelate, Archbishop William Temple).

[1] *Retrospect of an Unimportant Life,* vol. III (1950), p. vi.

It is significant that his delay in accepting the yoke of ordination was due to a fear of losing his soul in bondage to a party within the Church. In this state of mind he walked to the Norman church of Iffley, stood at the altar of the empty church, and there took a vow 'that I would never let considerations of my personal reputation and advantage influence my public course.' Recalling this decision, he added many years later: 'I was then poor and unknown; I knew that independence, which is the *heritage* of the powerful and wealthy, must be the *trophy* of the poor.'[1]

This virile honesty marked every stage of his life. It was characteristic that, when he published the first sermon he had preached as Head of the Oxford House settlement, he prefaced it with these words: 'I do not care one straw about popularity for I know that it is generally purchased by a sacrifice of the truth.'[2] When there was a tendency in the early years of the twentieth century for preachers to prepare sermons expounding Scripture without any reference to the principles of historical criticism, presumably to avoid worrying the congregations or even perhaps to avoid charges of heresy being levelled at the preacher himself, it was Henson as Rector of St. Margaret's who nailed his critical colours to the mast, and published his views in the volume *The Creed in the Pulpit* (1912). Similarly, when the obscure and zealously orthodox set up a hue and cry at his appointment as Bishop of Hereford and even tried to encourage his future clergy in disaffection, and the Archbishop of Canterbury besought him to give reassurances as to his orthodoxy, Henson remained silent.

[1] *Ibid.*, I (1942), p. 76.

[2] *Ibid.*, I, p. 27.

He contended that even though he could neither affirm nor deny the Virgin Birth of Christ, yet he firmly accepted the Incarnation, and that those who wished to find such statements could discover them in his books. He felt it was undignified to bow to the storm and unbecoming to a man of candour. Throughout his life, whether criticizing the Oxford Group, the Romanizing tendencies of Anglo-Catholics, the wilder forms of 'corybantic Christianity,' or the partisanship with which many clergy jumped on to the Socialist bandwagon, he stuck to his guns and stood by his friends.

For such an individualist of rectitude and generosity, the acceptance of a party badge, ecclesiastical or political, would have been as welcome as a straitjacket. The true intermediary was inevitably attacked by the Anglo-Catholics as strongly as by the Evangelicals. Yet his loneliness was his spiritual and moral strength. 'I hate and deplore religious division,' he said. 'Every High Churchman assumes that I must be a rigid "Catholic." I exalt individual responsibility and freedom. Every Dissenter claims me as an ally. But I am in neither camp—a "crossbench" man, abhorrent to all good partisans everywhere.'[1]

One can readily understand his admiration for those men of the 'middle way,' George Herbert and Richard Baxter of the seventeenth century, and Robertson of Brighton of the nineteenth century. In fact, part of his strength derived from his deep understanding of the history of the Anglican Communion.

It comes out clearly in these words in which as Father-in-God he commends to his sons in the faith:

[1] *Ibid.*, I, pp. 76–77.

'You are to be ordained in a very sacred place, for as you traverse this chapel you must pass over the grave of Bishop Cosin, and, as you kneel for the laying on of hands, you will be kneeling on the grave of Bishop Lightfoot. Very near will be Bishop Westcott's grave. I am addressing you now from a place where once was seen the frail but noble form of Bishop Butler. Think of it, my sons, and glory in your heritage as English clergymen. Cosin, Butler, Lightfoot, Westcott—the statesman, the philosopher, the scholar, the mystic—adding each one his distinctive glory to this famous see, remind you that you hold your ministry in a Church which has been illustrious in Christendom.' Like the Puritan divines, Henson lived in the fear of God and so was unafraid of men.

3 · *Varieties of Preaching*

A felicitous historical and apologetical writer, as well as a pungent diarist and essayist, and a brilliant disputant in both the House of Lords and in Convocation, Henson concentrated his gifts of mind and heart on preaching. He excelled in many different types of preaching and in varied contexts.

His sermons were prepared with the Greek New Testament open before him and not only was every word written in a careful hand, but even when he preached an old sermon again it was almost always altered to make its beginning suited to the particular parish in which he delivered it.[1] In his later years he wondered if perhaps he had not spent too much time in

[1] See the preface by C. J. Stranks to Henson's *Theology and Life*, pp. 7–8.

polishing and repolishing his sermons. In his earlier days he possessed the gift of extemporary speech; but had he been too fastidious in the choice of the right word and the telling epigram? Henson concluded that he had no alternative: 'Should I be able to face the Judge with a less troubled spirit? Or should I have degenerated into the type, so familiar in the religious world, which is not unfairly described as a WINDBAG?'[1]

On another occasion when he was placed, as retired bishop, immediately under the pulpit of a fashionable seaside church he had to endure a rhapsodical utterance on the theme that the first Pentecostal experience could be renewed in exact detail, down to experiences of cloven tongues of fire and the gift of speaking in diverse tongues. As Henson left, the preacher asked him, 'Was I too unorthodox for you?' The bishop replied: 'It was not its unorthodoxy which disturbed me, but its incredibility.' Henson commented in his journal: 'I came away from church with a vivid realization of the chasm that separates popular Christianity, whether Catholic or Protestant, from reasonable religion.'[2]

He preached with the very minimum of gesture and despised both rhetoric and rehearsal. In the latter connection, he quoted Tyrrell with appreciation: 'I can forgive a woman easily who paints, enamels, and dyes, but a preacher who practises his sermon before a cheval glass (as some of our French celebrities do) seems to me farther away from God and reality than the blackest atheist in existence.'[3]

[1] *Retrospect of an Unimportant Life*, III, p. 312.
[2] *Ibid.*, III, pp. 326–327.
[3] *Church and Parson in England* (1927), p. 144.

A good sermon has four essentials in his judgment: interest, intelligibility, relevance, and edification.[1] Interest commands and holds the attention; intelligibility assures it is understood; relevance is necessary for it to be effective; and edification ensures that it improves the hearer.

His own sermons were admirable illustrations of his teaching. Even the least controversial of them immediately gripped the interest of the congregation because they were concerned with the central issue of belief and ethics. His sermon structure was as lucid as his diction. He always commended his teaching by its utter reasonableness. His constant aim was to claim the primacy of Christian faith and duty, as he saw them.

The superficial observer might assume that his brusqueness of manner, and even occasional asperity, were the reflex of an intellectual snob. No judgment could be more mistaken. He rightly judged of himself that 'Nature had endowed me with a sceptical intellect, a sensitive conscience, a considerable power of self-expression in lucid and incisive speech, and a warm heart.'[2] It is most moving to reflect that after all his years of acclaim in the highest offices of the Church, he was to consider that 'the happiest years of my ministry were those in which, as the vicar of a great industrial parish, I was nearest to the people. Faces look out at me from the past—toil-worn faces radiant with love and confidence. Nothing of what men foolishly call success is worth comparison with the experiences which those faces recall.'[3] These words were spoken after fifty years in the sacred ministry.

[1] *Ibid.*, p. 140.
[2] *Retrospect*, I, p. 21.
[3] *Ad Clerum* (1937), p. 210.

His experience of preaching was extraordinarily rich and wide. In Bethnal Green and Barking Henson preached to artisans, skilled and unskilled. In Ilford Hospital he had a congregation of clerks and shop assistants. In Westminster he had an influential and educated congregation. In Durham he preached to all sorts and conditions of men and women, professional folk and miners, and not infrequently to the unemployed. In Hereford most of the congregations were rural. He preached to the academics in the universities and to the lawyers in the Inns of Court.

4 · *The Qualities of Henson's Preaching*

Henson had the capacity of the great preacher to identify himself with the capacities and interests of his hearers, without playing down to them. He had the right but different approach for a great commemorative occasion in a cathedral, for a 'political' sermon addressed to the members of Parliament attending St Margaret's Church, Westminster, or for a parochial sermon in Barking, Ilford, or in the dioceses of Hereford and Durham.

Wherever he preached, certain qualities would be marked. First, the choice of a text that would admirably summarize his message. Then a clear structure, usually making two, three or four cogent points. Thirdly, the sentences and the choice of words would be the lucid index of a clear and wise head. Every now and then there would be a memorably minted phrase or epigram that etched itself on the memory; frequently it would be ironic and caustic. And it would be unusual if Henson's candour did not prick some bubble of pretension or prepare a surprise.

Sometimes there is an incisive word for the clergy: 'If a slumberous habit of almost unconscious indolence is the besetting sin of the largely unemployed rural incumbent, a futile and fussy multiplication of engagements which rather obscures than interprets spiritual duty is the besetting sin of his urban brother.'[1] Another time he stalks larger prey, as on the Sunday in 1908 when the Bishops assembled for the Fifth Lambeth Conference received the Holy Communion in Westminster Abbey: 'Our prayer for those Bishops at Lambeth will be the prayer that they may be given grace of denominational self-suppression, that is, the power of a true spiritual perspective, the insight which distinguishes between the essentials and non-essentials of religion, which recognizes the truth even in novel and unwelcome forms and rises to obey the truth it sees.'[2]

On yet another occasion he shows how a self-regarding spirit has twisted the Beatitudes so that what they now mean is a parody of themselves:

> Blessed are they who have a high notion of their own rights, for they shall secure deference and high regard.
> Blessed are the light-hearted and the unthinking, for they shall enjoy life.
> Blessed are the ambitious, for they shall rise in the world.
> Blessed are the opportunists, for they shall escape disaster.
> Blessed are the close-fisted, for they shall make money.
> Blessed are the self-indulgent, for they shall make the most of life.

[1] *Retrospect*, III, p. 15.
[2] *Westminster Sermons* (1910), p. 95.

Blessed are the litigious and self-assertive, for they shall inherit the earth.

Blessed are the time-serving, for they shall be honoured.[1]

Henson rarely loses the severity of the prophet in the pulpit. Even when his theme is Easter, he resists any temptation to smother the message with lilies! His sermon is entitled 'Easter, the Festival of Other Worldism.' Its first two notes are enfranchisement and aspiration, but the third is responsibility. 'There is in the Easter message the note of solemn warning. Beyond the grace stands the Judge, and before Him must be laid open all the secrets of human lives.'[2]

He is not less the prophet in refusing to take the easy way of the 'Social Gospel.' Deep as his sympathy for the artisans was, he knew that men in the long run will weary of the partisan parson, and that 'only by the slow method of individual redemption can the Church contribute anything distinctive to social improvement.'[3] The perennial contribution of Christianity to the life of society, he insisted, is threefold. The Gospel brings to the world in its assurance of God's redemptive purpose for all men the gift of social hope. It also brings to those who receive it the conviction that social service is a religious duty. Finally, the Gospel also brings to everyone who receives it the conviction that personal righteousness is a social duty and the very condition for performing effective social service.[4]

Henson is not only the prophet, he is also the minister of consolation and the tutor in spirituality. His sermons

[1] *Ibid.*, p. 237. [2] *The Creed in the Pulpit*, p. 162.

[3] *Bishoprick Papers* (1946), p. 180.

[4] *Westminster Sermons*, No. XVIII, 'The Social Influence of Christianity.'

published in *Ad Clerum* and his ordination charges contained in *Church and Parson in England* provide a rich introduction to spiritual duty in preaching, celebrating the Sacraments, and visitation. His incidental sermons delivered to various parish churches in the diocese of Durham and recently collected under the title *Theology and Life* (1958) are admirable for their concise instruction on the Christian faith and life. They would be suitable in any church because of their relevance and wisdom.

The following are some of the pivotal topics he treats: The Source of Hope; The Conversion of St Paul; The Picture of a Christian Church; Christ the Author of Division and Peace; The Lordship of Jesus. It would be tempting to follow their intriguing development, and to note the unusual and apt quotations selected from a well-stored mind, the striking anecdotes, the memorable epigrams, and the arrow-like devout and direct conclusions.

It must suffice to let one sermon in this collection illustrate all. I select for summary the sermon with the rather unpromising title: 'Disinterested Service.' The text is I Peter 1.8: 'Whom not having seen, ye love.' Henson begins by referring to a *Hibbert Journal* article by Claude Montefiore entitled 'What a Jew thinks about Jesus,' in which Jowett of Balliol is quoted as saying that he cannot understand how Thomas à Kempis could feel a personal attachment to Christ since he had died so many centuries ago. It strikes Henson as odd that Jowett as an ordained minister of Christ should find any difficulty in this respect.

The transition is then made to St Peter who is also intrigued that thousands who have never seen the earthly Christ can love him even through persecution. But, says Henson, this can be said of Christians in every century since with equal truth. The secret of the Master's unique posthumous influence is the Resurrection. 'Indeed, nothing else can explain it. For the only condition under which personal influence can survive is contact.' The proof of the contact is that Christ stamps on his followers the likeness of himself and men cannot but 'take knowledge of them that they have been with Jesus.'

The Christian character is fully exhibited in him and derivatively so in his followers. His title is a servant and the lowest order of the ministry bears the same, as deacon, and the strongest impulse to service is the example of humility he showed when on the eve of the Passion he washed his disciples' feet.

Public service appeals to the patriotism and pride of men who receive the homage of their contemporaries. But personal service may be unnoticed, is often unattractive and even repulsive among the poor, the sick and the unfortunate. It only appeals to those who are filled with disinterested and serviceable love which perpetuates on earth the spirit of Jesus.

From this Henson passes to de Tocqueville's *Democracy in America* in which the prophet commented on American religion that it had been deeply secularized, exchanging the motives, inspirations and hopes of the next world for earth-born and earth-bound hopes. Is that not increasingly true of English religion in this day?

Religion cannot be presented as a way of gain: it is fitly symbolized by the Cross. Henson concludes with an episode in Joinville's *Life of St Louis* of France, which he heard of when a prisoner among the Moslems. A religious brother saw an old woman carrying a chafing-dish of fire in one hand and a cruse of water in the other. She said that she wanted to burn up heaven with fire and quench hell with water so that no man would do right for the reward of heaven or the fear of hell, but just to win the love of God.

The sermon ends: 'May God bless this Church with an unfailing succession of loving, devoted men and women who, in face of all difficulties and discouragements, will witness in character and service to the Presence with them of Jesus Christ, "Whom not having seen, they love."'

It can be seen, even in digested form, that this is a twenty-minute masterpiece on Christian ethics, inspired by Christ's own example.

For all his lucidity, profundity and relevance, Bishop Henson was not always appreciated. The truth can sting like iodine on an open wound; however healing the intent, it can be misconstrued. He sometimes thought he had only attained 'the dolorous distinction of a *succès de scandale*.'[1] His ecumenical concern, his criticism of Tractarian exclusiveness and of Evangelical heresy-hunting, which he occasionally described as the 'Protestant underworld,' were bound to make enemies. On one occasion when he was preaching in Westminster Abbey a Minor Canon, sitting directly under the pulpit, 'disclosed his disgust by ostentatiously reading a newspaper' and Henson frequently received letters that were more insulting than intelligent.

[1] *Retrospect*, III, p. 312.

Such prophetic spirits as his scorn the tact of the wily ecclesiastical diplomat and the mealy-mouthed mumbling of the time-server; but their sharpness sometimes gives needless offence. This is particularly the case when they speak the truth but not in love, and occasionally confuse their own irritability with Divine inspiration. Bishop Henson, as in his change from supporting the Establishment to wishing the Church disestablished, did not allow sufficiently for the public to appreciate the factors which had brought about the change, and hence was judged to be a prelatical equivalent of the Vicar of Bray. His rate of speaking was rapid, about 180 or 190 words a minute, his dislike of sentimentality acute, and his manner occasionally brusque—so that he was admired by many and loved by the few who had penetrated the dignified and daring exterior to the warm heart which it disguised.

What is chiefly significant, however, is that neither his love of scholarship nor the demands of administration in a vast diocese, ever deflected him from his primary commitment to preaching.

When his official portrait was painted as Bishop of Durham, Dr Henson decided that he would be apparelled in a preacher's gown rather than in the familiar red and white of his convocation dress. But, instead of holding the conventional book between his hands, he rather grasped the historic sword of his great Norman predecessor, Anthony Bek. That is a parable of his struggle for truth, and perhaps also of an unconcealed love of pugnacity for its own sake.

5 · The Paradoxical Personality of Inge

During his time as Dean of St Paul's Cathedral in London (1911–1934) Inge was, if not the most famous, certainly the most quoted clergyman in the modern world. He was wise as he was witty. Bernard Shaw regarded him as 'the greatest intellectual asset of the English Church.'[1] A perceptive journalist, Harold Begbie, declared that 'his intellect has the range of an Acton, his forthrightness is the match of Dr Johnson's, and his wit less biting than Voltaire's has the illuminating quality, if not the divine playfulness, of the wit of Socrates.'[2] Less exaggerated than Begbie's was the evaluation of the Earl of Oxford and Asquith, who, as Prime Minister, had recommended him for royal nomination as the Dean of St Paul's. 'He is,' said Asquith, 'a strange, isolated figure, with all the culture in the world, and a curiously developed gift of expression, but with kinks and twists both intellectual and temperamental. Still he is one of the few ecclesiastics in these days who is really interesting.'[3] His biographer, Canon Adam Fox of Westminster, claims that as a result of a combination of brains and personality Inge was 'the most famous ecclesiastic and one of the most famous writers of the time.'[4]

For all his eminence (and perhaps this is a clue to the fascination of his personality) Dean Inge was a paradox.

[1] Sidney Dark, *Five Deans* (1928), p. 211. Archbishop William Temple outshone Inge, however, intellectually.

[2] *Painted Windows* by 'A Gentleman with a Duster' (1922), p. 45.

[3] *Memories and Reflections* (1928), cited by Adam Fox in *Dean Inge* (1960), p. xiii.

[4] *Ibid.*, p. xiii.

J. H. Jowett: the photograph by which he is remembered at Carrs Lane Church, Birmingham

'Dick' Sheppard of St Martin-in-the-Fields

Dr H. H. Henson

W. R. Inge as Dean of St Paul's in 1923

It is unlikely that any housemaster at Eton, or Cambridge don at King's, or fellow member of the senior common room at Hertford College, Oxford, or even any of the three Judges who regularly heard him preach in the select congregation of All Saints', Ennismore Gardens, in London, would have predicted that Inge would become the religious oracle of England.[1]

He combined characteristics and aptitudes that are normally exclusive. He was a mystic and a critical savant. A famous preacher, who was not only the antithesis of the popular preacher as commonly conceived, he deplored the 'court-chaplains of King Demos' who accommodated their religion to the needs of the present and played shamelessly to the gallery. This renowned preacher had none of the arts of oratory, read almost every word from his manuscript, and even described preaching as 'trying to fill rows of narrow necked vessels by throwing buckets of water over them.'[2] The man who was a failure as an Eton schoolmaster because he could not keep discipline, yet believed that English society was disintegrating for lack of discipline and was his own sternest taskmaster. This passionate advocate of the new science of eugenics was disappointed that his own children did not emulate his own scholastic successes, although he later came to feel that two of his children were saints.[3]

[1] Inge went back to Eton as assistant master in 1884; afterwards he was Fellow at King's, Cambridge (1886–1888), Fellow and Tutor at Hertford College, Oxford (1889–1904), Vicar of All Saints', Ennismore Gardens (1905–1907), and Lady Margaret Professor of Divinity at Cambridge (1907–1911).

[2] *Goodness and Truth* (1958), pp. 5–6.

[3] His seraphic daughter Paula died as a saint at the age of 11. His son, Richard, although as a clergyman he could have been

The supposedly 'Gloomy Dean' (a title given him by the *Daily Mail*) repeatedly spoke of the joy of the Christian faith, and the so-called cynic thanked God for his marriage and his family as the chief of blessings. The chief paradox was that this intellectual ascetic, epigrammatist, ironist, classicist, philosopher and savant, was the chief exponent of the mystical tradition in the modern Anglican Church, and that the formidable exterior masked a man who could say as truly as St Paul that the motive of his life was, 'the love of Christ constraineth me.'

Inge was, indeed, an unlikely candidate for nomination as a prince of preachers, from several considerations. His was an exceptionally cloistered life, and he had only three years of parish experience. Apart from his ministry at All Saints', Ennismore Gardens, itself a very pleasant and select parish, Inge's life had been spent almost entirely in the company of university men. His own father was a Fellow and later Provost of Worcester College, Oxford, and his wife's uncle was the famous Spooner, Warden of New College, Oxford. He was both pupil and teacher at Eton, as at King's College, Cambridge. Moreover, he had the unusual distinction of being an honorary Fellow of three colleges: at King's and Jesus, Cambridge, and at Hertford, Oxford. He lived the life of a schoolmaster for four years and of a don and professor for twenty-two years and, even as Dean of St Paul's in the heart of the metropolis, he

exempted from military service, was burned to death trying to rescue a stunned pilot, who had crash-landed, from beneath a burning plane. See Adam Fox, *Dean Inge* (1960), pp. 184–185; 251–252; and *Personal Religion and the Life of Devotion* (1924), pp. 87–96.

had singularly few parochial responsibilities. His life until 1911 was among the intellectuals and leaders of the country, and he was frequently in the same company as host, after-dinner speaker, lecturer and preacher after that time. The point is that he knew little of middle-class life and nothing of the working classes, so he had not that deep sympathy with all kinds and conditions of men that is almost indispensable for a great preacher. A longer and diversified parish experience would have rectified what can only be considered a serious disadvantage.

Furthermore, his was an aloof, introverted personality. Only once (in recording the loss of his young daughter Paula in *Personal Religion and the Life of Devotion*) did Inge allow his tenderness to break through the veils of reserve.

Inge shatters the stereotype of great preaching in a third respect. Great preachers, though thoroughly well prepared, toss aside the manuscript in the pulpit in order to grapple in a face-to-face encounter with the souls of the congregation, that they may modify their pace or diction or add instances or illustrations to elicit understanding and acceptance. This was the concession Inge never made to his congregation. For this reason he is best thought of as a lecturer in the pulpit rather than a preacher. In giving up one advantage, that of immediacy, he gained another, that of a superb literary finish.

6 · *Reluctant Fame*

It is also strange that he, who despised popular preachers, became one. He described popular preachers as those who 'adulterate our message to suit the popular taste.'[1] The root cause of such preaching was, he believed, faithlessness and impatience: the Gospel was believed to be inadequate and God's slow methods were deemed inefficient. Such faithless impatience, in Inge's view, took two current forms. Many clergy rushed into political and social pronouncements, 'a task for which they were unprepared by any serious study of economics and political philosophy.'[2] Agitation was not the business of the Church. Indeed, to preach the 'Social Gospel' was, in his view, to fall prey to the very temptation in the wilderness which Christ had spurned, namely, of turning stones into bread for the masses. On this precise point Inge had written in the *Speculum Animae* of Christ: 'He will not make His way into men's hearts through their stomachs, or give His countenance to Platonic Republics or Socialistic Utopias.'[3]

The second form which popular preaching took was pandering to men's superficial wants, not their deeper needs. In his view it was a dereliction of ministerial duties to blunt the incisive demands of the Gospel, which is cruel in judgment that it may be kind in consolation. 'The average person,' he truly said, 'wants something less austerely moral, less intellectual, more exciting and amusing, than the Gospel of Christ.'[4] To provide such minimal wants was, in Inge's view, not preaching, but arrant exploitation. It should be clear, however, that it is not intelligence but sincerity that Inge regarded as the prime requirement in preaching. 'It is,' he insisted, 'God and not the speaker, who can make the poor sounds

[1] *Death the Gate of Life* (1935), p. 20.
[2] *Ibid.*, p. 21.
[3] *Ibid.*, p. 21.
[4] *The Gate of Life*, p. 22.

of the human voice the vehicles of grace, and it is the sincere word, not the clever one, which is most likely thus to be honoured.'[1] Certainly it was Inge's utter veracity, even on the most controversial issues, where ecclesiastical diplomats would have been silent, or have trimmed their sails to the wind, that helped to account for his renown. He would, however, have been the first to recognize the validity of Phillips Brooks' definition of preaching as 'truth through personality,' provided the emphasis was on *truth.* Indeed, he recognized that 'it is the religious teacher, not the religious lesson, that helps the pupil to believe.'[2] He became popular because he swam so boldly against the stream. Men who were tired of tranquillizers in the pulpit rallied to the Dean's tonic; sickened by popular sedatives they responded to the spur of his intellect.

One further proof that he was a famous preacher, almost despite himself, is seen in the eagerness and brilliance with which he taught the London masses who never entered the portals of Wren's masterpiece through the wider pulpit of journalism. A wag might remark that Dean Inge thought that he was the pillar of the Church, but he was only two columns in the *Evening Standard*; yet it was by these literary columns that he supported his pulpit reputation, and, it may be said, gained recognition for the Christian perspective in contemporary affairs.

7 · *Reasons for Renown*

What was the secret of Dean Inge's fame as a preacher? A large element in it was his outspokenness.

[1] *Speculum Animae*, p. 1.　　[2] *Ibid.*, p. 39.

For example, in a Cambridge University congregation which undoubtedly included many clerical collars, he reminded the undergraduates that Christ's enemies were 'the ecclesiastics, priests and scribes, the theologians and lawyers, and the formally strict traditionalists, the Pharisees. Organized Churches make no mistakes when their vital interests are threatened. A priest is never so happy as when he has a prophet to stone.'[1] To the same congregation, which undoubtedly included many stalwart defenders of the apostolic succession, he challenged the accepted ecclesiastical definition by saying: 'The only true apostolic succession is the lives of the saints.'[2] Even the lecturers did not escape his irony as he remarked that Christianity 'is a way of walking, not talking.'[3] Similarly, when he was leading a devotional retreat for clergymen at Wells Cathedral, he reminded them that those who had helped him most in life were not clergymen, nor even laymen, but women: 'It does not seem to me that clever books and brilliant sermons have done so much for me as those chance glimpses into characters far above my own.'[4] Authoritarianism and sacerdotalism were anathema to this apostle of liberty.

He can be equally direct with the laymen, parading an exquisite malady of the spirit: 'There is such a thing as vulgarity in the spiritual life. It would be better for some people if they thought less of their souls and how to save them.'[5] Candidness was the consuming fire for him, a devastating honesty. He told a group of English travellers in Bordighera, in a sermon on 'Truth in Love,' that

[1] *Things New and Old* (1933), p. 48.
[2] *Ibid.*, p. 57.
[3] *Ibid.*, p. 2.
[4] *Faith and Knowledge*, p. 228.
[5] *Ibid.*, p. 64.

'Intellectual honesty is not, I am afraid, an English virtue. We are too much disposed to regard compromise as a proof of common sense, and to apply the principles of the British Constitution to the world of thought. We rather pride ourselves on being illogical; our enemies naturally call us hypocritical. And we are terrible partisans. . . .'[1] What he considered to be the envy and utopianism that lay beneath Socialism were also targets of his preaching. In the pulpit he showed the relevance and superiority of Christianity to an external political reform by a profound definition: 'Real Christianity is a revolutionary idealism, which estranges the conservatives because it is revolutionary, and the revolutionary because it is idealistic.'[2] In brief, Inge committed himself to the cause of honest religion, because it was in line with the integrity of his life and because it was conspicuously lacking in the public utterances of the leaders of his own Church. On the latter he declared: 'Most of the leading Churchmen, though socially much in evidence, are intellectually in hiding.'[3]

His gift for terse, epigrammatic sayings was another factor in his success. This encapsulated wisdom, which is wit, gives his sermons their unique flavour. Arguing that the Christian mystic seeks, not flight, but fight, Inge insists that otherwise 'we shall grasp at infinity and find zero.'[4] Or, when asserting that the opposite of joy is boredom, he remarks that doctors should prescribe for sufferers from ennui not a rest-cure, but a 'work-cure.'[5] Christianity, because it is other-worldly in its

[1] *Ibid.*, p. 101.
[2] *Personal Religion and the Life of Devotion*, p. 81.
[3] *Labels and Libels*, p. 260.
[4] *Personal Religion and the Life of Devotion*, p. 56. [5] *Ibid.*, p. 67.

inspiration and its end, he defines as 'a radical optimism, behind a superficial pessimism.'[1] A typical epigrammatic statement contrasts the Greek anthropology with that of the present age: 'The Greeks prided themselves on being the degenerate descendants of gods, we on being the very creditable descendants of monkeys.'[2] His best epigram, for my choice, is applied to the dangers of doctrinal dilution and it is significant of Inge's self-criticism that this *bon mot* is the creation of a Liberal theologian. The admonition goes thus: 'If you marry the spirit of the generation, you will be a widow in the next.'[3] With it may be compared Dr Johnson's judgment of Addison, that 'he thinks justly, but he thinks faintly.' As a single example of Inge's irony, we may take Inge's appraisal of Ruskin: 'He was a protestant mediaevalist, who admired everything in the mediaeval cathedral except the altar.'[4]

An incandescent veracity, a brilliant turn of the epigram and irony, and the unusual combination of Christian scholar, moralist, and mystic, these three qualities together account for the uniqueness of Dean Inge's impress on the mind and heart of the age. Canon E. W. Barnes (later to be the controversial Bishop of Birmingham) discerned this unusual combination as he introduced Inge to a large London audience at the Peace Meeting at Caxton Hall in 1921: 'The Dean needs no

[1] *Ibid.*, p. 82.

[2] *Diary of a Dean, St Paul's 1911–1934* (1950), p. 190. It is part of his 1920 Oxford Romanes Lectures on 'The Idea of Progress' republished.

[3] *Ibid.*, p. 12.

[4] *Ibid.*, p. 221, a citation from his Cambridge Rede Lecture of 1922 on 'The Victorian Age.'

introduction to an English audience. Our people are often surprised that an intellect so keen and piercing into human affairs should yet belong to so great a divine and the greatest mystic of the age.'[1]

8 · *A Dean's Deficiencies*

Granting Inge the remarkable qualities which we have listed and illustrated, there were yet some serious defects in his preaching. His style of writing was described as 'frosty elegance' and there is something of the iceberg in Dean Inge's pulpit presence, even if the sunlight of an eternal mysticism occasionally breaks through the clouded northern skies. He might quote Keats, but unlike him he was not 'one for whom the miseries of the world are miseries and will not let him rest.' It is a disadvantage for any famous preacher if he can only bow to instead of embracing humanity in its poverty as well as affluence, in its simplicity as well as in its sophistication. Like the aborigines of Borneo, Dean Inge was a head-hunter, even if a very sophisticated one.

It is clear also that he was, for all his alleged pursuit of the Greek triad of eternal values, deficient in the appreciation of beauty. His taste for art was merely conventional and it was appropriate that he should be a trustee of the National Portrait Gallery, not of the more contemporary Tate. He seemed to share none of the delights of his predecessors in St Paul's Cathedral in the splendour of the ceremonial or the glory of the music. On the contrary, the entry in his diary on 28th May 1911 (his first Sunday in St Paul's) reads: 'Spent nearly

[1] *Ibid.*, p. 70.

the whole day in the Church 8–9; 10.30–1.15; 3.15–4.15; 7–8.30. I have never before had work to do which wounded my conscience, but those services seem to me a criminal waste of time. I have held different views at different times about the character and nature of the Creator of the Universe; but never at any time have I thought it at all probable that He is the kind of person who enjoys being serenaded!'[1]

He seemed, despite his Tractarian upbringing, utterly incapable of understanding the strong current of Anglo-Catholicism in the Church of England. Only in his later apologetic, in considering the themes of astronomy and the new cosmology (as in *God and the Astronomers*, 1933) did he overcome his aversion for Roman Catholicism by an appreciation of Thomistic philosophy. Other blind spots in his mental retina were the Irish and the Americans, apart from several individuals from these races whom he greatly admired. It seemed that it was the isolation and cloistral seclusion of this ascetic of the intellectual and clerical aristocracy to which these defects in appreciation must be attributed. In the last analysis it was his independence, even eccentricity of judgment, his swimming against the stream, which made him the interesting personality that he was. His critics, who seemed to wish him to demonstrate a cordial and undiscriminating ambiguity of opinion, would thus try to liquidate the entire *persona* of the outspoken Dean.

We may conclude that, even if he was greatly admired, he was also bitterly detested. One example of the bitterness of his opponents will suffice. It appears that in 1917 Inge had argued for realism instead of revenge in

[1] Fox, *Dean Inge*, p. 115.

the treatment of the defeated army. The result was that he received a letter from a virago three days later which said: 'I am praying for your death; I have been very successful in two other cases.'[1] On the other hand we might cite the entry in his diary for 13th October 1929:

> I preached the University Sermon at Cambridge. . . . I was well advertised; the *Granta* said: 'The Dean of Deans is coming to preach. Those who cannot come early had better bring their hassocks, for they will find no other seat in the Church.' It was so . . . there was not a vacant seat in the Church.[2]

Dean Inge was an oracle on subjects as disparate as Eugenics and Astronomy, Mysticism and Political Theory, Philosophy and Medicine. He was a gadfly in the Church of England (it has been said that his name rhymes with 'sting' not 'cringe'), stinging clergy and laity from their conventional comatoseness. He was guilty of some insensitivities, but never of platitude. Above all, he was single-minded in his pursuit of truth (and he recognized his kinship with the scientists of the day who were intellectual ascetics).[3] Clichés, pretentiousness, insincerity, sentimentalism, obscurantism and ignorance were his ultimate foes. The essential Puritanism (which Inge shared with Henson) is expressed with simple dignity in *Vale*, and this is his farewell message: 'I have always tried to speak the truth, and to give honest work.'[4] That truth was the Christian revelation, appealing to mind, soul, and will, brilliantly expounded by the Christian scholar, mystic and moralist, that was William Ralph Inge, God's luminary in an age of dusk.

[1] *Diary of a Dean*, p. 42.
[2] *Ibid.*, p. 141. [3] *Vale* (1934), p. 98. [4] *Ibid.*, p. 2.

4

The Preaching of Truth Through Personality

'DICK' SHEPPARD & STUDDERT KENNEDY

THE preaching of 'truth through personality' is Bishop Phillips Brooks' admirable description of strongly marked characters graciously proclaiming the Gospel. Thomas Carlyle hit off another characteristic of this type of dynamic utterance—its direct, first-hand quality—in declaring that what the village of Ecclefechan needed was a minister who knew God other than by hearsay.

Two essential elements are required for the preaching of truth through personality: a striking personality wholly subordinated to God and absolute candour. A striking personality alone may be no more than a stunter or an exhibitionist who plays to the gallery. But the personality of originality and integrity used by God to manifest his joy and love is the truly *charismatic* preacher. His lively graciousness is the reflection of God's grace. From him the infection of Christian love and the confidence of faith are caught, as well as taught. Two original and lovable twentieth-century personalities in the English pulpit must now be studied.

'Dick' Sheppard & Studdert Kennedy

1 · *A New Image of the Anglican Ministry*

When the twentieth century dawned in Britain, it was heralded with fireworks and balloons, fitting symbols of confidence in the automatic progress of the human race. Within fifteen years the bland optimism had burst like shrapnel. The fireworks became Very lights eerily exposing the front-line trenches of no-man's-land and the inflated balloons were punctured on the barbed wire of Flanders. In the mood of despair, cynicism, fatalism, and hedonism that ensued, it was clear that the commonplaces of the traditional Christian faith and the complacency of the English Established Church were as out of date as episcopal gaiters and as irrelevant as gargoyles. The central questions were: Can the historic Christian faith be made vital again, and can the Church be humanized? Two men above all other ministers in the Church of England proved able to win and sustain the trust of the disillusioned masses. One of these highly unconventional clergymen was Geoffrey Antekell Studdert Kennedy, who had been given the bitter-sweet nickname of 'Woodbine Willie' by the privates of the British Expeditionary Force in France. He was the most admired of all the British military chaplains in France. The other unconventional parson was Hugh Richard Lawrie Sheppard—called by the multitude of his friends 'Dick'—who became the most famous parish priest of this century in England. The fact that both had nicknames was a proof of their acceptance with the common man.

During this difficult period there were, of course, other impressive figures in the Church of England, including bishops such as William Temple and Hensley Henson. Bishop Charles Gore, co-founder of the Community of the Resurrection, leader of the Anglo-Catholic party in the direction of Liberal Catholicism in the areas of Biblical criticism and socialism, and a great influence on William Temple, was the scholar-prophet. He was also a considerable preacher, even if the expository volumes of sermon-lectures he left do not do justice to his personal dynamism.[1] At Canterbury and York were Archbishops Davidson and Lang. The bench of bishops was far from being the sleeping compartment of the Church of England. Yet neither brilliant ecclesiastical statesmanship, nor even sound theological construction alone, would have convinced the laity of England of the relevance of the Christian faith and the usefulness of the Christian Church.

It is hardly an exaggeration to say, as Ernest H. Jeffs does: 'What saved the Church of England, so far as the respect and liking of the masses was concerned, were the personalities and work of two young rebels against ecclesiastical convention—"Dick" Sheppard and "Woodbine Willie." '[2] What St Francis did for the Church in

[1] See G. L. Prestige, *The Life of Charles Gore* (1935), and for evaluations of his theology James Carpenter, *Gore, A Study in Liberal Catholic Thought* (1960); Ragnar Ekström, *The Theology of Charles Gore* (Lund, 1944) and Archbishop A. M. Ramsey, *From Gore to Temple* (1960). For his lecture-expositions of Scripture see *The Sermon on the Mount* (1897); *St Paul's Epistle to the Romans* (2 vols., 1899, 1900); and *St Paul's Epistle to the Ephesians* (1898). However practical these expositions are, they are not cast in sermonic form, and a representative collection of Gore's sermons illustrating his wide variety of theological, social and ecclesiastical interests during a long life ought to be prepared.

[2] *Princes of the Modern Pulpit*, p. 155.

his day, in recalling it to the Divine simplicity of the imitation of Christ through his friars, these other experts in the understanding of the Humanity of God did for the Church of England, except that they founded no new religious order. Certainly they brought the Church into living touch with the people and inspired them with the conviction that Christianity was not an arid orthodoxy, but an alluring adventure of faith undertaken in love. Sheppard and Studdert Kennedy were 'Pre-eminently the pulpit voices of the new democracy.'[1]

2 · *Canon W. H. Elliott's Radio Ministry*

Another successful, if more conventional, preacher of 'truth through personality' who attained to fame a decade later as a renowned radio preacher was Canon W. H. Elliott. Coming from a simple, working-class background, severely hampered by hyper-thyroid in his youth and manhood, acutely unhappy at Oxford where he was an Exhibitioner at Brasenose College, he found his feet at the Ripon Clergy School and as senior curate of Leeds Parish Church. (The latter two institutions had also been the centres in which Studdert Kennedy was trained.)

Elliott was appointed Vicar of St Michael's, Chester Square, London, in 1930. During the Great Depression (or Slump) of the following year, he was asked by Sir John Reith, the Director-General of the British Broadcasting Corporation, to broadcast a late-evening service from his church each Thursday. The hope was that a

[1] *Ibid.*

short and informal talk, followed by Scripture lessons, prayers and a few well-known hymns, would comfort many dispirited and lonely people. It was successful beyond Elliott's wildest hopes. It continued, with a summer intermission of a month each year, for eight years, with an audience counted in the millions. It was discontinued in 1939, only when the B.B.C. was moved for war-time security from London to Bristol. By that time the vibrant reassurance of Elliott's voice and matter, his compassion expressed in moving stories of the struggles and sacrifices of the 'little people,' and his insistence on reality in religion, made his the single most popular pulpit voice in England.

In form and manner of delivery, if not always in content, his sermons had several qualities. They had an endearing intimacy at a time when outsiders were suspicious of men in clerical grey or black. Elliott extended the sympathy of a man who was himself no stranger to poverty and suffering. He rebelled against snobbishness, cruelty, and theological complexity, in such a way as to intrigue the ordinary listener. His happy informality of manner contrasted greatly with the stereotype of the dignified and remote Anglican clergyman of the day. Writing of the techniques of radio broadcasting, he urged that the microphone be thought of as an old friend. He claimed that it would be fatal to picture the listening millions and that the broadcaster should focus on the picture of one person, or a small group sitting around a fire. 'To them,' Canon Elliott added, 'he can speak conversationally and confidentially. If he can do that, then those who hear him, especially anyone listening alone, cannot avoid the impression that the voice

W. E. Sangster
at Westminster
Central Hall, 1952

Leslie D. Weatherhead broadcasting in New York

Archbishop
William Temple

Professor James Stewart

from the radio set is like a personal call on the telephone.'[1]

His popularity was proven by the flood of congratulatory letters he received and by the tangible responses to his appeals for charity, as also by the avidity with which the public read the more than fifty volumes of radio talks he published. His gospel of reassurance and consolation was often, however gratefully received, very sentimental. It generally lacked the sterner note of judgment, without which comfort is an ointment where egotism requires a radical surgery. Furthermore his statement of the Christian faith and its ethical demands was usually greatly over-simplified. In his later days his Christian spirituality was barely distinguished from Spiritualism,[2] as if the unconditional assurance of life after death was the whole truth about Christianity. However, like the two more notable exponents of truth through personality now to be considered in detail, he helped to change the image of the Anglican priesthood, so that dignity melted to humanity.

3 · *The Priest and the Padre*

In many ways Sheppard and Studdert Kennedy were astonishingly alike; it is no surprise to learn that for half a year they were colleagues on the staff of St Martin-in-the-Fields, known as 'the parish church of the

[1] W. H. Elliott's autobiography is *Undiscovered Ends* (1951). The citation is from p. 169. People, he judged, listened to his 35-minute sermons 'perhaps because I was simple and sincere' (*ibid.*, p. 160). King George V, who had appointed Elliott as one of his chaplains, greatly liked the man and his message.

[2] See, for example, *Rendezvous, The Life that some call Death* (1942).

British Empire.'[1] They were born in the same decade; Sheppard in 1880 and Kennedy in 1883. They were both sons of the Anglican clergy, Sheppard of a Canon of Windsor and Kennedy of a Vicar of a down-town Leeds parish. Both had unforgettable experiences of living among the desperately poor. Sheppard was first a chaplain and then Head of Oxford House settlement in Bethnal Green. Kennedy was a curate of Rugby parish church in an industrial neighbourhood, later became his father's curate in Leeds, and later still was Vicar of St Paul's, Worcester, where he had the cure of 3,000 souls in a squalid milieu.

Each suffered acutely from the prostration and torture of asthma. Each died before his time, exhausted by the demands on his nervous energy made by the poor and the perplexed and on his time by exacting lecturing and preaching schedules which sent them through the length and depth of England. Sheppard died at 57; while Kennedy died at 46.

There was also a striking similarity in their temperaments. Both were men who scorned pretentiousness. Intensely lovable, generous in time, money and possessions to the point of quixotry, they were also great practical jokers. They were also men of incandescent integrity, genuine humility and invincible courage.

They held a common conception of their task as preachers. First, they would rescue the pulpit from the obscurantism of professional jargon; secondly, they would rescue the teaching of the Church from social and

[1] So called because it is situated in Trafalgar Square where so many countries of the British Commonwealth have the offices of their High Commissioners, and because the overseas religious broadcasts of the B.B.C. originated from St Martin's.

political conservatism; and, finally, they would present Christ to their people as the companion of men and women in their hardships and sufferings and as the inspiration and dynamic for heroic living. Both struck the note of immediacy in the pulpit. It was a simple and passionate directness that employed colloquialisms, jokes, anecdotes and appeals to personal experience, all to bring congregations to a face-to-face encounter with God. Each was a prophet in presenting the Divine Revelation as the antidote to popular lies and delusions. Each was also the true priest and confessor, finding his courage, example and strength in the Sacrament of the Holy Communion.

In other and important ways they differed. Although Sheppard had written *The Impatience of a Parson*, he was not half as impatient and impetuous as Kennedy. However unconventional his diction, theology and approach might be, Sheppard was sufficiently acceptable to ecclesiastical authority to become after his twelve years' pastorate at St Martin's Dean of Canterbury and then a Canon of St Paul's Cathedral. Kennedy is unthinkable in either dignity. Moreover, 'Woodbine Willie' never tamed his language, even for the most exquisite or exalted ears. In place of Sheppard's occasional and mild colloquialisms, Kennedy consistently used slang, often expletives, and always the most explosive terms that were guaranteed to keep the most desultory hearer awake. Kennedy was also the more revolutionary in doctrine, being convinced that Patripassianism (the doctrine that God the Father actually suffers) was less a heresy than the essential meaning of the Gospel. While Kennedy used shock tactics, Sheppard tried to coax his hearers into the Kingdom of God. Sheppard's compassionate temperament also radiated the glad confidence of faith. For Kennedy, however, life in this present world was always under the Cross and while Christ's Resurrection was the proof of the ultimate victory of faith, he never seemed to find the serenity in the here and now he was sure would be his in the hereafter.

In their spheres of influence these popular preachers were also very different. Sheppard was the model parish priest in St Martin's for twelve trying years. Kennedy made his great reputation in the First World War as a military padre—at base, in various Army training schools in France, and at the Front. He, too, was an excellent parish priest, but his ministry was interrupted by his service overseas. Sheppard was the successful pioneer of religious broadcasting and his intimate and confidential technique made the ministry of St Martin's known to thousands whom he would never meet. Kennedy, while personally most compassionate, believed that social justice was the widest possible expression of Christian compassion and he devoted his post-war years as a 'Messenger' of the Industrial Christian Fellowship, lecturing on the implications of the Gospel for social, political and economic life throughout Britain.

Kennedy's mind was more acute and more richly stored than Sheppard's. His imagination also was richer, as is shown by the poems he published, which read like a Kipling converted to pacifism. Sheppard was deeply self-conscious, although in time he learned to turn this to advantage. This he did, for example, when beginning a sermon delivered before the University of Cambridge: 'What has an ordinary person with no intellectual attainments and with the sad memory of a misspent university career in which Fenners, the racquet court, the A.D.C. and the Pitt played parts wholly disproportionate to their real value, to offer to a congregation such as this?'[1] It was a disarming opening that elicited interest, but also an embarrassing one for the electors of the Select Preacher. Studdert Kennedy seems to have been both absent-minded and utterly unself-conscious. One suspects, however, that there was an occasional touch of Irish art in the apparent artlessness of his appeal. Although each stooped to conquer by his unconventionality, neither ever stooped to egotism. However different their gifts, they were the most trusted and admired parsons of their age in England.

4 · *'Dick' Sheppard*

'Dick' Sheppard concentrated on humanizing the Church and Studdert Kennedy on showing the relevance of the Gospel to the deepest needs of man and society. Two different pictures of the work of St Martin-in-the-Fields illumine the new image of the Church of England which Sheppard was trying to project on the screen of the laity. It was radically and necessarily different from the stereotype of the authoritarian, time-honoured and slightly musty institution, which was kept going for the pious and regular few and for the occasional use of the affluent and the professional groups. The ancient institution was to be redesigned as a centre of family life, a *home*. Sheppard wanted to make actual Francis Thompson's vision of a new Divine-human encounter in

[1] *The Best of Dick Sheppard*, ed. H. E. Luccock (1951), p. 80.

. . . the traffic of Jacob's ladder
Pitched betwixt Heaven and Charing Cross.

He imagined on his first Sunday in St Martin's the kind of church this might become:

> I saw a great and splendid church standing in the greatest square of the greatest city of the world. I stood on the west steps and saw what this church would be to the life of the people. There passed me into its warm inside, hundreds and hundreds of all sorts of people, going up to the temple of their Lord with all their difficulties, trials and sorrows. I saw it full of people, dropping in at all hours of the day and the night. It was never dark; it was lighted all night and all day, and often and often tired bits of humanity swept in. And I said to them as they passed, 'Where are you going?' And they said, 'This is our home. This is where we are going to learn of the love of Jesus Christ. This is the altar of the Lord, where all our peace lies. This is St Martin's. . . .'
>
> It was all reverent and all full of love and they never pushed me behind a pillar because I was poor. . . . They spoke to me of two words only, one was the word 'home' and the other was 'love'.[1]

This was, of course, the ideal; but what of the real St Martin's? The second picture is delineated by R. Ellis Roberts:

> St Martin's church became the church of the classes and the masses; the church for the cheerful and the desperate; the church for the healthy and the sick; of the young and old. It was a church in which the congregation was no more shocked at hearing the minister pray for the street-walkers than pray for school-teachers, for crooks than for the clergy, for blackguards than for bishops, no more shocked than

[1] R. Ellis Roberts, *H. R. L. Sheppard, Life and Letters* (1942), pp. 44–45.

> when the vicar laughed and told a funny story from the pulpit. It became a refuge for the unhappy and the home for the homeless. In short, it was a Christian church.[1]

St Martin's admirably exemplified the new conception of Christ's Church as a family centre. Like a true home, ready to welcome the returning sons and daughters, whether prodigals or paupers, the lights were always on and the doors were always open. There was always a bed in the crypt and meals in the refectory. An employment agency provided posts for the impoverished. Far from there being any forbidding restraint, there was only encouragement for the 'tired bits of humanity' that constantly 'swept in.' Sheppard's own marvellous capacity for friendship was the magnet that drew others dedicated to a genuine catholicity of charity. Besides the notable services of worship, St Martin's appealed to art-lovers, drama enthusiasts and the 'mad about music' fans, all in the Fellowship Guild, the *St Martin's Review* and the St Martin's Players.

Sheppard's sermons radiated the same joyous love of the brethren for Christ's sake. They were not remarkable for culture, intellectual or spiritual profundity, nor even for striking epigrams (the latter a characteristic of Kennedy's addresses). They evinced an unusual understanding of persons and an illimitable love for them, expressed in the most unaffected and unadorned style. His sermons are distinguished by their simple, earnest directness and sincerity—by the man-to-man frankness, mingled with concern. As Halford E. Luccock remarks: 'Sheppard always talked to a person; he never merely

[1] *Ibid.*, pp. 92–93.

sprayed the solar system with words.'[1] Moreover, his sermons dealt with the central and practical issues.

Above all he was anxious to avoid any taint of humbug or hypocrisy in his preaching. His candidness and compassion were the reflection of his conviction that 'if intellectual doubt has slain its tens, the Christian profession unrelated to practice has slain its tens of thousands.'[2] Max Beerbohm, a sensitive and often ironical spirit, writes of the impact of Sheppard's personality on him with a singular delicacy. He is recording a meeting with Sheppard at Portofino, where the exhausted priest was hoping to recover his strength and health: 'He radiated a youthfulness that was less that of an undergraduate than of a schoolboy. Nevertheless he made me feel younger than my years. And better than my character.'[3] These final words of the citation admirably define the confidence Sheppard gave to every man, that there were untapped resources of spirituality and compassion in his own self. He seemed to see, like his Master, the image of the King, which Christ would renew, in every world-soiled human coin, that others would have dismissed as too tarnished and rusty for use.

It is true that he often began a sermon with a joke, but it was almost always extraordinarily apt. When dealing with the endemic human defect of thinking too highly of ourselves and too poorly of others, he tells the following story which illuminates man's true condition: 'There was once a fashionable lady who went to a photographer. She was plain but thought she was beautiful. Said she to the photographer, "Young man, mind you

[1] Luccock, *op. cit.*, p. xix.
[2] *Ibid.*, p. 24.
[3] Roberts, *op. cit.*, p. 199.

do me justice," to which he replied, "Madam, it's not justice but mercy you need!" '[1] It is significant that this story was part of a radio broadcast to non-churchgoers. A conventional parson might have made the same point much less effectively (and lost half of his invisible audience) by retelling the parable of the Pharisee and the Publican.

If the impression has been given that Sheppard was merely a sincere and thorough-going sentimentalist, this would be false. He can bark as well as coax. The courteous priest was also very much the rebel. He was profoundly aware of the contrast between the values of Christ and society, as this ironical statement makes clear: 'Men, too, have brought their own prejudices with them as they sought to know Him, and have only found in Him what they were looking for—a revolutionary, a social reformer, a miracle worker, a physician, a kind-hearted philanthropist, an Oriental potentate, an upholder of the established order, and, sometimes, apparently, even the first Anglican clergyman.'[2] He was acutely impatient with the compromises of the Church of England and its trust in its own security in a rapidly changing world. 'We have played,' he said, 'for safety, position, and prestige too long. . . . We have been content to provide a peephole through which people could see God through a blizzard.'[3] The savage indignation which tore at the heart of Kennedy hardly touched Sheppard. More typical of his attitude is the whimsical self-depreciation that provokes the remark that 'any idea

[1] Luccock, *op. cit.*, p. 27.
[2] *The Human Parson* (1924), p. 98.
[3] Luccock, *op. cit.*, p. 162.

that a round collar is a slipped halo must be once and for all abandoned.'[1]

The difference between Sheppard and Kennedy can be seen in a compilation, *If I only had One Sermon to Preach* (1928), to which they and eighteen other well-known English preachers contributed. Sheppard chooses the inevitable text, 'Come unto Me all ye that labour and are heavy laden, and I will give you rest.' Studdert Kennedy's theme, blazing with social justice, is based on two texts, the practical 'Give us this day our daily bread' and the highly mystical, 'But My Father giveth you the true bread.' For Sheppard sacrificial love, Divine and human, is the clue to joy and peace. For Kennedy sacrificial love is the inspiration to struggle for social solidarity through toil, assisted by the wounded hands of Christ. He declares, 'The hands are wounded, for the struggle was a reality; but they will not always bleed, because love triumphs in the end.'[2] Even if Sheppard's sermons hardly do justice to the need to reconstruct all institutions and orders, so atomistic is his thinking, and even if he can descend to saccharine expressions on some occasions, yet his life was proof positive of his commitment to the task of society's redemption. He was Honorary Secretary of the Life and Liberty Movement of the Church of England, National President of the Brotherhood Movement in 1935, and best known as Leader of the Peace Pledge Union.

By his unconventional and compassionate ministry at St Martin's, as by his pioneering broadcast services, he changed the man-in-the-street's understanding of the Christian ministry. No merely muscular parson, nor

[1] *Ibid.*

[2] *Op. cit.*, p. 268.

even a hail-fellow-well-met type, nor the urbane and witty priest, nor the smooth-tongued orator, not yet the distant and mysterious celebrant of the liturgy, but simply and sincerely man's best friend for Christ's sake.

5 · '*Woodbine Willie*'

If Sheppard changed the man-in-the-street's image of an Anglican priest in one direction, Studdert Kennedy changed it in another direction. Sheppard depicted the priest as friend; Kennedy saw him as a fighter, heroic in battle and crusading for social justice. Both Michael Scott and Bishop Trevor Huddleston, as well as the present unconventional Bishops of Southwark, Woolwich and Middleton, and the leader of Christian Action, Canon Collins, must look back to Studdert Kennedy as the pioneer of their type of priesthood.

Geoffrey Studdert Kennedy assumed the great burden of trying to demonstrate in word and deed his conviction of the humanity of God, as well as of the relevance of the 'strong meat of the Gospel' for twentieth-century 'Hollow Men.' For this task he was superbly equipped by ability, training and experience.

Brought up in a northern industrial slum parish, he demanded to be sent to the Front in the war, so that his faith had to be fought for with all the gifts of courage, imagination and intelligence that he possessed. The Vicarage garden at St Mary's, Quarry Hill, Leeds, the playground of his youth, was surrounded by the Workhouse, the Board School, the Brick Quarry, and a public house.[1] Experience taught him how men's souls were

[1] *G. A. Studdert Kennedy By His Friends*, ed. J. K. Mozley (London, 1929), p. 40. See also William Purcell, *Woodbine Willie* (1962).

stunted by the bleak industrial environment, and how poverty and injustice chafed men's spirits like chains. In the same way he learned in the mud and blood of Flanders that a Deistic faith in a remotely benevolent God was as substantial as the disappearing Cheshire cat in *Alice in Wonderland*, and that a magical belief in immediate Divine protection was as effectual in bridging the chasm between Heaven and Hell as gossamer. No merely midsummer faith or piping *Pippa Passes* optimism would suffice. Only a crucified Christ could, in Baxter's words, lead men 'through no darker rooms than he went through before.'

He was fortunate in being trained at the Ripon Clergy School, where his disciplined Tractarian devotional life was complemented by the modernist quest to reconcile Biblical faith with modern knowledge. He claimed to have learned much from Dr H. D. A. Major's lectures on the philosophy of religion. Certainly, he also learned much of the art of communication from Dr Boyd Carpenter, the Bishop of Ripon and a superb preacher. Most important for him, his rigorously independent mind was allowed to develop in freedom and depth. He was equally fortunate in being able to develop at Rugby (where he was one of many curates on the staff of the parish church) his pastoral care for children and the down-and-outs, and to preach some of his very unconventional messages. On one occasion he is said to have enjoyed greatly the rebuke of Dr A. V. Baillie, his Rector, who said, 'Kennedy, I can stand one heresy from you each Sunday, but I cannot and will not stand two.'[1]

He was doubly blessed in having superiors who

[1] *Ibid.*, p. 60.

recognized his unique gifts, which goes to prove that the Church of England was far from being convention-ridden as is commonly supposed. Although not technically on the staff of the Vicar of Leeds (being the curate to his father), yet Dr Bickersteth encouraged him greatly. He urged Kennedy to speak in the great city square where his task was to out-argue anti-Christian demagogues and hecklers. Years later, Bickersteth reported, 'I can recollect none who more instantly caught the attention of upturned faces . . . than Geoffrey Studdert Kennedy.'[1] In this free-for-all forum he developed his mastery as a public speaker. Here he tried out the telling anecdotes, the staccato sentences like rapier thrusts, and the brilliant dialectical turns and the earthy diction that were the distinctive marks of his sermons and addresses.

Fortunate at Leeds, he was also fortunate at Worcester in having a sympathetic sponsor in authority. Hardly had he reached the cathedral city, when Dr W. Moore Ede, the Dean, invited him to address 2,000 raw Army recruits each Sunday morning in the cathedral. These he held spellbound.[2] To be sure he had unique gifts for popularization, but it must be rare for a young man to be so regularly encouraged by authority to use his talents to the full. It was the same again when he went to France as a military chaplain. His schedule was wisely planned by the Chaplain-General, so that times at the Front were intermingled with visits to the Army Schools. Kennedy did, indeed, grasp opportunity by the forelock, but its head never seemed to be beyond his grasp.

[1] *Ibid.*, p. 74. [2] *Ibid.*, p. 100.

The acuteness of his mind is attested by his obtaining a double first class honours in classics and divinity in the Third Year examinations at Trinity College, Dublin, in 1902, and by the honour of a silver medal two years later. He was a reader of deep and lengthy books by preference. His thought was incisive, though often undisciplined. His imagination was vivid. He had great moral candour and a vehement earnestness. These qualities, combined with a pungent style and fearlessness, meant that men who met him never forgot him. When the war ended, he was far and away the best known of the British military chaplains, and he thoroughly deserved the Military Cross awarded his gallantry.

Kennedy's advice to another chaplain is an excellent summary of his conception of the office:

> Live with the men, go where they go; make up your mind that you will share all their risks and more, if you can do any good. You can take it that the best place for a padre . . . is where there is most danger of death. Our first job is to go beyond the men in self-sacrifice and reckless devotion.
>
> . . . There is very little spiritual work—it is all muddled and mixed—but it is all spiritual. Take a box of fags in your haversack, and a great deal of love in your heart, and go up with them, live with them, talk with them. You can pray *with* them sometimes, but pray *for* them always.[1]

In most of his rhymes and addresses there were two insistent emphases. One was that God is involved with humanity in their sufferings. The other was that the Church, far from being the sanctifier of class distinctions, was to be the spur to social, political and economic reform.

[1] *Ibid.*, pp. 139–141.

Kennedy's primary concern was to refute the idea that the essence of faith was spiritless submission; rather it was, in Pauline phrase, to enter into the fellowship of Christ's sufferings. He satirized the older view in the lines:

This is the Gospel of the Christ.
  Submit whate'er betides
You cannot make the wrong world right
  'Tis God alone decides.

By contrast, Kennedy prays for a manlier imitation of Christ:

O by Thy Cross and Passion, Lord,
  By broken hearts that pant
For comfort and for love of Thee
  Deliver us from cant.[1]

Kennedy had joined the forces in the mood of chivalrous commitment, as this was expressed in the aspirational war poems of Rupert Brooke. Soon, however, he saw, like Wilfrid Owen, that the only poetry of war was in the pity of it. He then declared: 'Religion as an insurance policy against accident in the day of battle is discredited in the Army.' Not only do the sun and rain fall down on the just and unjust, but also the rain of shrapnel. Hence suffering is as inevitable as the Cross. It is man's misuse of freedom that brings wars, for 'a shell is just an iron sin.' God conquers sin by the way of the Cross, by the way of love, taking it upon Himself. So God 'makes an army of the Cross, an army of men and women who pledge themselves to fight with sin and gladly suffer in the fight, that by strife and suffering the

[1] *Lies!* (n.d.), pp. 132–133.

power of evil may be broken and the world redeemed.'[1] That was his philosophy in a day of tragedy.

It is necessary, he believed, to preserve the love of God even at the cost of denying his omnipotence. To recite the first article of the Apostles' Creed seemed to him to be blasphemously blaming God for all the ugliness and callousness of the world. Consequently he rejected the Aristotelian conception of a God incapable of suffering. He claimed that the glory of the Christian faith was its declaration that there was a Cross in the heart of the Father before there was a Cross on Calvary. For him the truest insight into the Divine nature was provided in the Incarnation, where God-as-Man meets and exalts men and is represented anew in the Sacrament of Sacrifice. Therefore, as his *Rough Rhymes* tell:

Father, if He, the Christ, be Thy Revealer,
  Truly the First Begotten of the Lord,
Then must Thou be a suff'rer and a Healer,
  Pierced to the heart by the sorrow of the sword. . . .

God, the God I love and worship,
  Reigns in sorrow on the Tree,
Broken, bleeding, but unconquered,
  Very God of God to me.

On my knees I fall and worship
  That great Cross that shines above,
For the very God of Heaven is not Power,
  But Power of Love.

His message is that as long as history lasts love must be suffering love; and only in heaven is love triumphant.

No Anglican clergyman since Scott Holland had sounded the trumpet of social justice to more rousing

[1] *The Hardest Way*, cited E. H. Jeffs, *op. cit.*, pp. 165–167.

effect than Studdert Kennedy. He was withering in his condemnation of those who met all plans to abolish or reduce poverty with superior smiles and the threadbare excuses of the impossibility of changing human nature and the misapplication of Christ's words, 'the poor are always with you.' 'There is,' he commented, 'more real blasphemy in these words than in the most lurid sergeant's speech that ever turned the air of Flanders blue. It is sheer blank atheism.'[1]

He was too religious a man to think that well-intentioned philanthropists, unassisted by Divine grace, could build the New Jerusalem out of the dark, Satanic mills, yet he warned the leaders of the Church that its rigid conservatism was forcing men to turn to the new *bonhomie*. The multitude, he cautioned, were revolting from a Church 'which damned souls to build churches, sweated work-people to endow charities, and manufactured prostitutes by low wages to build rescue homes for fallen women and buy a peerage.' The common people, he added, were nauseated by the religion of the upper classes 'who patronized God as the best of all policemen, the power that kept poor people in their places by threats of hell and promises of heaven.'[2] He sounds like an Amos with the tenderness of an Hosea. As 'Messenger' of the Industrial Christian Fellowship, he applied the radical teaching of Christ to war, to slums, class-warfare, industrialism, politics and the problems of marriage. Everywhere he used 'the unrestrained utterance of a soul in revolt.'[3]

So unconventional a preacher was bound to have many

[1] *Lies!*, p. 37.
[2] *Ibid.*, p. 108.
[3] J. K. Mozley, *op. cit.*, p. 167.

critics as well as thousands of admirers. In some cases the critics were justified. Kennedy definitely upset the balance of the Gospel, which is both criticism and comfort, by frequently over-emphasizing the judgment of God. (Sheppard's was the opposite defect, with the ever-present danger of sentimentality.) His shock tactics ultimately ceased to shock, like the man who was always crying, 'Wolf! Wolf!' His language was too muddled with slang and expletives, which tended not only to distract from his message in drawing attention to the speaker, but was felt to be *passé* in the years of peace.

Similarly, his teaching was too lop-sided in his failure to balance sacrifice with hope. It is true that he had a wide and deep understanding of the Revelation of God: which he acknowledged in the beauty of Nature and of artistic creation, in the call to noble endeavour heard in the conscience and in social reform, as well as in the dark glory of Christ's Cross. Though he recalled with singular realism that Christ had said, 'In this world ye shall have tribulation,' he seemed to forget the completing clause: 'But be of good cheer, for I have overcome the world.' Jesus was more Victim than Victor for Kennedy. Like the great modern French painter Georges Rouault, his portrait of the crucified depicted a swollen-lipped, blood-smeared and thorn-crowned Jesus, against menacing leaden skies. There is suggested only in the faintest smudged aureole the risen Christ who tore open the sepulchre and destroyed death. Kennedy was, of course, reacting against the idyllic Galilean teacher and social prophet of the 'New Theology.' The result of this swinging of the pendulum of his thought in a realistic direction was that his preaching lacked what Jeffs has called 'inward sunshine,' or what I should prefer to term the serenity and liberation of the Christian hope. Thus 'the wounds and scars of battle were too plainly manifest in the man who stood up, with sad mouth and dark and burning eyes, to tell the people of his hard-won discoveries.'[1] Jeffs added: 'He was the saddest preacher I have ever known.'[2]

Yet in all his teaching in sermons and addresses Studdert Kennedy had shown himself an expert in the Humanity of God and suitably was himself a very human divine. God was seen anew by thousands, not as a remote Potentate of inscrutable ways, but as the Father of Our Lord Jesus Christ, and as man's compassionate Companion involved in their afflictions and their agonies and committed to the establishment of a Kingdom of holy love in men's social relations. Kennedy translated religious terminology into the speech of the trenches and the market-place. His life as well as his lips made devotion to God and man a reality where otherwise (in the war and in the slums) they might, but for his witness, have seemed utterly irrelevant.

[1] Jeffs, *op. cit.*, p. 167. [2] *Ibid.*, p. 160.

5

Liturgical Preaching

MONSIGNOR RONALD KNOX

KNOX and Inge are two outstanding examples of wits in the modern English pulpit, though very different. If Inge was, in truth, the 'gloomy Dean,' Knox was certainly the merry Monsignor, a fountain of gaiety and grace. G. K. Chesterton suggests this in his quatrain *The Namesake,* which contrasts the dour, determined Scottish Reformer, John Knox, with his effervescent opposite, Ronald Knox.

Mary of Holyrood may smile indeed,
Knowing what grim historic shade it shocks
To see wit, laughter and the Popish creed
Cluster and sparkle in the name of Knox.[1]

Ronald Knox's life, writings and sermons shatter the stereotype that a priest-preacher must be dull, conventional, and flat, because he is a man under authority. In fact, Knox is immensely entertaining, highly original, and *sparkling.* Sparkling, as stars on a frosty night, in his profound clarity and holy austerity; sparkling, like champagne, in his buoyant sense of the joy of life. If the similes seem contradictory, we may take refuge in

[1] *The Collected Poems of G. K. Chesterton* (1927), p. 15.

the thought that Knox was himself a paradox in which the goal of other-worldliness did not interfere with his full appreciation of the joys of friendship. He was a foe alike of grudging Puritanism and diluting Modernism.

1 · *Man of Many Parts*

His heredity, his environment and his achievements were all remarkable. Born in 1888, the grandson of Bishop French of Lahore (a heroic Protestant counterpart of Charles de Foucauld),[1] the son of the future Evangelical Bishop of Manchester, and brother of a future Editor of *Punch*, the most remarkable features of his life were its variety and versatility. The variety is to be found in his change of religious allegiance, as he moved from an Evangelical Anglican boyhood to an Anglo-Catholic adolescence and, after much disquietude, to the Roman Church in which he was received in 1917. Variety is also seen in his several occupations or in differing tasks in the same vocation.

He had a brilliant career at Eton (where he was first King's Scholar) and Oxford (where he was senior Scholar of his year at Balliol College, was elected President of the Union in 1909 and gained a first class honours degree in classical, philosophical and historical studies, and many university prizes). This was what had been forecast for the boy who was accurately reported to have been translating Virgil into fluent English at six and improbably to have made Greek puns at four. He was a Fellow and Lecturer in Classics at Trinity College,

[1] The official biography is Evelyn Waugh, *Ronald Knox* (1959). The reference is to p. 26.

Oxford, in 1910, and to these duties he added that of Chaplain, after ordination in the Church of England in 1912. Then, as the First World War took away most of his students to the trenches (and to death), he became for a time classics master at Shrewsbury School.

After his reception into the Roman Church (in which he was ordained priest in 1919), Knox taught Latin and New Testament Studies at St Edmund's College, Ware (1919–1926), and was Roman Catholic Chaplain to Oxford undergraduates (1926–1939). At the age of 51 he was preparing to devote his remaining years exclusively to literary work, with the opportunity of occasional special preaching at week-ends, when the Second World War broke out. During these years he combined the great work of preparing the Knox translation of the New Testament and Old Testament with the unlikely duties of chaplain and instructor to the girls of the School of Assumptionist Nuns which had been evacuated to Aldenham Hall, the Shropshire country home of his great friends, Lord and Lady Acton. His last years were spent in Mells, the Somerset seat of his other great friends, Lord and Lady Oxford.

His versatility is even more striking than the variety of duties he fulfilled. He was a brilliant debater and dialectician; an original satirist; an astute writer of detective stories and novelist; a detonating broadcaster; a felicitous translator of Greek and Latin lyrics and epigrams,[1] as well as of hymns and pre-eminently of the Scriptures; a perceptive historian; and a preacher of insight into the ways of God with undergraduates, priests, aristocrats and schoolgirls.

[1] See Ronald Knox, *In Three Tongues* (ed. L. E. Eyres, 1959).

Such was his renown as a witty debater that, as an undergraduate, he had the unique distinction of being quoted in a leading article in *The Times* of London. Referring to an inexplicable change in the policy of the government of the day, Knox had quipped: 'The honourable gentlemen have turned their backs on their country and now they have the effrontery to say their country is behind them.'[1] The same wit, now at the service of religion, gained him a national reputation in a brilliant satire in which, imitating Dryden's *Absalom and Achitophel*, he protested against the confusion of the traditional Anglican faith with the vapours of philosophical idealism and its erosion by the acids of Biblical criticism. What makes *Absolute and Abitofhell* so remarkable, apart from its wit, is that Knox satirized a forthcoming book whose seven clerical authors, being Oxford dons, he knew well, but the proofs of which he had never seen. Each of the seven authors of *Foundations* were perfectly hit off as was their failure to agree. The Primate, an apostle of decency rather than of dogma, exemplified the spirit of accommodation, and is pilloried thus:

> When suave politeness, temp'ring bigot Zeal,
> Corrected, 'I believe,' to 'One does feel.'[2]

How admirably Knox contrasts the intentions of the authors to make the Bible more meaningful while they merely multiply the human sources and dissipate the Divine authority of Scripture which was accepted by their forefathers; who

[1] Nathaniel Micklem, *The Box and the Puppets* (1957), pp. 34–35.

[2] *Absolute and Abitofhell*, which first appeared in *The Oxford Magazine* in November 1912, was reissued in *Essays in Satire* (1928), pp. 81–88, and in *In Three Tongues* (1959), pp. 112–117.

. . . were content MARK, MATTHEW, LUKE and JOHN
Should bless th'old-fashion'd Beds they lay upon:
But we, for ev'ry one of theirs have two,
And trust the Watchfulness of Blessed Q.[1]

The more serious refutation of *Foundations* appeared in 1913, entitled *Some Loose Stones*.

Knox's imitation of Swift's irony appeared to perfection in his prose tract, *Reunion All Around*, with the engaging sub-title, 'Or Jael's Hammer Laid Aside and the Milk of Human Kindness Beaten up into Butter and Served in a Lordly Dish, Being a Plea for the Inclusion within the Church of England of all Mahometans, Jews, Buddhists, Brahmins, Papists and Atheists, submitted to the Consideration of the British Public.' The argument takes the form of reducing religious toleration to the point of absurdity—sheer indifference. Mohammed, in his attacks on Mariolatry and on unduly strict views of marriage, appears as the first Protestant; while Bishops are said to exist to control doctrines and keep them unscriptural, to forbid high ceremonial and thus enable the disobedient clergy 'to snatch a fearful joy' and taste the spice of martyrdom lacking since the abolition of Roman amphitheatre! This astonishing work was completed in four days.

Like G. K. Chesterton, that other Roman Catholic publicist, journalist, wit and master of paradox, Knox was a writer of detective stories. *The Viaduct Murder* (1925) was the first and *Double Cross Purposes* (1937) the sixth and final detective story. These were ingenious exercises in logic, with the necessary clues with which an intelligent man could solve them. They had neither the

[1] *Ibid.*

theological implications of the short stories of Chesterton's Father Brown, whose uncommon sense is masked as apparent *naïveté*, nor the theological, romantic, and literary allusiveness of Dorothy Sayers' Lord Peter Wimsey series of novels, which might be termed Who-Donne-its. His masterpiece of fiction is, however, *Let Dons Delight* (1939), which is his farewell both to Oxford and to secular literature. The reader eavesdrops on the conversations of the fellows of St Simon Magus college, as they discuss the living issues of their day, at half-century intervals, from the time of the Armada to Munich. The continuing theme is the gradual displacement of theology and the consequent loss of direction, as autonomous disciplines emerge and the increasing bewilderment of the dons until they become merely obscure specialists. But it is all garnished with wit, as with the locutions, mannerisms and topics appropriate to the periods and the characters portrayed. Another admirable essay in fiction is *Barchester Pilgrimage*, which brings Trollope up to date.

His career as a broadcaster was brief, brilliant and terrifying. He was more aware of the disadvantages than of the possible gains to religion in the early days of radio. The general syncretism it encouraged (which Chesterton had said was religion literally going to *pot*), the nuisance unless the broadcaster lived near one of the studios, the impossibility of ever again using a broadcast sermon, and his preference for personal encounter with his hearers without any need of laborious replies to correspondents; all accounted for his lukewarmness.[1] His terrifying success came in 1926 in the notorious

[1] Evelyn Waugh, *op. cit.*, p. 190.

'Broadcast from the Barricades,'[1] which had the same kind of effect as the Orson Welles simulation of the landing of the Martians in the United States about a decade later.

Believing that many Protestant 'converts' were disappointed at losing opportunities for congregational singing, and that this, in turn, was due to the literary mediocrity of many Roman Catholic hymns, Knox attempted to rectify this as a member of the committee appointed to prepare a revision of the *Westminster Hymnal*. He not only persuaded his colleagues to incorporate the Catholic hymns of Chesterton, Lionel Johnson, Francis Thompson, and others, but produced four original hymns and 47 of a total of 107 translations from the Latin, only nine of which were the work of living writers.[2] Incomparably his finest work in translation, however, was the Knox translation of the New (1945) and the Old Testament (1949). In the panegyric preached in Westminster Cathedral at the Solemn Requiem Mass for Knox on 28th August 1957, Father Martin D'Arcy hinted at the meaning of the 'long companionship with the word of God, so close to the Holy Spirit,' suggesting that it led to 'his ever-growing gentleness and charity.'[3] Certainly, few Roman Catholics can ever have preached such consistently Biblically based sermons as Knox did, for this was a characteristic of his long before his almost exclusive concentration on translating the Scriptures.

His major work as a historian is, in effect, a claim that the Roman Catholic Church is the middle way between

[1] *Ibid.*, pp. 190–192.
[2] Waugh, *op. cit.*, p. 253.
[3] *Ibid.*, p. 333.

the exaggerations of religious fervour and scepticism, as he studied the varieties of religion in the seventeenth and eighteenth centuries in *Enthusiasm* (1950). He could be counted on to produce at least one superb work in every literary *genre* that he tried, with the exception of detective stories. That statement is as true of several volumes of his distinct types of sermons as of his works of apologetics, translations, novels, and satires. A man of many parts, he played each role superlatively well.

2 · *Types of Sermons*

It is not proposed to attempt an account of the changing development of the thought or style of Monsignor Knox's sermons, and for two reasons. The first is that many of them have not yet appeared in print, but are likely to do so, so that such a study would be premature. The second reason is even more compelling: Knox was ever revising and refining his sermons, so that when they eventually appeared in print, in many cases several years after he had first preached them, they were the finished rather than the developing product of his meditation.[1] The implication is that their author wished to be judged by the finished work, which is entirely his right.

The aim will be to refer briefly to his Anglo-Catholic sermons, produced while he was still a priest in the Anglican Church, and then to consider his apologetical and doctrinal sermons prepared for his conference with

[1] Mr Evelyn Waugh insists that the study of the sermons of Knox, which are undated except for the occasional sermons, 're-quires, and will no doubt in good time receive, the attention of a team of research workers.' *Ibid.*, p. 186.

the Catholic undergraduates at Oxford University, and, more fully, the liturgical sermons of his mature age. The latter, as will be argued later, are the most considerable in number, importance and type that he composed.

Monsignor Knox may, in several ways, be likened to Cardinal Newman. Both were brought up as Evangelicals of the Church of England; both found a temporary (Newman a longer) lodging in the High Church wing of the Church of England; both sought for authority and found it in the Roman Church. Both were Fellow Chaplains, and later Honorary Fellows, of Trinity College, Oxford. Both wrote spiritual autobiographies, Newman the famous *Apologia Pro Vita Sua* and Knox *A Spiritual Aeneid*. Newman fought a life-long battle with Liberalism, Knox with Modernism. In many ways Knox tried to complete projects or take a part in them which were judged premature by the Hierarchy in Newman's time, such as a new translation from the Vulgate or establishing a Roman Catholic chaplaincy in Oxford. But the relatively few Anglo-Catholic sermons that Knox published are not to be compared in maturity, depth, moral or psychological insight with the eight volumes of Newman's *Parochial and Plain Sermons*. Knox's mature sermons, however, almost demand such a comparison.

Knox's earliest sermons are, indeed, frank, ingenious, and apt in the application of Biblical passages to the condition of the Church of England of his day; and there are individual passages of great beauty, as of religious insight and ardour.[1] Even so, if we consider the best of

[1] For evidence, see *The Church in Bondage* (1914), pp. 24 and 69–71.

them, as published in *The Church of Bondage* (1914), they are marred by a partisan and often polemical spirit, by mistaking facetiousness for wit, and by an occasional triviality of anecdote or allusion.[1] Sometimes one gets the impression that R. A. Hilary Knox, as the author then styled himself, is enjoying a hearty bout of ecclesiastical 'gamesmanship.' The point in referring to these unequal sermons is that the improvement of the Catholic sermons may be appreciated by contrast. They may be distinguished as the work of Knox only because they are never dull.

A selection of the sermons of an apologetical and doctrinal nature, demanded by the duties of a Roman Catholic Chaplain for undergraduates at Oxford University, is contained in two volumes, *In Soft Garments* (1942) and in *The Hidden Stream* (1952). The latter, the fruit of his return to visit the Chaplaincy, after he had retired from the office, contains more varied and wittier occasional sermons, but the former is the staple of the sermon diet for the 'conferences' between 1926–1938 when Knox was resident Chaplain. With deference to the professional theologians, Knox described the addresses of *In Soft Garments* as attempts 'to deal, unprofessionally, with some of the hesitations that naturally occur to us Catholics when we compare our intellectual commitments with the current thought of the day.'[2]

To venture a purely personal opinion, the liveliest addresses in the book seem to be those dealing with

[1] For evidence of unfair polemicism, see *op. cit.*, pp. 18–19; for triviality, see the anecdote on p. 11, or the references to the Elizabethan Settlement of the Church of England on pp. 4–5.

[2] *In Soft Garments* (1942), p. vii. See Knox's criticism of his preaching in those days in *A Spiritual Aeneid* (1918), p. 105.

highly practical issues, respectively the gain and loss of Faith, and questions of Divorce and Marriage. It is not only that abstract doctrine does not seem greatly to excite Knox's mind (as it did Newman's), but that he feels more at home in day-to-day questions of the Christian life and finds more scope in such subjects for exercising his irony and psychological insight. He clinches the argument that a plurality of wives or husbands is a declension from primitive monogamy and is atavistic today, by insisting 'it is absurd to allow free love unless you allow free hate.'[1] Typically Knoxian is an ironical passage about unselfish bachelors, whom he describes as 'the unselfish people who want to spare several unborn souls the misery of not being brought up at Harrow.'[2]

3 · *Liturgical Preaching*

Knox's very versatility and variety in preaching make it difficult to confine it within a single descriptive category. It might be simpler to call him an 'Ecclesiastical Preacher,' for he was always the faithful exponent of the teaching of the Catholic Church. Such a description, however, hardly brings to mind his distinctive and original quality, nor does it do justice to that great humility which was the work of grace in an extremely gifted intelligence and that glad adoration that was the treble above the bass of the awe of his devotion.

'Liturgical Preaching,' as a category exemplified by

[1] *In Soft Garments*, p. 190.

[2] *Ibid.*, p. 104. See also an ingenious illustration of the difference between a formal and a material sin on p. 113.

Monsignor Knox, is a reminder that the Revelation of God in Holy Scripture is proclaimed within the context of worship and aims not only at the illumination of the mind and the elevation of the heart, but at the consecration of the will in the grace-empowered imitation of Christ. It is also a reminder that his sermons were preached in the context of the cycle of the Christian Year, affording opportunities to study the many facets of the Incarnation of God and stimulating the faithful to imitation of the saints, themselves eminent imitators of God. Above all, liturgical preaching at its best always recalls that Deep calls to deep and Sacrifice to sacrifice. In all Knox's wit and inventiveness, in his brilliance and aptness of illustration and allusion, the solemn joy of the Liturgy is never forgotten. These sermons enable the people of God to see that they must *live* the Liturgy in the spirit of glad obedience.

One possible objection remains to the use of this term to describe the primary emphasis of the sermons of Knox. It is the inference that Knox might have been a faddist in matters of ceremonial and vestments. Nothing could be further from the truth. He believed, indeed, that every action and every phrase in the Liturgy had its important meaning. But so far was he from feeling that inner pride and outer pomp mattered, that he ever insisted in his Eucharistic teaching and in his retreats for priests that the priest was God's *slave* or *tool* in the Mass,[1] who should be humble because of the extraordinary privilege to which he is called. One does not decorate a spanner. It may be remembered that *The Mass in Slow Motion* is a series of meditations on *Low*

[1] *The Mass in Slow Motion* (1948), p. 112.

Mass, and appropriately so, since Monsignor Knox spoke like an angel, but sang like a rook.[1]

His most popular book of liturgical sermons was *The Mass in Slow Motion* (1948) which ran to nine impressions in eleven years. It is doubly remarkable. It is, on the one hand, a vivid, moving and often profound set of reflections on the meaning of the Christian life as these are suggested by the successive parts of the Mass. It is, on the other hand, a triumph of communication that it should have been prepared for and presented successfully to a girls' school evacuated from London to Shropshire in the Second World War. It is an astonishing work in its capacity to blend the sense of the supernatural with the conversational tone and to inculcate theological and spiritual instruction by analogies drawn from inkstains and ladders in stockings. The measure of the achievement is so great that one is forced to find the most outrageous parallels to hint at it, such as, that this is Ronald Searle supernaturalized, or St Trinian's sanctified!

One Priest's Mass, the alternative title that Knox thought of using, is an indication of the freshness of his interpretation of the central and uniform rite of Latin Christendom. The Introduction is a breathlessly brilliant summary of the whole, an appetizer for the rich and leisurely feast that follows. Of the Collects he says simply, 'It's nice to have a lot of different subjects of conversation when you are going to talk to God.'[2] On

[1] *Ibid.*, p x: '. . . it is a long time since I had to sing High Mass, and when I did, the only thought I can remember entertaining, was a vivid hope that I might die before we got to the Preface.'

[2] *Ibid.*, p. xi.

the clause in the Creed 'and was made man,' he comments, 'and the splendid dramatic moment of *Et homo factus est*, with the noise of kicking and scraping behind you, where rheumatic knees are being laboriously bent in honour of God made Man.'[1] Next there is the brilliant image of the Preface, 'with the various ranks of Angels flashing past us like the names of suburban stations as we draw closer to the heart of the great capital.'[2] Then comes the amazed wonder and of the Consecration itself: 'You elevate the Host, the Chalice; or are they trying to fly upwards out of your hands? You hardly know, it is so strange.'[3] The conclusion of the Introduction is: 'So much of drama, every day of our lives; and we, how little we are thrilled by it!'[4]

The companion volumes, *The Creed in Slow Motion* and *The Gospel in Slow Motion*, exhibit the same aptness of illustration and clarity of instruction, but do not—since they are primarily doctrinal expositions and the meeting of simple difficulties—lend themselves to the devotional and mystical treatment of *The Mass in Slow Motion*, of which Knox was such a master. But here, too, one is astonished by the illustrations. For example, Knox uses the Loch Ness monster, an inquisitive boy in a train, children's games, a dog-eared book, a young widow, an indulgent father, a spoiled child, a battering-ram, sacks of coal, making a rabbit-hutch, writing a poem, peeping behind a curtain at a Christmas-tree, the planet Venus, a libel action, earwigs and wart-hogs, in the first 36 pages of *The Creed in Slow Motion*.[5] One

[1] *Ibid.*, p. xiii. [2] *Ibid.*, p. xv.
[3] *Ibid.*, p. xvii. [4] *Ibid.*, p. xviii.
[5] *The Creed in Slow Motion* (1949). For illustrations see, respectively, pp. 11, 13, 16, 19, 22, 24, 25, 29 (twice), 31, 33, 34.

instance must suffice of the astonishing rapport between the great translator (who was then at his task of 'seven years' hard labour') and the schoolgirls he instructed. He describes Divine revelation as a special kind of hide-and-seek between God and us. Moreover, he believed that the childlike (not childish) faculty of wonder and trust is the best receiving-set for the message of Divine revelation, as taught by Christ himself.

Knox's subtlest and most profound liturgical preaching is found in sermons he delivered to Father Kearney's congregation in London's theatreland each year at the Festival of Corpus Christi and which were collected and published as *The Window in the Wall, Reflections on the Holy Eucharist* (1956), and in the addresses which he gave to conferences of priests, published as *The Priestly Life, A Retreat* (1958).

The title of *The Window in the Wall* is itself a fine leap of the imagination. Knox, using allegorical exegesis, takes a text from the second chapter of *Canticles* about the lover who seeks a glimpse of the beloved, 'looking through each window in turn,' and interprets this as Christ looking for the faithful soul. This, again, 'brings to mind a fancy which I have often had before now—in looking at the Sacred Host enthroned in the monstrance.' The fancy is 'that the glittering Disc of whiteness which we see occupying that round opening, is not reflecting the light of the candles in front of it, but shining with a light of its own, a light not of this world. . . .'[1] This is the veiled glory of the Eucharistic Christ, a curtained window, which 'lets our world communicate with the world of the supernatural.'[2] The call of the Beloved is

[1] *The Window in the Wall*, p. 2. [2] *Ibid.*, p. 4.

from the stupefaction of the senses and from anxieties. The medicine of Holy Communion 'enables the enfeebled soul to look steadily at the divine light, to breathe deeply of the unfamiliar air,' until such time as 'God calls us, too, to himself, and makes us glad with the beauty of his unveiled presence.'[1]

The suggestiveness of this volume consists in the various aspects of the Sacrament which Monsignor Knox considers, and which he conveys with crystalline clarity. The Eucharist is seen as the focusing point in which eternity breaks through into time, the spiritual life through the material life, and Christ into human nature.[2] It is also the Sacrament of unity and peace,[3] doubly significant in our time of racial bitterness, international wars, and of refugees who die by inches; thus the heavenly altar of which the earthly altar is an analogue is the true centre of the Church. As the name 'Eucharist' signifies, it is the Sacrifice of Thanksgiving,[4] for our creation and renewal in Christ. It is the Sacrament of Christ's continuing humility,[5] requiring and eliciting the humble obedience of his followers. The Holy Communion is also the inexhaustible iron-ration of the pilgrim, the real Bread that nourishes his soul.[6] It is the Sacrament of probing self-examination.[7] It is also the Sacrament that prepares for life and for death.[8] Supremely, the Holy Eucharist is the Sacrament of Christ's love,[9] manifesting his unchanging friendship and his pity for the multitude, and the Sacrament of Sacrifice.[10]

[1] *Ibid.*, p. 6.
[2] *Ibid.*, sermons 1 and 4.
[3] *Ibid.*, sermons 2, 8, 14.
[4] *Ibid.*, sermon 5.
[5] *Ibid.*, sermons 6, 9, 10, 16.
[6] *Ibid.*, sermons 3, 7, 13, 17.
[7] *Ibid.*, sermon 11.
[8] *Ibid.*, sermon 19.
[9] *Ibid.*, sermons 18 and 20.
[10] *Ibid.*, sermons 12 and 15.

The Protestant will differ from the Catholic in his attempted explanation of what is ultimately the mystery of Christ's presence in Holy Communion, but he would be singularly insensitive if he did not see strongly evangelical elements in Monsignor Knox's presentations: the majestic humility of the Incarnation and the Passion, the centrality of Christ's supreme Sacrifice for the sins of the world and his strengthening and sanctifying of his Church by this Sacramental Food, and his challenge to his followers to suffer with him. Are not such emphases common to Catholic, Orthodox, and Protestant? These are appeals that echo, as so often in Monsignor Knox, the very accents of the New Testament.

All his mature writings reflect what he calls the 'eucharistic attitude.' This he illustrates from Michelangelo's Adam in the Sistine Chapel frescoes, 'that recumbent figure, stretching out one hand, at the full length of the arm, towards the Creator, as if an acknowledgment of its utter dependence, its creaturely reliance, on him.'[1]

The Priestly Life consists of a series of contemplative addresses to busy priests gathered in retreats. The first of them, on 'Energy and Repose,' begins with St Augustine's vivid phrase about the nature of God as *semper agens*, *semper quietus*, always active, yet always at rest, which is mirrored in God's providence in Nature, and still more clearly in the earthly life of Christ, and in his continuing grace in the Sacrament. It is characteristic of the life of the Church, active in the missionaries, priests, theologians, great ecclesiastics, yet quietly powerful in

[1] *Ibid.*, p. 34.

the cells of her praying celibates. Then there follows a passage of eloquence reminiscent of Cardinal Newman for its crescendo of interest, dramatic contrast, superb image, measured cadences, and convincing close (and there could be no higher praise):

> For if you would approach near to the innermost secret of her life, you must go, not to the palaces of Pope or bishop, not to the courts of ecclesiastical tribunals, or the lecture rooms of learned theologians. You must go to the cells of Carthusians and Poor Clares, if you want to know what the Church really is. Shut off from the noise of the world and its dusty disputes, sheltered by their protecting walls from public inquisitiveness and from the blare of advertisement, these cloistered souls find a peace which is, if we would but realize it, the breath of the Church's life, the source of her triumphs, the solace of her despair. Look at a man or a horse racing; and then remember that behind all that tremendous display of outward activity there is one tiny valve which beats all unseen, all unheard, within the breast; and if that beating were to cease, all the external activities would cease with it. Something of the same importance belongs to those homes of silence and recollectedness where men and women serve God in holy religion: there lies the heart of the Church. Their restfulness is her secret life; the powerhouse from which all her restless activity must spring. Go elsewhere, and you will see the rippling of her muscles; it is in the hours of contemplation that you will hear the beating of her heart.[1]

Such, in alternation between restless activity and quiet contemplation, should be the life of the priests. The other addresses almost all sustain this high standard of spirituality and psychological insight expressed in subtle prose.

[1] *The Priestly Life; A Retreat* (1958), p. 7.

Another charming side of Monsignor Knox is seen in the 24 wedding addresses collected in *Bridegroom and Bride* (1957). His services were required many times because he had been a Chaplain of undergraduates for thirteen years and of schoolgirls for four years. In the Preface he says, accounting for the concise brevity of these addresses, that he was asked to preach at a fashionable wedding by the Earl Marshal of England, and was told: 'You know, the kind of thing for which five minutes is too short and ten is too long.' Since friendship demanded that he should compose a separate address for each occasion, he decided 'to give them that form of burial which befits one's own faded manuscripts —publication.'

Certain central ideas on the Catholic view of marriage naturally repeat themselves in these pages. Knox insists that it is not blind Cupid, but clear-seeing God who is the Matchmaker. The charity and hope of young love is not destroyed but supernaturalized by grace, and therefore will enable groom and bride to gain greater unity in joy and sorrow. Above all, the importance of marriage is that it is the making of a new cell of humanity and the earthly home is to be a type of the heavenly home.

Knox gallantly defends the ardour of the young against the worldliness of the old: 'The cynic will tell you that married happiness is a matter of give and take. Do not believe him; it is a matter of give and give.'[1] With what delicacy of understanding does Monsignor Knox suggest to the married pair that their parents and friends will not grudge them the glory and fulfilment of the hour, but are bound to think that they will live more for one another,

[1] *Bridegroom and Bride*, p. 26.

and less for them, so that 'your wedding, for them, is an unwedding.' Whenever possible, he makes allusions to the local scene, and, in one case, in the Church of St Mary on the Quay, the name suggests the title, the development, the atmosphere and the ending of the address. With delightful fancy he asserts that the Virgin Mary's obedient response to the Annunciation exhibited a naval promptitude. The humour, fancy, wit, gaiety, and deep humanity of Knox are perhaps most clearly expressed in this volume and in *The Mass in Slow Motion*, but almost every sermon he preached exhibits the eucharistic attitude—a grateful, humble, joyous and trustful dependence upon God and confidence in the sufficiency of his providence and grace.

4 · *Method and Style*

Knox, like the consummate stylist that he was, preached from a typewritten manuscript.[1] He could do no other, with his sense of the exact word in the right order. Moreover, this practice safeguarded him from the possibilities of exaggeration and indiscretion, and from any fear that his fertile, darting mind might run away from him. He fully rehearsed his manuscript, which was marked with appropriate elocutionary signs,[2] until he was almost word perfect.

The structure of his sermons with their close progression; the natural lucidity of his thoughts; the vividness, aptness and originality of his images; the intriguing

[1] Evelyn Waugh, *Life*, p. 120.
[2] *Ibid.*, p. 242; Mr Waugh says 'that it is a unique gift of his to give by a sort of vocal legerdemain the impression, while reading, that he was still talking simply and directly to his hearers.'

beginnings and pointed endings; the whimsicality of his wit and the manliness of his monitions; his adaptations of diction and illustration to suit the varied needs of the special groups such as schoolboys at St Edmund's, schoolgirls at Aldenham, Oxford undergraduates and priests, and of special occasions like society weddings and panegyrics in Westminster Cathedral; all together represent a remarkable and flexible command of the art of English rhetoric. Many of these qualities have been already noticed in brief citations from his sermons.

Like Cardinal Newman, Knox's reliance on Scripture in his preaching was considerable. He also shared Newman's habit of searching out the various levels of meaning in Scripture. He did not use a text as a pretext, as a merely ornamental quotation, or as a mere introduction. On the contrary, his text (occasionally he collated two or three texts) in its context was usually the theme of his sermons. His Biblical translations enabled him to discover delicate nuances and refined subtleties of meaning that the customary translations had obscured. The Biblical basis of his preaching supplied authority to all his sermons. His quiet conversational tone was the appropriate index of a mind and heart obedient to Divine Revelation and a spirit that had learned sanctity through suffering. The brilliance of his sermon lies partly, like Donne's, in the juxtaposition of thoughts rarely associated;[1] partly in the unerringly apt illustrations; partly in epigrams and wit; and partly in the clear but unobtrusive structure.

[1] As in likening the window in the monstrance to that through which the lover in *Canticles* sought his beloved, or as in comparing Ruth's gleaning to the Christian's reception of the Eucharist. (See sermons 1 and 2 of *A Window in the Wall.*)

For those who like sermons to be a historical and theological exposition of the Scriptures, many of Knox's sermons are too allegorical. In some cases, the theological approach may seem so arbitrary as to find foreshadowings of the New Testament in the Old where there are only shadows. Sometimes, even in the Catholic sermons, the easy but fatal transition from lightheartedness to levity is made;[1] but this is the occupational hazard of a fertile, original and witty mind. There are very few polemical misrepresentations of other Christian denominations or movements that have survived his polishing of manuscripts.

The final impression is of a great preacher, of a brilliant mind and imagination first captured and controlled, then liberated by grace to become an effective cultural attaché of Christ's court and Kingdom, and of a priest who entered into the fellowship of Christ and his sufferings, and who remained courteous until his last breath.

As he lay on his death-bed, momentarily recovering consciousness after a three-day coma, he was asked whether he would like some passage of his own translation of the New Testament to be read to him. He answered faintly but clearly, 'No.' Then, following a long pause, he added, in words that recalled the idiom of his youth, 'Awfully jolly of you to suggest it, though.' Those were his last words.[2]

[1] For an unfortunate example, see *Bridegroom and Bride*, p. 69: 'Eastertide is rich in the feasts of martyrs; it was in Spring, perhaps, you got the best bookings for the amphitheatre.'

[2] Evelyn Waugh, *Life*, p. 333.

6

Psychological Preaching

LESLIE D. WEATHERHEAD

DR Leslie Dixon Weatherhead, who was born in London in 1893 and who attained the widest fame as Minister of London's City Temple from 1936 to 1960, is unrivalled as a twentieth-century physician of souls and preacher of the integration of personality through Christ and the Beloved Community, the Church.

1 · *Renown and Influence*

This reputation has been solidly achieved by preeminence in three ways. An early and convinced advocate of the necessity for ministers to collaborate with medical doctors and psychiatrists, he has pioneered in the establishment of psychological clinics in connection with two important churches where he has exercised his longest ministries. The first was at Brunswick Methodist Church, Leeds, where he was pastor and preacher to a large and influential congregation from 1925 to 1936. The second was at the City Temple for the ensuing 24 years. It may be doubted, therefore, whether any other minister has a more scientific knowledge of the frustrations, fears, anxieties and disintegrations of the human personality, and of the way to overcome them through scientific and religious techniques of healing, than Dr Weatherhead. His experience is based, therefore, quite literally on thousands of case-histories.

His renown has been even more widespread in the remarkable success of the books he has written correlating Christianity and Psychology, of which four are the most famous: *Psychology and Life*, *Psychology in Service of the Soul* (1929), *The Mastery of Sex through Psychology and Religion* (1932), and the crowning work, *Psychology, Religion and Healing* (1951), an authoritative and critical survey 'of all the non-physical methods of healing, with an examination of the principles underlying them and the techniques employed to express them, together with some conclusions regarding further investigation and action in this field.'[1]

Psychology, Religion and Healing impresses the non-technical reader with the author's remarkable objectivity in expounding psychological theories with which, as a Christian, he can have little affinity (for example, Freud's pansexualism), his Pauline capacity to be 'all things to all' psychologists in order that he may save some—patients, and, supremely, his unconcealed conviction that Christ, the unique Son of God and Saviour, cannot be reduced to the dimensions of a great Faith-healer, nor can radiant health be anything but a by-product of the Christian faith and way of life.

The third avenue by which Dr Weatherhead has attained distinction is as a preacher, and, it should be perceived, not only as a psychological preacher. In the Preface to a collection of sermons, *That Immortal Sea*

[1] The sub-title of his book.

(1953), Dr Weatherhead indicates his range: 'I have tried to choose, from the many sermons I am called upon to prepare, those which illustrate a wide variety: theological, expository, evangelistic, philosophical, psychological, and so on.'[1] Dr Weatherhead is, it must be insisted on, a preacher of the full-orbed Gospel who is both an apologist of great ability and a superb literary craftsman. Even if all his psychological sermons were to be eliminated, he would still command attention since his other sermons (which are the vast majority) are among the best examples of modern preaching.

Nevertheless, if we look to his unique contribution to the modern ministry, we shall find it in his expertise as a physician of souls in Church-related clinics and as a preacher of the integrating love of Christ. Dr Weatherhead has demonstrated in pulpit and clinic that the love of God in Christ excludes anxiety and that Christian faith excludes fear. He has also shown the inspirational power of Christian worship and fellowship which makes the introvert look upward to God and outward to a needy world of service and the extrovert look within to discover his guilt and upward to discover his forgiveness and potentialities in God.

2 · *A Pioneer in Religious Psychology*

The most impressive Christian pioneers are the most courageous. Out of the nettle danger they pluck the flowers of safety. They blunt the edge of criticism by

[1] *That Immortal Sea* (1953), Preface, p. 7. He adds that he has preached topical sermons on suitable occasions, but that he has not published them because they 'date' rapidly.

accepting its validity. Such a pioneer was the distinguished Anglican Victorian divine, Frederick Denison Maurice, the founder of the Christian Socialists. He recognized the writing on the wall in 1848, the year of turbulent revolutions, and saw that social justice was a Christian, not merely a secular and socialist ideal. He saw that a Church only standing for the social and economic *status quo* would be swept away, as he discerned Marx the prophet in the guise of Marx the agitator. In the same way Dr Weatherhead[1] responded positively to the challenge of the 'New Psychology' and continued to believe that the psycho-analyst might benefit instead of replacing the priest. It took considerable courage since the father of modern psycho-analysis, Freud, had written of the future of religion as *The Future of an Illusion*, as if belief in the Heavenly Father were merely the symptom of man's unwillingness to stand on his own feet and his projection of the comforting illusion of a God on the empty screen of the heavens. Moreover, the assertion of Freud that the greatest driving force in man was the sexual instinct and the deterministic concepts of the Behaviourists seemed to eliminate the role of religion, even if Jung made place for God. In brief, it was Weatherhead's distinction to recognize in an enemy a potential ally.

What, then, has Dr Weatherhead learned from his

[1] Weatherhead was not alone, of course, in the belief that psychology could be made an ally of religion. Other English theologians who shared this view were W. B. Selbie, L. W. Grensted and T. W. Pym. Psychologists in England who were convinced of the value of co-operation between psychology and religion included J. A. Hadfield, C. H. Valentine (both of whom had received a theological training) and William Brown.

attempt to correlate psychology and religion? In the first place, he has been convinced that both disciplines recognize the paralysing effect of guilt and the inordinate importance of confession. The psycho-analyst has indeed probed the dimensions of guilt in the neuroses and obsessions of the patient in a deeper way than was open to the religious confessor. For his deep analysis probes back into the subconscious and even into the unconscious layers of the mind, sometimes tracing back the guilt to an incident in early childhood. Such concealed feelings cause a type of mental obstruction that prevents the mind and often the body from attaining to the confident integration that spells health and wholeness. But while the psycho-analyst helps the patient to achieve acceptance, the religious psychologist in the name of Christ is able to offer not merely acceptance but the forgiveness of God, the restoration of a confident relationship with him and with his fellow-men. Dr Weatherhead knows that forgiveness is a profoundly healing experience. Moreover, the religious psychologist can introduce the forgiven soul into the invigorating fellowship of other redeemed and forgiven souls. This removal from the isolation of a paralysed self into the heart of a forgiven and forgiving community is also part of the progress of integration. But Dr Weatherhead knows that some Churches and some forms of worship can weaken rather than strengthen the patient. They can merely encourage the egotism of the soul which seeks an escape from the rigours of reality in the aesthetic evasion provided by a lovely but seemingly irrelevant liturgy. Or, on the other hand, a confessor may so emphasize the negative aspect of sin, without a correlative stress on the victory of faith, that the patient becomes more engulfed and immured in his sins and, ultimately, more despairing, as his introspection is exaggerated.[1]

Secondly, Dr Weatherhead recognizes the positive importance of Christian worship, for it inculcates the *worthiness* of God in Christ. He writes: 'Thus in worship, when we express the emotion of admiration for those qualities which God personifies, we are remade in His image, and the more we can look away from ourselves to Him, the more we can benefit, paradoxical as it may sound.'[2] He is fond of citing Moffatt's translation of Philippians 4.8 because it expresses the importance of true Christian worship for concentrating on the positive: 'Whatsoever is true, or worthwhile, or just, or attractive, or high-minded, keep on thinking about these things.' In true worship the constant emphasis on the unconditional and unchanging love of God to men (as opposed to the hatred that breeds neuroses), the sheer generosity of his grace in Christ (as opposed to the envy and jealousy that the sick soul feeds on), the radiant confidence of trust which is faith (as opposed to the fear and suspicion that suppurate in the mind), is itself a reconditioning and therapeutic process.

In the third place, Dr Weatherhead finds that in the genuine Christian community, which is outgoing in its concern for the world, there is provided a community of altruism, as well as a community of appreciation, both of which are needed to develop an integrated personality. On the latter point he says decisively: 'One of the

[1] *Psychology, Religion and Healing*, pp. 450–451. See also *Psychology in Service of the Soul*, p. 82.

[2] *Ibid.*, p. 453.

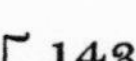

greatest needs of personality is to be loved.'[1] This is peculiarly the case in our modern civilization, where in the vast cities, the personality becomes reduced to a pigmy unit, being a mere unit of production or consumption, a statistic or a 'hand.' The place where he can find significance and appreciation is in the Beloved Community, the Church. But also while the Church's inward glance is directed at Christ and at its own loving fellowship, its outward glance and mission is towards the world. The mature personality must find an outlet in altruism. Indeed, Dr Weatherhead suggests that 'perhaps the personality is most fully integrated in those people whose lives are devoted to one all-consuming altruistic purpose in which bodily powers, mental energies—including all the instincts and all the healthy emotions—and spiritual aspirations find their full expression.'[2] It is literally true that 'He that loseth his life for my sake and the Gospel's, shall find it.' Thus in sharing the missionary and social work of the Christian Church the introvert becomes outward-looking and the extrovert uses his gifts not for mere geniality and self-expression, but for the benefit and satisfaction of others.

Fourthly, Weatherhead recognizes the great value of the practice of intercession for the sick. His complaint is, however, that it is practised in most churches vaguely, casually and without expectation of any results. Experience over many years convinces him that there are certain essential conditions to fulfil before intercession for the sick is likely to be rewarded. One is that the patient must be assured of the genuine love and concern of those who pray for him. Another is that the intercessors must

[1] *Ibid.*, p. 466. [2] *Ibid.*, pp. 466–467.

be able to identify themselves imaginatively with the patient and be utterly and serenely confident of his recovery through the instrumentality of their prayers. In the City Temple it was Dr Weatherhead's custom to intercede for three or four sick persons in one service. He would supply some details about the patient to assist the congregation's concentration and say, 'In imagination go into the ward and stand beside her bed. Do not pray that she may become better, because that is putting her cure into the future. Believe that at this very moment Christ is touching her life, and that His healing power is being made manifest in her body now. Believe that He can work more powerfully in the atmosphere of our faith and love.'[1] This power of intercession is not a substitute for medicine or for psychiatry but an additional and co-operating power. There is no doubt that Dr Weatherhead's ministry has provided powerful confirmation of the effectiveness of intercessory prayer.

In the fifth place, Dr Weatherhead realizes that 'preaching aims at providing the conditions in which conversion can happen.' He is well aware that conversion 'cannot be engineered by man in cold blood.'[2] It is neither deserved nor won; it is a gift of God in response to man's need. But the community hearing God's Word of challenge, consolation and consecration is the context of conversion. Here, indeed, the preacher is enabled by the power of the Holy Spirit to make real the transforming friendship of Christ. Here the questing soul finds its peace, fulfilment and completion in God. Here the egotist experiences what Chalmers termed 'the expulsive power of a new affection.'

[1] *Ibid.*, p. 241.

[2] *Ibid.*, p. 467.

Finally, Dr Weatherhead has much detailed teaching on the insights of psychology and religion which cannot even be mentioned, far less contained in this brief study. But what is most impressive cumulatively is his recognition of certain limitations in religious and psychological healing. No fanatic, he recognizes that much 'garage work'—as he calls the physical healing methods of the general medical practitioner—still needs to be done. He also insists that while the healing ministry of Christ entitles the Christian to believe that sickness is not to be received in resignation as the will of God (since God wills for his children the abundant life, with the maximum physical, mental and spiritual health) yet there are persons who in uncured sickness have manifested the flowers of spirituality and have been saints in their suffering. He is rightly insistent, also, that health is only a by-product of the worship and service of God, for he truly observes that 'worship is ruined if it is conceived as toadying, or *using* God for our own ends.'[1] Nevertheless, while much may be learned, Dr Weatherhead believes, from the mental mechanisms which Christ used in his healing miracles, 'we shall not be able to do the things He did by becoming cleverer psychologists.'[2] His power was the supernatural power of the Son of God. To compare Christ's power with the power of the slow and patient psychotherapist is like comparing 'the power of an oxyacetylene flame' with 'the power of rust to eat through an iron bar.'[3] Dr Weatherhead believes that the supreme healing power is the Person of Christ himself, which has not been

[1] *Ibid.*, p. 453. Cf. also p. 465.
[2] *Ibid.*, p. 78.
[3] *Ibid.*, p. 488.

withheld, but rather unappropriated. 'When the Church returns to her early devotion to Christ and creates united fellowships, even faintly like the small body of men who went out in the power of the Risen Christ and His Spirit to turn the world upside down, then a power more potent to heal than any atomic bomb to destroy will once more surge through sick souls and minds and bodies. It will be His own power and recognised as such.'[1]

Thus in Dr Weatherhead's mind the pastor, the preacher and the religious psychologist are not three vocations but three aspects of the same calling. Their conjoint task is to channel by compassionate word and action the integrating love of God in Christ and in his Church. Weatherhead's own life is an admirable example of sublimation. He writes, 'I had wanted to be a medical missionary, but neither my family nor I could afford the cost of medical training.'[2] In closing that door, God opened for him a wider and more effectual channel as a physician of souls in the 'Age of Anxiety.'

3 · *Sermon-craft*

Whether the minister or layman shares Dr Weatherhead's convictions about the importance of psychology in the service of the soul or not, he is not likely to question the helpfulness of his representation of the central themes of Christian faith and duty or his consummate artistry in sermon-craft.

That Immortal Sea (1953) demonstrates Weatherhead's versatility of theme and treatment. Four are concerned with practical problems: acquisitiveness, worry,

[1] *Ibid.*, p. 495.

[2] *Ibid.*, p. xxiii.

true and untrue selves, and the confidence necessary to face old age. A well-argued sermon on the forbidding theme, 'Foreknowledge, Free Will, and Fate,' insists on a distinction between the direct and permissive will of God, and 'Is life a matter of luck?' also gives grounds for belief in the Divine providence. The evangelical sermons are concerned with the utterly unconventional love of Christ, the power of the risen and crucified Christ, and the contrast with human callousness and Christ's total concern for humanity. Other sermons, such as 'This Haunted World,' are mystical and devotional in character. Some exceptionally able apologetical sermons are included, particularly the ironically titled 'The Advantages of Atheism' and 'Whose Voice shall I Trust?' which examines critically the counter-claims of the cynic and materialist in comparison with the believer in God.

Dr Weatherhead's craft in sermon-writing might be missed by the reader or hearer of these sermons so naturally is the interest caught and held. In fact, however, this art conceals great art. An analysis of the citations and references reveals an astonishing apparatus of illustration and exemplification. There are 31 references to personal experience or to the experiences of those known personally to the preacher. They vary from letters written to him after a broadcast sermon to a conversation with Dr C. E. M. Joad's vicar; from boyhood reminiscences to the conversation of 'dear old ladies' in a boarding-house; from army memories of India to walks in the English countryside; from troubled men and women to those who have conquered their temptations. Clearly, the ex-combat officer, the former padre, the psychotherapist and confidant, the man who has lived in the industrial cities of the north and gathered distinguished members in the metropolitan church, is able to open the widest windows of experience to his congregation and this has interest and relevance, as of first-hand observation and common-sense judgment on the lessons of life.

The second largest class of references in *That Immortal Sea* consists of literary citations. There are 37 separate references, made to 27 different authors. The most frequent are Tennyson, Browning, Vaughan and Shakespeare. Others apt, but recondite and far from conventional, are to Georges Sand, Richard Jefferies, Charles Morgan, Nevile Shute, Galsworthy, De La Mare and Traherne. Clearly, the psychologist is determined to bring before his people 'Whatsoever things are of good report.' And his own style with its clarity and cogency, its occasional epigrammatic summary and affectionate touch, owes much to companying with the great names in English literature. It is not surprising that a preacher who believes that admiration and reverence are the heart of worship should return so often to the poets who evoke these qualities.

The third largest class of illustrative material consists of anecdotes, of which there are 19 in this volume, to complement the references to personal experience. What makes them impressive is the variety of callings which they illustrate—their extroverted quality which prevents worship from being too ingrowing. A missionary candidate, a Hebridean seaman, a soldier in Burma, sacrificial coal-miners, two intrepid explorers, aeronautical pioneers, doctors, musicians, an American journalist, an artist of renown, a general, and slum-dwellers are only some of the witnesses whom Dr Weatherhead calls to the bar to offer their testimonies positively or negatively to the power of religious faith. Here, again, the fetid, hothouse atmosphere of a self-regarding church is overcome by opening its windows to the winds of the world.

The fourth class of references is to foreign lands. There are 17 of these, and while they also serve to hold the interest (since travellers' tales are usually fascinating), they have a second purpose—to widen the horizons of the local church until they are coextensive with the world. Palestine and India have the priority of interest, as in most of Dr Weatherhead's sermons, because these he has lived in. (From 1919–1922 he was minister of the English Methodist Church in Madras and as a combatant officer and chaplain he became familiar with the Near East; also he visited Palestine in 1934.)

The other groups of references are less important. There are 9 references to theologians from Augustine to C. H. Dodd, 10 to thinkers as varied as Von Hügel and Bertrand Russell, 9 to preachers and ministers, and 3 to psychologists. What is much more important is Weatherhead's interest in philology and the consistent concern to interpret the New Testament from the Greek. This exegetical carefulness and linguistic accuracy are most characteristic. For example in his book on the parables, *In Quest of a Kingdom* (1934), there are 28 references to 16 different Biblical commentators.

His most recent volume, *Key Next Door and Other City Temple Sermons* (1960), provides a selection of 26 sermons preached at the close of his 24-year ministry at the City Temple. It discloses a new Weatherhead in several respects. For one thing he is here seen as a preacher on special occasions, for nine of the sermons were prepared for Christmas Day, the New Year, Holy Week, Pentecost, Harvest Festival, Bible Sunday, Missionary Sunday, Armistice Sunday, and it is probable that the two final sermons were preached at Eastertide. These sermons demonstrate that Dr Weatherhead is not in the least cramped by the set theme, but that he preaches on it without the least diminution of interest, relevance or cogency.

Of even greater interest is the changed proportion of the different categories of sermons in his selection. While *Over His Own Signature* (1955) was exclusively dedicated to sermons on the devotional life, and there were only three sermons of doctrinal type in *That Immortal Sea*, there are no less than 11 doctrinal sermons in *Key Next Door* and only two sermons on the spiritual life. The number of apologetical sermons is increased to six, as compared with four in *That Immortal Sea*. There are also four psychological sermons and two ethical sermons.

A third most interesting emphasis in this volume is on the primary importance of absolute candour in religion. The Preface indicates Dr Weatherhead's concern above all 'to be mentally honest and realistic,' his dissatisfaction with theological clichés and glib affirmations, and his increasing awareness of the utter disparity between the mind of Christ and many hymns and even passages of Scripture. He made it a special discipline while spending two periods in hospital in 1956 to test 'poetic imagery, beautiful language, traditional theology, religious words made familiar by centuries of repetition' by the canons of 'sincerity and truth and realistic usefulness to the hearer.'[1] The result is that a cutting wind of truth blows away the autumnal leaves of discarded traditions and even the cyclone of iconoclasm whirls through some of the sermons. It is most invigorating, and all the more impressive because Dr Weatherhead's concern is always to build up new structures of faith where he detonates faulty foundations.

This intellectual zest of his may well reflect the post-Christian situation in modern England, where the Christians are necessarily a valiant minority swimming against the scientific and sociological tides of secularism. Another indication of his concern to argue for theism and for the Christian interpretation of life's meaning and destiny instead of merely reaffirming the Christian faith, is the vast number of intelligent witnesses, scientists, theologians, leaders of art and music, whether contemporary or past, that he brings forward as advocates of his case.

4 · *The Secret of Success*

How are we to account for the great popularity of Dr Weatherhead as a person and as a preacher? Clearly, the first facet of his success must be found in his own winsome and radiant personality. Here the preacher of the primacy of 'transforming friendship' is himself an admirable illustration of the candid compassion of the Christian disciple. He has said that the new psychology has the same practical aim as the New Testament,

[1] *Over His Own Signature* (1955), Preface.

namely 'the facing up to life bravely and the making of it that vigorous, radiant, confident, healthful thing God meant it to be.'[1] Each adjective is applicable to the impression of quiet and serene confidence that he gives in the pulpit.

Not only does Dr Weatherhead look friendly, but he cultivates the techniques of a confidant in the pulpit in a great variety of ways. It may be the conversational casualness with which he introduces the topic of his sermon, such as 'I wonder how your New Year resolutions are getting on?'[2] or the naturalness of the title of a sermon on Divine Providence—'Is Life a Matter of Luck?'[3] It may be the vast number of references to his own experience, usually introduced in the most modest and natural fashion. It may be the refusal to use technical theological terms—the determined avoidance of pedantry and dogmatism. It may be the use of homely analogies and of colloquial English, with the occasional slang term. It may well be the catholicity of attitude which is not only ecumenical in spirit, but even allows that God uses religions other than Christianity as avenues to him.[4] It could also be the candour with which old shibboleths are dismissed. Certainly it would have to include the characteristic tenderness of his mood, and his whimsical sense of humour. The offensive pietist with his bland assurance that God covers him with a special insurance policy is delightfully satirized by citing the following limerick:

[1] *Psychology in Service of the Soul* (1929), p. xxiii.
[2] *Key Next Door*, p. 60.
[3] *That Immortal Sea*, p. 166.
[4] *Key Next Door*, pp. 152 f. 'Is Christianity the Only Way to God?'

There was a young lady of Ryde,
Who was carried away by the tide,
    A man-eating shark
    Was heard to remark,
'I knew that the Lord would provide!'[1]

The constant sympathy for the difficulties of modern life, the conviction that the dullest lives can have significance through the ennobling grasp of Christ's handshake, the concentration on understanding and forgiving rather than criticizing, are all exceptionally endearing qualities. But not even all of these factors explain the immediacy with which Weatherhead establishes a remarkable rapport with his congregation, as with his readers. There is no disputing that it is an asset of cardinal importance.

It is, in the second place, a great advantage for a preacher to have a distinctive quality in his own ministry. Dr Weatherhead's, as we have indicated, is that of religious psychology. He speaks with the authority of a physician of souls.

Thirdly, the wide range of personal experiences and the breadth of his reading in literature, psychology, and history, bring before the listener or reader of his sermons a vast and variegated human panorama, a type of modern Canterbury Pilgrimage. A man with such wide interests is bound to enlarge the vision and outlook of his congregation or literary audience. He might say, of his twenty-four years at the City Temple, with Dr Johnson, 'Sir, when a man is tired of London, he is tired of life.' His interest in the human family is untiring and it is motivated by a desire to understand, never to condemn or belittle.

[1] *Ibid.*, p. 114.

In the fourth place, his sermons always have a clear plan, and these patterns are extremely varied. One may take the form of a simple contrast, as in 'Babel or Jerusalem?' setting off the chaos of Babel against the unity of the primitive Christian community at Pentecost, or comparing the world of appearance with the world of reality as in 'This Haunted World.' It may have a three-fold structure as in 'Whose Voice shall I Trust?' where materialist, cynic and theist make their competing claims for attention. His Christological sermon, 'Master and Lord,' the ninth in the devotional series *Over His Own Signature*, makes four major points to establish Our Lord's claim to Divinity. In the intriguingly titled sermon, 'The Advantages of Atheism,' he makes no less than twelve separate points as dents in the atheist's armour, which are also links in the chain of the Christian's defence. These twelve 'incredibles' for the atheist are twelve unanswerable questions which are more credible on the Christian hypothesis. Like every eminent preacher Weatherhead is clear and flexible in his planning, using whatever shape the text or topic or the heads of argument dictate. But each point is made clearly and cogently before proceeding with the next. It is *vertebral* sermon-making.

Fifthly, he has the great preacher's gift for putting abstract thought into direct speech and into concrete images. As an example we may take his clarification of the promise of Jesus: 'I will give you the spirit of truth and he shall guide you into all truth.' Weatherhead explains:

> *You cannot be guided anywhere if you refuse to move.* Do not scorn the uneducated heathen because of his metal image.

Ask yourself whether a creed or hymn has not too often been a metal image, causing you either to stop thinking or to use words and mean either nothing at all or else something which the words certainly do not say, a species of mental juggling which the man in the street calls downright hypocrisy. 'You say the words,' he says, 'but you do not mean them. You mean something else.' I can understand his scorn. It is as though a chemist learned in boyhood Dalton's Atomic Hypothesis that an atom is the smallest conceivable part of an element, and that when the discovery of electrons burst on the chemist's horizon, he refused to stop chanting Dalton's Atomic Theory once a week, but inwardly said to himself, 'Of course, by "atom" I mean "electron."' No one, for example, who chants, 'I believe in the resurrection of the body,' means what their first author meant.[1]

In the sixth place, Dr Weatherhead has a strong visual imagination, and there is more than a tincture of the romantic in his make-up. This may be seen in the visual titles of his book of sermons: each conveys a clearly defined image. He has also an almost Victorian delight in the grandeur of landscape and it is not surprising that Wordsworth is one of his favourite poets. Listen to him conjuring up the vision of the isolated John of Patmos watching the dawn by the seashore:

Above him the stars flashed like gems in the splendour of the velvet night, at its darkest just before the dawn. It was early on the Lord's day and he longed to worship with those he had been compelled to leave. He turned toward Jerusalem, far in the east, and behold the darkness was breaking. He had had his back to it, gazing mournfully at the black, hostile sea as yet unillumined by the dawn. But now the great splendour had begun. The colour spread across the

[1] *Over His Own Signature*, p. 60.

sky. Daffodil first with gleams of pale green and primrose light, then the faintest pastel pink rapidly deepening to crimson and gold. John thought of the temple in Jerusalem catching the gleams in its golden dome as God's day of worship began. As a great wave crashed behind him, he turned at the noise and it seemed to shout to him, in a trumpet voice of majesty and assurance, 'I am Alpha and Omega, the first and the last.'[1]

He is perhaps happier in less ambitious effects, in simple analogies in which he is fertile. As, for example, in his psychological illustration of the frustrated man who asked to have a major instinct removed, which Weatherhead regards as tantamount to 'a motorist who had his engine removed from his car and proceeded to push it.'[2] Or when he translates the urgent relevance in the term 'gospel': '"Good news," said a friend of mine, "is that which can be shouted across a street." Thus—The war's over! The baby's born! Susan's out of danger! The strike's settled! Here is my bit of good news for you: GOD WILL RECEIVE YOU—NOW!'[3] Other evidence of Weatherhead's strongly visual imagination which he can transfer to his hearer's or reader's mental screen is provided by the many memorable cameos and word-pictures in which his sermons abound. His frequent word-transparencies or snapshots of Palestinian shepherds and householders,[4] of life in the Arabian

[1] *Ibid.*, pp. 142–143. This is 'Vistavision' writing rather than good literature, but it is admirable for popular purposes. More disciplined and sensitive writing would have avoided the archaism of 'behold,' the ugly repetition of 'had had,' and the commonplace 'gazing mournfully,' and might have toned down some of the more blatant 'gorgeous Technicolor' effects.

[2] *That Immortal Sea*, p. 153.

[3] *In Quest of a Kingdom*, p. 73.

[4] *Ibid.*, p. 191.

desert or in an Indian bazaar or mission-station,[1] all exemplify the use of this gift.

Most important of all, Weatherhead chooses the central Christian themes and relates them in most relevant fashion to the daily needs of men and women. Here his understanding of theology's message and psychology's diagnosis admirably complement each other: God and man are related as closely as gift to need. Man's guilt is obliterated by God's forgiveness and the Kingdom of God is defined as the kingdom of rectified and restored relationships, both vertical and horizontal.[2] *This is the Victory* is a series of sermons written in wartime when the tide of battle was not going notably in Britain's favour and when faith was the only antidote to pessimism and despair. Faith is itself nurtured by the 'perfect love' which 'casteth out fear.'

Above all, both in *The Plain Man Looks at the Cross* (1945) and in *Personalities of the Passion* (1942), as well as innumerable single sermons, Dr Weatherhead never fails to see afresh the staggering generosity of God's seeking and saving love in Christ constantly and unconditionally for the last, the least and the lost. This love which is victorious over sin, suffering and death is the cure for anxiety in this life, as the Resurrection is the cure for the fear of death. This is the holy love that makes a man divinely dissatisfied with his own poor level of achievement; it is the same love of Christ which constrains him to helpful altruism. It is the *power* of Christ's love, mediated by his Church, which enables

[1] *Ibid.*, p. 107.

[2] Weatherhead's most extended treatment of Christian social relationships is found in his book *In Quest of a Kingdom*. Generally speaking, he is not greatly concerned with Christian social action.

him to walk with a pilgrim's confidence and to endure hardship like a good soldier of Jesus Christ, as one of 'the happy band of pilgrims' and part of the Church militant on earth. Christ's and the Church's friendship is the ending of man's endemic loneliness, in modern rootless living. This love 'which couldn't care more' is the Christian's example and encouragement. It can look death, disease, suffering, despair, and doubt in the eyes in the power of the Crucified and Risen Christ, the Guide, the Revealer, the Companion, the Pioneer, the Teacher, the Healer and the Saviour of Humanity. Dr Weatherhead's is a high, not a reduced Christology, and he speaks of Our Lord in all those roles which we have listed. But it is chiefly as Friend, Healer and Saviour that our preacher thinks of him, for he knows that modern man's desperate loneliness cries for a Friend, that his anxieties and obsessive fears call out for a Healer, and his degradation and failure demand a Saviour. It is Weatherhead's distinction to have provided as the aim of each of his services of worship 'a glimpse of Christ.'[1]

[1] It should be noted that in Dr Weatherhead's services the worship as well as the sermon is planned as an integral whole. He pays particular tribute to Dr Eric Thiman, distinguished organist of the City Temple, and to the choir because their music provided 'an atmosphere in which preaching came easy,' and 'in church I had the immense asset of preaching at a point of the service when the minds and hearts of the congregation—a congregation that I knew and loved—had been prepared for my message by three-quarters of an hour of worship.' (*Key Next Door*, p. 7.)

5 · *A Final Evaluation and Critique*

For all his deserved popularity and his immense influence, Dr Weatherhead is not every man's indispensable preacher. For the hundreds who respond to his wooing notes, to his tenderness and sympathy, there must also be the tens who occasionally find him mawkish and even sentimental. Even though his most recent volume of sermons displays a more virile, realistic and even iconoclastic tendency and a determination to think through and face the commonest criticisms of Christianity, yet even here occasionally the pathos degenerates into bathos. In a Christmas sermon he speaks of the strangeness of the gifts of the three Magi for the Christ child, and then continues: 'I do not mean to be in the least irreverent, but did no one give Him a soft, woolly, cuddly toy, the ancient equivalent of a teddy-bear? Did no one give Him a rattle? Did no one treat Him as a little baby thing?'[1] Here R. W. Dale's rebuke would be apt—that this is to 'forget that Christ is King, that He is not to be fondled but to be reverenced.'[2]

The more serious, though not entirely justified, charge would be that Dr Weatherhead preaches more of the comfort than the criticism of the Gospel. This may, indeed, be the appropriate way to preach the Gospel in twentieth-century England when Christians are few and need to be encouraged, for the world will provide more than enough criticisms of Christians. Indeed, Dr Weatherhead could point to sermons on the 'Harsh

[1] *Ibid.*, p. 213.
[2] *The Laws of Christ for Common Life* (1884), p. 271.

Words of Jesus'[1] and to his insistence that Christ's friendship is always *transforming* as discipleship matures, however *accepting* in its beginnings. The criticism would, however, be more relevant if it were directed to the paucity of Christian social teaching in Dr Weatherhead's sermons. Here, too, he could enter a *caveat*, that when England was nearing the end of the Second World War and considering the reconstruction of the nation that would alone do justice to the men who had died for her on the battlefield, he produced a whole series of sermons on the rectified relationships that the Kingdom of God demands, which he published as *In Quest of a Kingdom*. As his psychology is an individual psychology (and only in the most subordinate and secondary sense a social psychology), so is his theology a personal theology, and he regards the Church as a community of the like-minded in their commitment to service, except that unlike the Rotarians they do not try to do good by stealth. Rarely do we hear in him the denunciation of the prophet or envision a kingdom of social justice. There is the call to altruism as the completion of the balanced human personality; there is the command for an outgoing philanthropy; but never the insistence with Silvester Horne, that 'the ballot-box is the sacrament of brotherhood' or that political and economic structures must be refashioned to approximate to the mind of Christ. This is a curious lack in a preacher who in so many other ways insists that the Gospel meets modern humanity at its points of deepest need. It is appropriate to cite the caution of Dr Reinhold Niebuhr: 'No degree of goodwill alone can cure a deficiency in glandular

[1] *Key Next Door*, p. 70.

secretions; and no moral idealism can overcome a basic mechanical defect in the social structure.'[1]

Dr Weatherhead has frequently warned his hearers about the effects of negative thinking. This evaluation must, in justice, end on the note of appreciation. More than most preachers of his day he has been always ready to supply—in the title of one of his books—a *Prescription for Anxiety* (1956). He has harnessed the theoretical and practical insights of modern psychology to the integrating imperatives and dynamics of the Christian Gospel, which he has most simply defined as 'the acceptance of Christ's friendship.'[2] Yet he has never limited himself to psychological preaching. He has been equally concerned with the culture and discipline of the spiritual life in public and private worship, with the doctrinal sermons that expound the nature of God in Christ and the Divine purpose for mankind, and, increasingly in recent years, with bringing the doubting or daunted intellect into the captivity of Christ. His preaching is marked by profound compassion, a comradely interest in all types and conditions of humanity, a sustained encouragement of all who are trying to live as disciples of Christ, and a variety of interest that have carried him triumphantly through a ministry in the 'goldfish bowl' of London's City Temple for twenty-four difficult years in history.

'Our membership,' writes Dr Weatherhead, 'includes a cabinet minister, and others of rank, position and authority, and also the lowliest and the poorest—people who have been unemployed, people who have been in prison.' It also includes Harley Street doctors, highly

[1] *The Interpretation of Christian Ethics*, p. 192.
[2] *Key Next Door*, p. 37.

placed civil servants, professors and lawyers, students, 'with artisans, youngsters just beginning a career, nurses, clerks, typists, young business men and women, postmen, and policemen.'[1] In the days of peace it is not unusual to find fourteen different nationalities in one service. Dr Weatherhead's great achievement is to have gathered, held and helped so scattered and so socially variegated a congregation through unusually testing times and to have commended to them the Gospel with singular freshness, clarity and relevance for a quarter of a century.

[1] *The Significance of Silence*, p. 9. A short biography of *Dr Leslie Weatherhead* by C. Maitland was published in 1960, the year of his retirement.

7

Distinguished Lay Preaching

B. L. MANNING & C. S. LEWIS

ONE very remarkable feature of the twentieth century is that some of the best defenders of the Christian faith in England have been laymen whose grasp of theology and gift of communication many a clergyman might envy. To recall the names of G. K. Chesterton and Hilaire Belloc, T. S. Eliot and Dorothy Sayers, Charles Williams and C. S. Lewis, T. R. Glover and B. L. Manning is to be aware of the debt of Christian apologetics to laymen.

The reasons for selecting Manning and Lewis from among this distinguished company are twofold. In the first place, they alone (with the exception of the Baptist historian and Public Orator of Cambridge University, T. R. Glover) mounted the stairs of the pulpit to testify to their Christian faith and only they published their sermons and addresses. In the second place, their sermons and addresses represent through Manning the faith of a Free Churchman and through Lewis the faith of an Anglican. Dr Nathaniel Micklem, the Principal-Emeritus of Mansfield, Oxford, who was able to call on the services of many of the leading preachers in Britain for the Chapel of Mansfield College, has told that it was crowded consistently only when Bernard Manning and C. S. Lewis occupied the pulpit.[1]

It is clear that they both had a special gift for commending the reasonableness and relevance of the Christian Gospel to sophisticated undergraduates. The attraction was, in part, a sense that these men were not professional clergymen and presumably had no theological axe to grind. It was also a recognition that they were acknowledged experts in their respective fields of history and literature, who spoke with vigour and wit. Perhaps the greatest reason for their appeal, however, was that they were unyielding defenders and exponents of Christian orthodoxy, although neither was a literalist. At a time when most intellectuals trying to explain the faith only succeeded in explaining it away, Manning and Lewis presented central and historical Christianity. Theirs was neither a diluted version of the Faith, nor a denominationally distorted variant of it. In short, they both abhorred an accommodation of the faith to modernism. Far from being the apostles of a sanctified common sense, they preached the doctrines of the Holy Trinity, the Incarnation of Jesus Christ both Divine and human, Christ's effectual sacrifice and his glorious Resurrection. Lewis, indeed, went further in recapturing by his vivid concepts of heaven and hell the eternal seriousness of Christian decision with its abiding eschatological alternatives.

[1] See his *The Box and the Puppets* (1957) for a lively and candid account of his Principalship at Mansfield. The information on the popularity of both Manning and Lewis as preachers was conveyed in a letter to the writer, his former student, in May of 1960.

1 · *Similarities in Approach and Interests*

The likenesses between these different men are worth pondering because they are many. Each was a university teacher held in high repute. Manning was Fellow, subsequently Bursar and finally Senior Tutor of Jesus College, Cambridge, and University Lecturer in History at Cambridge and, for a time, Lecturer in Historical Geography at London University. Lewis was briefly a Tutor in Philosophy, then a Fellow and Tutor in English Literature of Magdalen College, Oxford, and University Lecturer in English, until he became the first occupant of the new Chair of Mediaeval and Renaissance Literature in Cambridge University.

Each had, moreover, won acclaim in his special field. Manning's earliest book, *The People's Faith in the Time of Wyclif* (1919), was an expansion of the Thirlwall dissertation Prize of the University of Cambridge. Its value was that it examined the nature of religion through the three great media of its transmission in medieval times—the Sermon, Confessions, and the Mass—and manifested a rare ecumenical spirit, while also showing that Dissent was not a merely modern phenomenon. The seal of his authority as an historian was set by the invitation to write two chapters in the seventh volume of the *Cambridge Mediaeval History*. C. S. Lewis has won even more brilliant renown as an English scholar. *The Allegory of Love,* which gained the Hawthornden Prize in 1936, has already become a classic in the interpretation of medieval literature, *A Preface to Paradise Lost* (1942) is a famous commentary on Milton, and the invitation to him to write a volume on the sixteenth century in the *Oxford History of English Literature* was the accolade of his peers.

What is remarkable in both cases, however, is that each man seemed to value his responsibility as a Christian apologist as highly as his reputation in his special field. Both Manning and Lewis have used the insights of their special fields to illumine the Christian contributions to culture.

Manning's historical gifts were used to demonstrate in *The Making of Modern English Religion* (1929) the irrigation of the national life by the river of the Christian religion. His *Essays in Orthodox Dissent* (1939) is both a reminder that faith becomes enervated when detached from orthodoxy and a Congregational Calvinist's attempt to recall his countrymen to their Free Church legacy. *The Hymns of Wesley and Watts* (1942) makes a brilliant plea for these writers as providing a 'Dissenting Use' or ritual which saved the Free Churches from a dilution of the faith in the days of Deism by being their sung Creeds. His final contribution to the Free Church tradition was *The History of the Protestant Dissenting Deputies*, the representatives of the Congregationalists, Baptists, and Presbyterians, who had direct access to the throne, and whose duty it was to be watchdogs of the unestablished Churches in England.

Manning's sermons and addresses, the first fruits of which appeared under the title, *A Layman in the Ministry* (1942), were published after his death and revealed that this distinguished scholar had been throughout his life a faithful preacher of the Gospel in village churches in Cambridgeshire and in his father's former church at Ravenstonedale. It was his hope, had his health permitted, to have been ordained a Congregational minister. His great loyalty to the Congregational and Free Church tradition, however, did not make him unappreciative of the Roman Catholic and Anglican traditions. His first book was a proof of his appreciation of the former, for it ended with the words, 'the mediaeval Church is the mother of us all.' His biographer and friend, Dr F. Brittain, significantly an Anglican High Churchman, insists that the dominating characteristic of his life was loyalty and that this embraced an appreciation for the hymns of Charles Wesley 'and a great veneration for the Book of Common Prayer.'[1]

To an even greater degree the major part of Lewis's published work, including his two autobiographies, his novels and his allegories, is a commendation of the Christian faith to the reason and the imagination. He has faced the difficult problems of competing philosophies when in *The Pilgrim's Regress* (1933) he expounds and exposes successively Rationalism, Aestheticism for its own sake, Freudianism, Totalitarianism, the Scepticism of cultured Worldliness, Esotericism, Pantheism, until his tired pilgrim (and weary reader) returns to a demanding but satisfying Christianity. He grapples with the difficulties of innocent suffering in *The Problem of Pain* (1940) and the contradiction between the modern scientific 'closed universe' and the invasions of it by supernatural power in *Miracles: A Preliminary Study* (1949). Peculiarly difficult Christian eschatological doctrines such as the Devil and heaven and hell are brilliantly restated in *The Screwtape Letters* (1942) and

[1] See F. Brittain, *Bernard Lord Manning, A Memoir* (n.d.), p. 19. See also pp. 1, 82 f., 86 f.

The Great Divorce (1946). The broadcast addresses, published together as *Mere Christianity* (1952), constitute a sparkling and comprehensive survey of Christian orthodoxy in belief and behaviour, defending (as one minor example of a concept unsympathetic to the modern mind) the Christian virtue of chastity. Even the 'Scientifiction' shows the effective baptism of his mind by Christianity, as, for example, when in *Perelandra* (1943) Lewis portrays an unfallen Eve, who resists temptation, as a central figure in 'Paradise retained.'[1] His two other books in the genre of space myths, *Out of the Silent Planet* (1939) and *That Hideous Strength* (1945), anticipate Armageddon as they present with marvellous conviction the titanic struggles between the forces of goodness and evil. Recent books include *Reflections on the Psalms* (1957) and *The Four Loves* (1960). By the perceptive use of the subtle weapons of reason and imagination Lewis has become the most successful popular apologist for Christianity in modern England. His vocation is teaching English literature, but his avocation is clearly that of Christian apologist.

Each, as we have noted, is an apologist for classical and orthodox Christianity, not for any modern 'Christianity-and-water.'[2] Manning presents his Christian orthodoxy because it alone appears to him to offer realism. He cries to the optimists, who merely whistle in the dark with their trust in automatic progress and live in a house that is all doors and windows and, therefore, fit only for summer living, and to the despairing

[1] A phrase of Chad Walsh in his exciting study of *C. S. Lewis: Apostle to the Skeptics* (1949), p. 42.

[2] *Mere Christianity*, p. 33.

pessimists, whose house has neither doors nor windows, 'a plague on both your houses.' For him the supreme relevance of the Gospel is that it defeats both death and evil in the presentation of the sacrificial death and glorious Resurrection of Jesus Christ.[1] The Gospel is good news because: 'To personal evil, it says forgiveness; to all evil, redemption and renewal. To a cursed world it brings the Cross, and the Passion of the Crucified.'[2] Moreover, he insists that the proof that the Gospel does not evade death is the earliest summary of the Faith: 'Jesus and the Resurrection.'[3] He ever followed the advice he gave in an address to theological students: 'What will make your preaching effectual is strong dogmatic preaching on the central things.'[4]

'Central Christianity' would be an equally apposite description of C. S. Lewis's aim. For him also the foe is modernism—the accommodation of classical and orthodox Christianity to the spirit of the present age. It is significant that both authors dislike Unitarian hymns which seem to them to confound the City of God, brought in by Divine grace, with the City of Man which is to be built by human hands. In the preface to *Mere Christianity*, Lewis explains that in his broadcast talks his aim was not to expound something 'I could call "my religion", but to expound "mere" Christianity, which is what it is and what it was long before I was born and whether I like it or not.'[5] His justification is that the Highest Common Factor of belief between Christians, Roman Catholic, Anglican, and Free Church

[1] *A Layman in the Ministry*, 1st sermon ('Wisdom's House').
[2] *Ibid.*, p. 10.
[3] *Ibid.*, p. 9.
[4] *Ibid.*, p. 150.
[5] *Op. cit.*, pp. vi–viii.

is far greater than their differences. This 'common Christianity' of all 'who believe that there is one God and that Jesus Christ is His only Son' turns out to be not only 'positive but pungent' and is divided from all non-Christian beliefs by the abyss which dwarfs differences between denominations. Further, Lewis believed that to stress the minor differences in belief would, rather than attract, only repel the uncommitted. There is, therefore, both in C. S. Lewis and B. L. Manning a strong ecumenical concern, yet each layman stands firmly within his own tradition, respectively Anglican and Congregationalist.

The final similarity between both apologists is a clear-headed wisdom—the obverse of which is an abhorrence of sentimentality which finds expression in piercing satire and wit. Of modern pantheistic hymns and the trite uplift of some modern pulpits, Manning says, with characteristic scorn:

> The hymns are not paraphrases, nor are they charged in every line with Scriptural content. They discuss mountain scenery (with special reference to sunsets), psychological disorders and political programmes. The preaching of the Word has degenerated into flabby platitudes about the dangers of the international situation or the benevolent commonplaces of Ella Wheeler Wilcox expressed even more prosaically than in her poetry.[1]

One thinks of Manning's occasional dislike of Anglican arrogance which was exhibited in the refusal to call the Free Church denominations 'Churches,' to which he retaliated by referring to the Episcopal Communion in England as 'the Anglican body.'[2] Equally characteristic

[1] *Essays in Orthodox Dissent*, p. 61.
[2] F. Brittain, *op. cit.*, p. v, and *A Layman in the Ministry*, p. 154.

was his immediate rapport with a mixed group at a conference in an address which began: 'As you get older and greyer and balder and bigger about the girth (if you are a man), or (if you are a woman) as you take the necessary precautions to prevent any of these things happening . . .'[1] His salty caution to theological students is well worth repetition: 'Do not fancy that your predecessors have reduced your congregation to an irreducible minimum.'[2] This was the index of the honesty and manliness of Bernard Manning's loyalty to Christ and his Gospel, and the Hapsburg jaw and gruff manner concealed a great love of humanity and added spice to his preaching and writing.

C. S. Lewis writes, when he wishes, with the irony of a Dean Swift. His most sustained essay in satire is the sophisticated study of the Machiavellian tactics of evil, *The Screwtape Letters*. His writings are jewelled with witty epigrams. One thinks of his comment in the sermon *Learning in War-time* on those who say that to study at such a time is fiddling while Rome burns: 'But to the Christian the true tragedy of Nero must be not that he fiddled while the city was on fire, but that he fiddled on the brink of Hell.' Or, again, one recalls the surprising turn by which he illustrated the importance of prudence as a virtue: 'The proper motto is not, "Be good, sweet maid, and let who can be clever," but, "Be good, sweet maid, and don't forget that this involves being as clever as you can." '[3]

[1] F. Brittain, p. 72.
[2] *A Layman in the Ministry*, p. 143.
[3] *Mere Christianity*, p. 61.

2 · *Different Routes to God*

Important as the likenesses between Manning and Lewis are, the differences between them are striking. This is true of their dissimilar routes to Christian commitment, of their Churchmanship, of their temperaments, and of their fame.

Manning is an admirable example of the 'once-born' Christian, Lewis of the 'twice-born.' For Manning there never was a time when he wasn't a Christian. His growing 'into Christ' was as steady as the increase in light from dawn to midday. Born the son of a Methodist schoolmaster who later prepared for the Congregational ministry, he came under the influence of Anglicanism in the College Chapel at Jesus College (whose most eminent theological alumnus was Archbishop Cranmer, the architect-in-chief of the Book of Common Prayer). Manning's loyalties broadened, while always remaining deep. He was a Congregationalist High Churchman who shared a love of the hymns of Charles Wesley with a remarkable appreciation of the Anglican Liturgy. But he never seems to have known the meaning of doubt. His was a steady 'Pilgrim's Progress.'

Lewis, on the other hand, fittingly called his first essay in autobiography, 'Pilgrim's Regress.' Like a mental prodigal son, he had lived on the husks provided by a variety of substitutes for Christianity until he found his path through Idealism to Theism and thence back to Christianity. He was, indeed, a Christian almost against his will. The conclusion of his quest is described in terms that rival Augustine's for honesty and a sense of the inexorable Divine Will:

> You must picture me alone in that room in Magdalen, night after night, feeling, when my mind lifted even for a second from my work, the steady, unrelenting approach of Him whom I so earnestly desired not to meet. That which I greatly feared had at last come upon me. In the Trinity Term of 1929 I gave in, and admitted that God was God, and knelt and prayed: perhaps, that night, the most dejected and reluctant convert in all England. I did not then see what is now the most shining and obvious thing; the Divine humility that will accept a convert even on such terms. The Prodigal Son at least walked home on his own feet.[1]

The different routes taken by these two men to God have determined the different approaches of their public defences of the Christian faith. Manning in his addresses and sermons concentrates almost exclusively on expounding and defending the Faith to the committed and the half-committed. Lewis fulfils the same task in his sermons, which are, interestingly enough, of a far higher intellectual level than his broadcast talks. But his success as an apologist is undoubtedly due to his exposés of competitive philosophical claimants for the mind of the modern man. His many years in the 'far country' (and the 'Waste Land' as Eliot has called it) have furnished him with the secrets of enemy-occupied territory. As Augustine knew the deceiving allure of the Manichees and the Sceptics and the near-truth of Neo-Platonism from within, so had Lewis experienced the successive attractions and disillusionments of several modern gods that failed. Moreover, he believed that the romantic quest of each individual is fulfilled in the vision of God which is the beatitude of the saints, so that all earthly

[1] *Surprised by Joy* (1955), p. 215.

loves and enthusiasms necessarily fail. In thus recognizing the place of the desires and instincts in the human make-up, he does not commit the common mistake of the Christian philosopher (and of the rigid anti-Christian rationalist) who reduces the personality to grey matter.

This suggests a difference in temperament between the two apologists. Though each is a shy man, devoted to books and the company of congenial minds (and Manning remained a bachelor and Lewis married only in middle age), Manning's is a rational, precise, and humorous mind, but Lewis has a mind like a rapier and his imagination is a flaming sword. Manning was, indeed, a double first class honours man in history, but Lewis attained a triple first (in both parts of the 'Greats' which was a philosophical, historical, and linguistic study of the civilizations of Greece and Rome, with a further 'first' in English). No quantitative comparison is implied here, but it will be noticed that Lewis is highly competent in philosophy and history as he is in the imaginative interpretation of literature. The sustained quality of Lewis's imagination is, in the last analysis, a great and original gift. But how superbly he has trained it! No Christian living is able to bring abstract concepts dancing into life as he has done. The characterization in his allegories has developed greatly from the rather wooden puppets of *Pilgrim's Regress.* There are the believable ghosts and Bright Spirits of Heaven in *The Great Divorce,* the devious sub-demons of *The Screwtape Letters* (credible only because we recognize their squalid rationalizations inside ourselves), and the marvellously imagined landscapes and supernatural beings in his space myths, of which *Perelandra* is the most hauntingly beautiful.

Manning and Lewis also differ in the degree of their attachment to the institutional life of the Church. For a Free Churchman Manning is surprisingly 'High' and, for an Anglican, Lewis's ecclesiology is unexpectedly 'Low.' Manning is a Congregationalist and a Calvinist who values the Church as the people of God, as a community divinely created and providentially sustained.[1] He is deeply appreciative of its worship, and supremely of its Sacraments. His sermons abound with appreciation for the Lord's Supper.[2] He is also a devotee of genuinely corporate hymns that sing the articles of the Christian faith.

Lewis, by contrast, found ecclesiasticism so repugnant that he averred: 'I had as little wish to be in the Church as in the zoo.'[3] His dislike of the Social Gospel, of totalitarianisms of any kind, and even the local congregation defined as 'just that selection of his neighbors whom he had hitherto avoided,'[4] are several indications of his natural misanthropy, as well as his dislike of being classified. His fullest study of the Church is contained in his address on 'Membership.' Here his chief concern is to distinguish Christian corporateness from mere collectivism, as he posits for the

[1] *Essays in Orthodox Dissent*, p. 29, reads: 'You cannot have for ever or for long the Christian experience of God without the Divine Society that is the result, the assurance, and the vehicle of that experience.'

[2] See *A Layman in the Ministry*, sermon 15.

[3] *Surprised by Joy*, p. 220.

[4] *The Screwtape Letters*, p. 16. Since these are the words of a Devil's minion, Lewis *knows* that this is the temptation of pride; but, presumably, this is how he *feels*.

Church a membership of complementaries as contrasted with the monotonous and flat units of a collective. He seems to recognize the need for democracy as a dyke against human irresponsibility in the holders of power, but it is significant that he insists that 'in the Church we recover our real inequalities and are refreshed.' He is most excited by the prospect of everlasting individuality which every Christian within the Church should enjoy; 'in it the individual person will outlive the universe.' The Church, in fact, is the laboratory for learning the science of Christianity through brotherhood.[1] He seems to accept, rather than to justify, the Sacraments, as he says: 'There are three things that spread the Christ life among us: baptism, belief, and that mysterious action which different Christians call by different names—Holy Communion, the Mass, the Lord's Supper.'[2] On such important matters as the Communion of Saints or the meaning of the Holy Communion, Lewis has little to say. On the subject of Apostolic Succession, he remains dumb. One may judge that it is as a mystical, not an institutional community, that he values the Church. It is clear that he would have been happier with Bernard of Clairvaux than with Cyprian, the polemical Augustine, Calvin or John Wesley. Manning, by contrast, would have made the rejected of Lewis his elect companions.

In terms of fame, finally, Manning's was a much smaller world than that of Lewis. Lewis's lectures at Oxford, as well as Cambridge, have been so largely attended that often no standing room could be found in

[1] *Mere Christianity*, p. 131.

[2] *Ibid.*, p. 48. Lewis adds: 'I cannot myself see why these things should be the conductors of the new kind of life' (p. 49), but that he accepts them on authority.

the most commodious lecture rooms. His broadcast audiences are to be counted in millions. His literary clientèle is even more varied and vaster for it includes the average Christians, the professional teachers of English in colleges and schools, the schoolchildren, and even the most sophisticated moderns (as in the case of *The Screwtape Letters*).

Manning was known only within the University of Cambridge and within Congregational circles. But those who knew him admired his deep and generous loyalty and his friendship given to a whole generation of Indian students (to whom he was official adviser at Cambridge). He was read and appreciated by surrounding dons, ministers and undergraduates.

3 · *Manning as Preacher*

The clearest distinction between the approaches of Manning and Lewis can be discerned in the form and content of their preaching. Manning is convinced that the only right that he has to proclaim the Gospel is by submitting himself to the discipline of understanding, obeying, and expounding the Revelation of God in Holy Scripture. His sermons are all expository, whereas Lewis's are topical.

Manning defines preaching in a way which makes it, as he practised it, sacramental: 'The preaching of the Word is an act of God for men; it is not men helping or hindering or boring each other.'[1] He insists that it must be interesting, and that it can only be so if it brings the Gospel of God to bear on the perennial and pressing

[1] *A Layman in the Ministry*, p. 141.

needs of men. Thus the Gospel is only truly preached where a man knows intimately the conversation and interests of his flock. Furthermore, true preaching will drop the lazy habit of using technical, theological terms. As an example he suggests the following:

> 'If a man die, shall he live again?'—that is a question which interests almost everyone; but if you begin your Easter sermon, 'I propose this morning to ask you to consider with me some familiar aspects of the doctrine of immortality,' you have already convinced many of us that this is no concern of ours.[1]

Moreover, according to Manning, the primary business of the preacher is 'the cure of souls, not the instruction of intellects.'[2] Here, of course, he differs from Lewis, who is more concerned to reach the outsider or the uncommitted, and therefore must use the intellect if only as a catalyst of obstacles preventing the reception of the Faith, or as a dissuasive from accepting some alternative philosophy of life. Manning, then, confines himself to corroborating the faith of the committed and in applying the promise and condemnation of the Gospel to the Christian congregation.

What makes his printed sermons so attractive is that they are preached rarely to the intellectuals and sophisticates of the universities, but chiefly to average middle-class town or socially mixed rural congregations. They would be listened to by any kind of congregation, high-brow or low-brow. He never talks down to his congregation, but always addresses them with urgency, clarity and relevance. He ranges through the Old and New

[1] *Ibid.*, p. 145. [2] *Ibid.*, p. 146.

Testaments and, if his is an Old Testament theme, we can be sure that in the application he will transpose the theme into specifically Christian terms.

Manning's eagle eye searches the Old Testament for parallels to our own time. He finds them in Jabez and his sorrow, in Achan the war-time profiteer, and in the way God made the Valley of Trouble into a Door of Hope (as he brings Resurrection out of Crucifixion). In 'The Harvest of Beth-Shemesh' he notes that the Christian equivalent to the Jewish Ark, as the symbol of God's presence, is the sacred elements in the Holy Communion, and he distinguishes between irreligious and irreverent then and now. 'Jeroboam and His Sin' is a brilliant account of mixed political and religious motives, and a searching analysis of conscience. He commends 'Jehu and His Zeal' in another sermon and shows how the Christian has greater cause for gratitude than Jehu. In 'Ezekiel and God's Glory' he keeps a fine sense of the Mystery of God, whose prophet foretold more than he knew in black days; we have our private black days, yet he claims that our faith is not a lie, as the Resurrection proves. 'Ezra and Being Ashamed' is an admirable sermon on the importance of loyalty, on keeping any taint of self-pity out of our shame, and on the Divine forgiveness and renewal. In 'The Harvest of the World' Manning reaffirms, in days in which the world's foundations shook, the Divine overruling. Our God is too tiny: 'We think of God as Master and Lord of churches, chapels, and the religious people; but not a Master and Lord of the whole world, of all that we fear and hate and are right to fear and hate. We do not think of God as Master of Germany, Russia and Japan, of secularism and materialism and international finance. But none of this is beyond His control.'[1]

Manning's perceptiveness may be appreciated if one sermon is more fully summarized. 'The Tower of Siloam' is a profound analysis of the problem of innocent suffering, appreciating yet distinguishing the Old Testament and the New Testament answers. It ends in the typical manner of Manning's sermons with several practical conclusions. The first is a reminder of our duty: however good the cause may be, we cannot be excused from helping it. Secondly, since wrongdoing causes harm to innocents, we should be doubly careful about the way we live. In the third place, 'God's reach does not end, though our sight ends, with death. That is one meaning of the Resurrection.'[2] The same sermon includes the following masterly summary of the meaning of the Cross of Christ: 'He died to show us that when God is in the sufferer the suffering can be, beyond all human intention or belief, turned to blessing. It is a mystery, but a certainty. . . . To bear evil, with God beside us, is to help to rid the world of it.'[3] Clearly, each sermon of Manning's is a declaration and application of the earliest Christian creed: 'Jesus and His Resurrection.'

So far the impression has been given perhaps that Manning's sermons are solid, orthodox divinity and eminently practical, but possibly uninspired. This would be not only to forget his humour, epigrams, vivid illustrations and literary citations, but also the inspired insights to which he can attain. Some of the latter are found in 'Pilate and His Cowardice.' His first comment on Pilate's 'What is truth?' is to ask: 'Is it a sneer or an

[1] *Ibid.*, pp. 76–77. [2] *Ibid.*, p. 86. [3] *Ibid.*, p. 85.

honest inquiry? Is it a joke in the worst of taste, as Lord Byron thought? It is all three.'[1] Then Manning scales the heights: 'Have you ever thought what the answer was? The Answer stood before him. Our Lord once said: "I am the Truth—the Way, the Truth and the Life." That is why the question is so remarkable: the man who asked it had the answer before him. He did not know because he would not face the real issue of the moment.'[2] Then Manning puts us in Pilate's shoes, but promises that Christ will guide those who, in courage, seek his way.

'Three Men and Saint Paul' is a superb analysis of Festus (a man trying to be good without religion), Agrippa (the man who is interested in religion but ashamed to admit it to his friends), and Felix (the man who thought that he could postpone religious commitment), and, consequently, of many who live on the grey frontier and in the dusk between the Church with its Faith and the World with its scepticism. 'Treasure and Earthen Vessels' is a study of the Gospel in the Church, and how a mercenary Church may repel men who seek the Gospel and a heavily institutional Church may lose the Gospel in the monotony and earthiness of its tasks. The proof of whether the Church has the Gospel is if its members have the daring faith that makes them unafraid of all skeletons in all cupboards and a Divine discontent with all present achievement. 'Some Other Man' proclaims, through the story of Philip and the Ethiopian eunuch, the Joy of the Christian life, when Christ is not a remote hearsay hero, but the Wisdom and Power of God.

[1] *Ibid.*, p. 87.

[2] *Ibid.*, pp. 89–90.

A Layman in the Ministry concludes with two remarkable sermons and two equally remarkable addresses. The first is on 'The Lord's Supper'; the second on 'Does this Generation need the Gospel?'; the third on 'Effectual Preaching: the Reflexions of one Hearer,' and the last is 'A Charge to the Church at its Minister's Ordination.' These are too freighted with wisdom and psychological insight for rapid summary, but some glint of the gold can be conveyed by a short sample of each. 'If the Bibles were all burnt and no more could be printed we should still have one thing to take us back to Christ: this Supper.'[1] Arguing that men have today a sense of communal or social sin, rather than of personal sin, and thus are overburdened by the overwhelming calls to shoulder personal responsibilities for world problems so that moral apathy prevails, Manning reminds his hearers: 'The Gospel comes to call us to a life not of responsibility, but of gratitude. The Gospel reduces public morality to its true proportions, and makes it a manageable matter.'[2] Consider his august definition of preaching: 'It is a manifestation of the Incarnate Word, from the Written Word by the Spoken Word; it is a most solemn act of worship, in which the thing given—the Gospel of the Son of God—overshadows and even transfigures the preacher by whom it is declared.'[3] Finally, there is part of the moving peroration of his Charge to the Church:

> The Word was made flesh and dwelt among us; and we beheld His glory; Who His own Self bare our sins in His own Body on the tree. He is risen. He hath abolished death and hath brought life and immortality to light through the

[1] *Ibid.*, p. 121. [2] *Ibid.*, p. 129. [3] *Ibid.*, p. 138.

Gospel. If these things are true (and if they are not what are we doing here when we might be doing so much else?), if these things are true, the world is for us a quite different place from the world of other people. We shall convince the world, not by arguing with it or lecturing it, but by making it envious: envious of the life that is life indeed.[1]

If theological fidelity and psychological penetration characterize the content of Manning's sermons, their technique is—through an art that conceals art—not unimportant. Like all good preaching it is a subordination of the personality to the message ('I must decrease, He must increase'), and it abounds in illustrations that are pointed and brief, rather than ornate and distracting.[2] Unobtrusively and aptly the citations from literature take their natural places in the sermons. Swinburne, Edward FitzGerald, Dante, Tennyson, De Quincey, Jeremy Taylor, William Blake, Meredith, Wordsworth, and Milton all stir the imagination. Latimer, Ridley, Cranmer, Oliver Cromwell, Stresemann ('For ten years since 1919 Europe has been suffering from men who meant well') and the Marquis of Salisbury all bring their tribute of truth. And Manning has his own distinctive epigrams that stab like a stiletto.

One of them recalls the startling and luminous honesty which was his most dominant characteristic. 'Most of our motives are mixed: the question is what are they mixed with?'[3] Two passages come to mind which have

[1] *Ibid.*, p. 160.

[2] For evidence, see *ibid.*, pp. 5 ff. for the Houses of Optimism, Pessimism and Wisdom; pp. 12–13 for inspirational flashes in dull Biblical chapters like the glimpse through the slit window in a medieval corkscrew tower; p. 110 for historical sites as a stimulus to recollection.

[3] *Ibid.*, p. 53 ('Jehu and His Zeal').

the bracing austerity of the landscape, winds and men of the Westmorland that he loved. The first passage is a calm look at the face of death in war-time. Recognizing its grim reality, he yet insists that it is a governing fact of life: it is inexorable and must be faced alone. War only underlines this truth, which Western civilization has tried to hide in maudlin fashion in time of peace. But the Gospel always comes to grips with it in the Crucifixion, while in the Resurrection it defeats it.[1]

The second passage takes a cold, steely look at the hardships of the ministry. The minister assumes poverty and the sarcasm of the world ('a bare living wage or less, the cold shoulder of the fashionable world, the indifference and inattention of the world at large, the scorn of the successful, the insolence of the social climber'), and is even warned to expect St Paul's reward at the hands of the Corinthians ('to be instructed by the ignorant, to be patronized by the vulgarian, to be set right by fools, to be gossiped about by the feather-brained, to have his work spoilt by the spiteful, and to be a spectacle unto the world and to angels and to men.') Then, with holy indignation arising, Manning reaches his terrifying climax, as sword-thrust follows sword-thrust into the calloused consciences of the complacent congregation:

> But what no young man who has put his whole life on the altar can expect—for until he has experienced it for himself he can not conceive it—is the coldness, the callousness, and the deadness of those for whom he looks for help, for support both in the work of the Church and in the daily quickening of his own spirit. The gates of hell, the whole world lying in the arms of the evil one, this will not daunt

[1] *Ibid.*, pp. 8–10.

him; but it is when he sees the abomination of desolation standing where it ought not—indifference, worldliness, heartlessness in you the Body of Christ, it is then that the cold fear paralyses his soul, the fear that the whole business is a mockery and the shadow of a name. If this be Christ's Body, it is a dead body, and Christ is dead. You are still in your sins; then He is not risen. The faith is vain; and the man who has renounced all else to preach it is of all men most pitiable. Having preached to others he feels himself a castaway. In such an hour the Saviour can still save His servant, but do you envy the Church that plunges a man into that pit?[1]

Manning's great quality is his searing honesty which comes from the unshakable loyalty to a holy God with whom he has made an everlasting covenant. It is the strength of a more charitable Puritanism.

4 · *Lewis as Preacher*

As we have seen earlier, Lewis is cast more congenially in the role of apologist than of preacher. Moreover, it is part of his great versatility that he can approach the outsider or the mildly interested inquirer, the genuine but simple seeker, and the sophisticated sceptic. For the straightforward inquirer he provides a conversational, simple and logical presentation of Christianity, through the broadcast talks published in full as *Mere Christianity*. For the interested but doubtful he provides answers to the major obstacles to belief in *The Problem of Pain* and *Miracles*. The indirect or oblique approach through philosophy is provided in the planetary novels, and through satire he probes the weaknesses in the sceptic's

[1] *Ibid.*, pp. 156–157.

defences in *The Screwtape Letters*. It is an impressive and formidable array of weapons in defence of Christianity.

Our concern with him is, however, in the important but rarely practised role of preacher. The only volume of sermons and addresses he has published appeared in England under the title of *Transposition and Other Addresses* and in the United States as *The Weight of Glory and Other Addresses* (1949). The high level of these sermons is a tribute to the intelligence of his Christian audiences which they may not have deserved.

All were preached or delivered to intelligent audiences. 'The Weight of Glory' and 'Learning in War-time' were both preached in the University Church of St Mary the Virgin in Oxford, and 'Transposition' was preached in the Chapel of Mansfield College, Oxford. The two addresses, 'Membership' and 'The Inner Ring,' were delivered, respectively, to the Society of St Alban and St Sergius, and to the faculty and students of King's College in the University of London.

Their outstanding qualities as sermons or addresses are more easily catalogued than imitated. The clear distinctions, careful arguments, pellucid clarity, fertility of illustrations, pithy epigrams, the deep wisdom and insight into the will of God and the nature of man, the candidness that is piercing, the presentation of central themes and abiding issues, as well as the loyal exposition of ageless and unpopular religious and moral truth in contrast to current fashions, are some of the pre-eminent characteristics of the sermons and addresses.

The sermon on 'Learning in War-time' answers the question: 'What is the use of beginning a task which we have so little chance of finishing?' Lewis parries the question by asking one which is even more fundamental, whether in peace or war. The Christian must ask 'How is it right, or even psychologically possible, for creatures who are every moment advancing to either heaven or hell, to spend any fraction of the little time allowed them in this world on such comparative trivialities as literature and art, mathematics or biology?'[1] He insists that life has never been normal, and that insects seek material security first, not men. 'They propound mathematical theorems in beleaguered cities, conduct metaphysical arguments in condemned cells, make jokes on scaffolds, discuss the latest poem while advancing to the walls of Quebec, and comb their hair at Thermopylae. This is not *panache*: it is our nature.'[2] The answer is that, while the whole of life ought to be religious, yet this means doing the same duties as before conversion with a new spirit, and the whole of one's life should most definitely not be devoted to the finite war effort. As for war, it is in the defence of the oppressed like life-saving, but 'the rescue of drowning men is, then, a duty worth dying for, but not worth living for.'[3] There is then a place for culture even in national crisis and in the urgency of the Christian life, but culture is not in any sense spiritually meritorious in its own right. 'The work of Beethoven, and the work of a charwoman, become spiritual precisely on the same condition, that of being offered to God, of being done humbly "as to the Lord." '[4] Thus, those who have the talent for learning (as their inclination and their presence in Oxford suggest) should pursue the search for knowledge as such and beauty as such in confidence that they

[1] *The Weight of Glory*, p. 44.
[2] *Ibid.*, p. 45.
[3] *Ibid.*, p. 47.
[4] *Ibid.*, pp. 48–49.

are advancing to the vision of God themselves or indirectly helping others to do so. The danger is that we may come to love *our* knowing more than the truth, and only humility can deliver us from such pride and reputation-hunting. For the Christian, moreover, the life of learning has also certain indirect values. One of them is clearly the duty of the educated Christian to defend 'our educated brethren who have, under God, no defence but us against the intellectual attacks of the heathen.'[1]

There are, so the practical preacher reminds his congregation, three defences from three enemies who strike at the life of learning in war-time. The enemy is excitement—a tendency to think about the war instead of our work; the second is the sense of frustration and incompleteness; the third is fear of death and pain. He warns that the first enemy only takes a different form in war-time, and favourable conditions never come, so true scholars do the best they can. The second enemy is routed by leaving the future in the hands of God and by recognizing that 'the present is the only time in which any duty can be done or any grace received.' As for fear, Lewis by cool reason dissipates the magnified illusions of the imaginations. He startles with the statement (of one who was wounded in battle himself in World War I): 'a battlefield is one of the very few places where one has a reasonable prospect of dying with no pain at all.'[2] The fine conclusion is, as ever, eschatological. 'If we thought we were building up a heaven on earth, if we looked for something that would turn the present world from a place of pilgrimage into a permanent city satisfying the soul of man, we are disillusioned and not a

[1] *Ibid.*, p. 50. [2] *Ibid.*, p. 53.

moment too soon. But if we thought that for some souls, and at some times, the life of learning, humbly offered to God, was, in its own small way, one of the appointed approaches to the Divine reality and the Divine beauty which we hope to enjoy hereafter, we can think so still.'[1] In this sermon there is, indeed, 'infinite riches in a little room.'

However, that tribute paid, one must confess that Lewis is obviously much happier as a writer or broadcaster than as a preacher. Generally, one misses the zest and fascination of the apologist of *Mere Christianity* in these sermons and addresses. In them Lewis is a chained falcon, however high he may occasionally soar. They are not his best genre.

Manning, by comparison, is equally happy in preaching to university and village congregations, and his humanity is everywhere engagingly present, and he sets himself out to expound Scripture as an exegete, so that his sermons have a structure and an authority that Lewis's do not have. As an apologist, however, Lewis wins hands down.

5 · *Appraisals*

Both men had the courage of their deep Christian convictions and were content to swim strongly against the stream of current fashion by proclaiming a Christian realism that takes seriously man's nature as crucifier, yet redeemable. For both men the Resurrection was the central Christian doctrine, but for Lewis, as for Dante, heaven and hell are not only irrevocable alternative destinies of the human soul but men choose them daily.

[1] *Ibid.*, p. 54.

It is Lewis's great distinction that he has repristinated eschatological categories in our secular century by a *tour de force* of imagination. Manning seemed content with Reinhold Niebuhr's judgment that it is no business of the Christian to be concerned with either the furniture of heaven or the temperature of hell, and to leave the issue to God in faith.

Their greatest claim to distinction is that, although scholars of renown in their own field, they have been exponents and defenders of the Christian faith. Manning preached to the committed and to the formal churchgoers, Lewis reached the much wider circle outside the Church or merely on the edge of it by his brilliant broadcasts and his allegories, dreams, letters, and space fiction.

They both, of course, have their critics. To have espoused classical Christian orthodoxy in the twentieth century involved Lewis in the charge that he used modernist apologetics to defend a fundamentalist theology. Manning was accused of living in the fifteenth and eighteenth centuries (the ages, respectively, of Wyclif and Wesley, his favourites). Each would have rebutted the charge by accusing their critics of mistaking the spirit of the present age for the ageless Gospel of Christ. In short, both believed that to be modernist was to be a traitor to the Christian tradition. They considered the essential task of a defender of the beleaguered Faith in a post-Christian or pagan age to preserve it, and if possible to increase the number of the adherents of the Faith, rather than to dilute it.

They have both been criticized for their apparent indifference to the struggle for social justice. Here they may both have been more aware of the dangers than the possibilities of reconstruction. Lewis certainly has committed himself to the view that the 'Christians who did the most for the present world were those who thought the most of the next.'[1] Yet this attitude might very easily lead to a pietistical or ascetical withdrawal from the world and thus refuse any social and corporate witness to the Gospel of God.

Lewis, as the more famous man, is naturally a larger target for the critics, and has been accused of an occasional sleight-of-hand in his apologetics, of evading rather than answering objections. One rather glaring example is found in *Mere Christianity*.[2] Both Lewis and Manning have been accused of misanthropy because of their use of irony, satire and sarcasm. Sarcasm is often the don's delight with which he may win an argument and lose a disciple. But equally satire is the strongest weapon for deflating pomposity and sentimentality and both are enemies of a genuine humility. My judgment is that Manning and Lewis used satire as a defence of the weak in face of the glutinous arrogance of the strong secularists of the age. Honesty compels the admission that Manning seems to be more charitable than Lewis, but I cannot know what temperamental difficulties each had to contend with and with what success the pride of each was tamed by grace.

Most of all are we impressed with the way these two laymen of our time preached or lectured or wrote to the glory of God, to the confutation of his foes and the

[1] *Mere Christianity*, p. 106.

[2] *Ibid.*, p. 32. Here the atheist's serious objections are dismissed cavalierly, first, by declaring his philosophy too simple, and second, by the assertion that 'If the whole universe had no meaning, then we should never have found out it has no meaning.'

confirmation of the faith of his friends. Though neither was ordained, Manning was a true, faithful, and incisive preacher of the Gospel, and Lewis is an exciting, imaginative, subtle and versatile defender of the Christian Faith and brilliant expositor of the primacy and ultimacy of the attainment of the Vision of God as man's true end.

8

Expository Preaching

CAMPBELL MORGAN, W. E. SANGSTER, & J. S. STEWART

THE sustained exposition of Scripture is at once both the oldest and the newest type of preaching. It seems new only because so much preaching of an apologetical, moral, or topical type in the past sixty years has been so marginal and more an accommodation to culture than a confrontation of culture by the Word of the living God. It is not only desperately needed, but also deeply appreciated. The proof for this statement is the fact that the two largest congregations in contemporary London are drawn by rigorously expository preachers. One is the congregation which meets in Westminster Chapel under the ministry of Dr Martyn Lloyd-Jones,[1] the former Harley Street physician, and the other is All Souls', Langham Place, where the Rector is the Rev. John R. W. Stott,[2] a Cambridge

[1] For two excellent but different examples of expository preaching by Dr Lloyd-Jones see his running exposition in two volumes of *Studies in the Sermon on the Mount* (1959–1960), and for a correlation of the Gospel to universal need his *The Plight of Man and the Power of God* (1942), based on the first chapter of Romans.

[2] J. R. W. Stott provides a series of expository addresses on the first three chapters of the Book of Revelation in *What Christ Thinks of the Church* (1958) and an invitation to Christian commitment on a

University double first class honours graduate in modern languages and theology. The two men rejoice in the Evangelical succession in which they stand, counting St Paul, Luther, Calvin, the great Puritan divines, Wesley, Whitefield, and Spurgeon, and Temple Gairdner among their predecessors.

1 · *A Description*

One of the most recent defences, descriptions and exemplifications of expository preaching comes from the hand of the Director of the newly established College of Preachers in the Church of England, the Rev. D. W. Cleverley Ford. It is modestly titled, *An Expository Preacher's Notebook* (1960).

It is there argued that four reasons recommend expository preaching. First, because the Church has no other 'primary source-book . . . for the saving acts of God in Christ.'[1] Secondly, because the sermon is a part of worship, and in a liturgical communion such as the Church of England is, the liturgy is thoroughly informed by the Bible in its lections and in its keeping of the fasts and festivals of the Christian Year. Thirdly, this type of preaching 'sustains the pulpit' by the inexhaustible variety of materials, by attaching Divine truth to Bible stories, and by enabling the exposition of the Scripture to stab the mind and heart of the congregation with a sense of relevance which is an act of illumination and

Scriptural and Christological basis in *Basic Christianity* (1958). He has also published the perceptive *Preacher's Portrait* (1962), a series of word studies on New Testament conceptions of the preacher as steward, herald, witness, father, and servant.

[1] p. 4.

revelation. Finally, expository preaching enables the 'preacher to speak with an authority without which his preaching is insipid.' The true 'Ministry of the Word' confronts the congregation, not with teaching about God, but by God himself with transforming power.[1]

Cleverley Ford asks why expository preaching has become 'a lost art in the mid-twentieth century'—the latter, incidentally, an overstatement as our selection of three renowned expository preachers will show. A decay of Bible reading, the lessening of the authority of the Bible for many clergy trained in a critical approach, and the demand for briefer sermons in our time, are three parts of his answer. His most constructive suggestions, however, consist in an analysis of six different kinds of expository preaching and in the helpful provision of examples of his own expository sermons. In sum, expository sermons, expounding and applying the Scriptures, may take any of the six following forms: (1) summarizing the whole sweep of the Bible, and expounding the saving acts of God in history; (2) expounding a single book of the Bible; (3) expounding a single chapter or passage of the Bible, corresponding to a lesson at worship; (4) expounding one verse; (5) expounding a central Bible word, such as 'Grace' or 'Faith' or 'Sin' and (6) illuminating the life of a Bible character, such as Saul, David, Solomon.

Three masters of expository preaching have been chosen for special attention in this chapter. Between them these varied personalities exemplify every one of the six kinds of expository preaching in Mr Cleverley Ford's analysis.

[1] *Ibid.*, p. 14.

Dr Campbell Morgan was the master of detailed book-by-book analysis and application of the Scripture; he also occasionally preached on Bible characters. In his evangelical sermons to vast concourses of people he also occasionally preached on the whole plan of salvation. Thus, he exemplified the first, second, and sixth kinds of expository preaching.

Dr W. E. Sangster excelled in doctrinal preaching which selected a significant text or group of texts as a summary of the Christian gospel. Occasionally, he also selected a central word in the Biblical vocabulary for extended treatment. He also, from time to time, expounded the scope of God's initiative in salvation. Thus, he used the first, fourth, and fifth kinds of expository preaching.

Dr James Stewart is both a textual and a contextual preacher, as well as an exponent of the mighty acts of God in redeeming the race. Thus he is an expert in the first, third and fourth kinds of expository preaching.

What unites these three preachers, however, is a common conception of the august role of the preacher as a *herald of God*. He is supremely the ambassador of the King of Kings, announcing through the authority of his calling and ordination by God the good news of Christ's victory over the world and offering the grace of pardon to repentant rebels.[1]

[1] See Morgan's impressive address on his preaching jubilee in John Harries, *G. Campbell Morgan, The Man and his Ministry* (1930), p. 240; and Sangster's *Power of Preaching* (1958), p. 102, and *The Craft of the Sermon* (1954), pp. 22, 33.

2 · *G. Campbell Morgan*

Campbell Morgan was a remarkable man for many reasons. Rejected by the Birmingham committee that examined local preachers to see if they were worthy to be recommended to the Methodist Conference in Britain for theological training, this man who taught himself and whose only degrees were honorary became the President of Cheshunt College, Cambridge, the theological seminary of the Congregationalists in that ancient university city, while retaining the office of minister of Westminster Chapel. A minister of such integrity that he was more than a hero to his valet—in fact, each of his four sons was ordained to the Christian ministry. At a time of relativism in theology and in ethics, when 'sermonettes were preached for Christianettes' (as he phrased it), he preached sermons from 45 to 60 minutes long, explaining the Biblical revelation, without ever toning down its high demands or lessening its authority. By his Biblical lectures which were closely argued and rarely made any concessions to illustration or humour (though his pictorial sense and whimsy were considerable), he gathered and held from 1,500 to 2,000 people for years in his Westminster Chapel Friday Night Bible School.[1]

To how many men is it given to return to the scene of their former ministerial triumphs after an interval of thirty years and to repeat the experience? Yet Dr Campbell Morgan was the exception. First ministering with conspicuous success at Westminster Chapel from 1904 to 1914, after an influential period in the United States as itinerating evangelist and Biblical lecturer, and,

[1] Harries, *op. cit.*, p. 91.

later, as settled minister, he returned to the ministry of Westminster Chapel in 1933 and sustained a great expository teaching until 1943, retiring through ill health at the age of eighty!

What makes his ministerial career so significant is that he was the ordinary man (except for his deep, bell-toned voice) made extraordinary by his consecration to the task and his painstaking studies. For example, he would never attempt to expound a book of the Bible until he had read it in the original language and in English at least fifty times.[1] Moreover, he proves conclusively the varied spiritual wealth that is at the disposal of the preacher who mines the deep lodes of the Bible. He also demonstrates the pertinacity of the true evangelist. By the end of July 1929 he had travelled over 714,000 miles, crossed the Atlantic 49 times, and preached 20,000 sermons.[2]

How are we to account for the great and sustained response to what many would have regarded as Dr Morgan's old-fashioned preaching? He was a conservative expositor preaching to conservatives. That is only partly true, for his Westminster congregation contained many who were neither conservative nor even convinced Christians. He was a man of great conviction who knew that preaching involved more than interesting or educating his hearers, but fighting with them until their wills surrendered to the claim of Christ. 'The preacher,' he said, 'is not merely asking a congregation to discuss a situation, and consider a proposition, or give attention to a theory. We are out to storm the citadel of the will and to capture it for Jesus Christ.'[3] Yet this never led to

[1] *Ibid.*, p. 199. [2] *Ibid.*, p. 227. [3] *Ibid.*, p. 245.

histrionic emotionalism or irrationalism, for the cogency of his exposition depended on the clarity and cumulative testimony of Biblical teaching in the light of alternative views of life. He admirably expressed the relation of faith and reason in the statement: 'The faith that does not come from reason is to be doubted, and the reason that does not lead to faith is to be feared.'[1] Furthermore, he knew the supreme source-book of the Christian faith better than most men of his day. It is the consentient witness of evangelical preachers that only as the Bible speaks to their own souls by meditation and obedience can it be preached effectively. Morgan, Sangster and Stewart concur in this judgment, based on identical experience.

Dr Martyn Lloyd-Jones, a distinguished colleague and successor of Dr Campbell Morgan in the Westminster pulpit, has shrewdly explained that Morgan's success is also partly attributable to the fact that he came into influence exactly at the time that he was most needed. Here he does not merely mean that a preacher's business is not to catch the spirit of the age, but to know it and correct it. Rather Dr Lloyd-Jones claims that his teaching ministry was the complement of the work of the famous evangelists, Moody and Sankey. Campbell Morgan was able to build up the new converts in the Christian faith and life. 'The evangelists had done their work; it was the time for the teacher, and God sent him.'[2] Certainly, this would help to explain the eager throng of missionaries, ministers, Sunday-school teachers and workers, who thronged to his mid-week Bible expositions which he inaugurated in 1895, in Westminster Road Congregational Church, Birmingham,

[1] *Ibid.*, p. 201. [2] *Ibid.*, pp. 329–330.

which were continued at New Court Congregational Church, Tollington Park, London, from 1897 to 1901, as in the Northfield Extension work for the next three years, and which reached their climax with the famous 'Friday Night Bible School' he began at Westminster Chapel on 4th November 1904. Its fruits were to be found in the monumental series of books called collectively *The Analysed Bible.*

His gaunt and ascetic appearance, the voice so perfectly modulated that even a whisper could be heard in the upper gallery of Westminster Chapel, the simplicity and purity of his English prose, the moral passion, the vivid imagination, the utter submergence of the man in the message—none of these observations entirely explains the success of Campbell Morgan.

Nor is his success to be attributed to the ingenuity in interpretation, though this was a great gift of his. Once, for example, he was preaching on the Book of Job and found it possible partly to exempt Job's three comforters from the commonplace criticisms of them. In Campbell Morgan's brief at least three things might be said on their behalf. It was remarkable that they came to see such a notoriously God-forsaken man. Further, what they said was in front of Job, not behind his back. And they showed astonishing restraint in keeping their mouths shut for seven days and seven nights![1] Morgan's success, under God, is almost entirely due to the method.

It was the result of the unremitting toil of submitting himself to the discipline of studying the Bible with the aid of the original languages, and with the benefit of the

[1] Edgar DeWitt Jones, *American Preachers of Today, Intimate Appraisals of Thirty-Two Leaders* (1933), p. 286.

best commentaries, only after he had allowed the Scriptures to make their first-hand impact on his mind and heart. Describing his own method, he said: 'Two things are vital, first personal first-hand work on the text, and then all scholarly aids available. I never take down a commentary until I have done the first-hand work and have made my outline. To turn to commentaries first is to create a second-hand mentality. I speak freely from a brief most carefully prepared.'[1] Moreover, this was only possible for one who was utterly convinced that in Christ are all the treasures of wisdom and knowledge because he is the Wisdom or Logos of God in the flesh. 'I am,' said Campbell Morgan, 'a disciple to the truth, but for me the truth is final in Christ, and I think that conviction is the true secret of Christian preaching.'[2]

It is fitting to illustrate his gifts by analysis of the first Psalm on which he preached a sermon entitled 'The Psalm of the Two Ways.'[3] The text sums up the entire teaching of the Psalm and comes from the sixth verse: 'Jehovah knoweth the way of the righteous; but the way of the ungodly shall perish.' The first three verses describe the way of the righteous, the fourth and fifth the way of the wicked, and the sixth is the summation. The idea that righteousness pays and wickedness does not is thought old-fashioned today, yet has generally been accepted by people born and brought up in the light of the Biblical Revelation. It went out of fashion only in the closing days of the last century.

Yet newness is not a guarantee of truth. Despite some

[1] Harold Murray, *Campbell Morgan, Bible Teacher* (*c.* 1938), p. 88.

[2] John Harries, *op. cit.*, p. 240.

[3] *Famous English Sermons*, ed. Ashley Sampson (1940), pp. 353–366.

of its follies, the preacher is grateful to have been brought up a Victorian.

With that apologetical statement, he returns to the Psalm. He points out that the Psalmist's diagnosis of the way of the wicked as denying morality, living in conformity with the denial, and unanimous in scoffing at goodness, is true of the modern situation. The wicked are 'like chaff which the wind driveth away.' 'Some day,' says Campbell Morgan, 'when the wind blows up a hurricane, look at a tree planted, rooted; and then at some chaff. . . . Thank God there are winds of God blowing all over human history, winds of God blowing today, trying, testing, sweeping winds, and they carry away the chaff.' Then he recalls that John the Baptist said the Christ ('your Lord and mine, our blessed and adorable Redeemer') shall come with his fan in his hand to gather the wheat in his garner and destroy the chaff in the unquenchable fire.

Positively, the man who walks in God's way delights in God's law, meditates on it day and night, indeed soliloquizes about it. He is 'like a tree planted by the streams of water that bringeth forth its fruit in season.' Unlike the wicked man in Psalm 37.35 who spreads himself like the green bay-tree in its native soil, he spreads by the water, the source of life. Again, as the man in Psalm 52, he is like 'a green olive tree in the house of God,' trusting 'in the loving-kindness of God for ever,' or like the palm-tree or the cedar of Lebanon, flourishing in God's courts, bringing forth fruit in old age (Psalm 92.12 ff.). Finally, the good man shall prosper in whatever he does, even if he seems to fail. Joseph was prosperous in Pharaoh's prison, Job in darkness, and

Christ prospered in his crucified hands. It looks as if the evil prosper, but the man of God really prospers 'for he marches through the passing phases of time to the lasting destiny and glory of eternity.'

This is a superb sermon in its structure, simplicity, fidelity to the spirit and letter of the passage of Scripture selected, in its allusions to other apt Scriptural passages, in its drawing forth of the meaning of the Biblical imagery, and in its proclamation of the Cross, and in its final robust assurance of the Resurrection.

Dr Campbell Morgan was himself a sturdy oak in what often must have seemed a forest of swaying liberal birches and willows bending to the winds of change. It may seem ungrateful to one who has given so much strength and support to many thousands to mention that there are rare occasional flaws even in his exposition or his personality. In the sermons just considered, does he not put fancy in the place of fact, when he implies that the Scripture intends us to find a subtle distinction between the bay-tree rooted in its own soil, as contrasted with the tree that is nourished by the river? At any rate, there seems to be some point in the ambiguous tribute of one who knew his preaching and said: 'Morgan can get more out of a familiar passage of Scripture that I didn't know was there, and some things that I am not yet certain are there, than any man I know.'[1] Others found him lacking in cordiality,[2] perhaps because he insisted on keeping the full quota of hours of study even when travelling in a train. Certainly, he was far from being a spoil-sport at home, but his own ideal

[1] Edgar DeWitt Jones, *op. cit.*, p. 283.
[2] Jill Morgan, *A Man of the Word* (1951), p. 253.

setting as he once described it would be 'a house buried in the woods, a quick transit to a crowded church—and back to the woods.'[1]

A man cannot, perhaps should not, switch temperaments and his best contribution is made by *being himself* for the glory of God. It is, however, disappointing to learn that Campbell Morgan was unduly dejected if he could not always command a vast congregation. Even in this man who toiled more than any other in his generation to unsheathe the sword of the Word of God, instead of blunting its impact by compromise, the old Adam had not been entirely subdued. Nevertheless, his preaching, lecturing and writing were lamps in the dusk of the twentieth century. His writings continue to illumine Holy Scripture like searchlights.[2]

3 · *W. E. Sangster*

Dr Sangster was an evangelical greatheart, whose intellect matched his spirituality. His method was not that of detailed, running exposition of lengthy passages of Scripture like Dr Campbell Morgan. Rather he expounded the central themes of Scripture in a breathtakingly rapid and succinct way. He differs from Morgan as telegrams from treatises; his sermons are very like

[1] Harold Murray, *op. cit.*, p. 66.

[2] From a vast output the following are selected as of unusual importance: *The Westminster Pulpit* (11 volumes); *Searchlights from the Word* (1,188 sermon suggestions from Genesis to Revelation, 1926); *The Analysed Bible* (10 volumes); the companion volumes of *The Crises of the Christ* (1903) and *The Teaching of Christ; Parables and Metaphors of Our Lord; Great Chapters of the Bible; Notes on the Psalms;* and *God's Last Word to Man* (exposition of Epistle to the Hebrews).

Greetings telegrams, admirably embroidered with imagery which does not detract from the urgency of his communication of the good news. Moreover, if he is theologically conservative, he is well read in philosophy, history, literature and is remarkably perceptive in practical psychology.

Like Morgan, his is a saga of unexpected development. Born in 1900 of working-class parents in the east end of London,[1] he became a local preacher while serving in the British Army during the First World War. His athletic hobby was boxing, and he had the robust frame necessary. He found the blasphemy and bawdy talk of the mess-room equally repugnant, but admired the courage and mutual concern of the soldiers. The Methodist Conference sent him to Richmond College for theological training. Afterwards he served Methodist churches in North Wales until he was called to Brunswick Church, Leeds, to succeed Leslie D. Weatherhead.

His longest and most memorable ministry was at the Central Hall, Westminster, where he succeeded the veteran Dr T. Dinsdale Young. He came in the inauspicious month of August 1939 and remained there until 1955, when he was appointed as the head of the Home Mission Department of the Methodist Church of Great Britain. He died in 1960 after two years of suffering, with extraordinary courage, from the inexorable approach of progressive muscular atrophy. One Easter Day, near the end of his life, being unable to walk or even speak, he wrote to his daughter: 'It is terrible to wake up on Easter morning and have no voice with

[1] See the vivid pamphlet *W.E.S., A Daughter's Tribute* (1960), and *Doctor Sangster* by his son (1962).

which to shout, "He is risen!"—but it would be still more terrible to have a voice and not want to shout.'[1]

He was in his physical and preaching prime when he came to Central Hall, Westminster, to a sorely depleted congregation. In 1940 the bombing of London began, and what would have seemed the slamming of it, was to him the opening of the door of opportunity. The vast basement was reinforced and Dr Sangster immediately threw it open to the homeless folk from the slums of Pimlico, and hundreds of them used it as an almost permanent home. Sangster and his family insisted on making their home there also and in occupying only one cramped room. This they shared for five long years. It was typical of Sangster's realism and compassion. His wife organized a canteen, providing economical food each night. Dr Sangster moved in and out among the shelter-dwellers with unfailing interest and zeal, telling his incomparable stories as only he could. 'Service before services,' was his motto. He would offer religion only when it was genuinely desired. As might be expected he was soon asked to take evening prayers. These, with a weekly lecture on current affairs, and a Saturday concert, were the highlights in the life of that vast basement shelter.[2] On Sundays he preached to enlarging congregations that contained many men and women of the lower middle class, a number of university students, and several professional families.

Most surprising product of all in these years—the work of what hours he could spare from his exacting duties—was the successful preparation of a London University doctoral dissertation, subsequently published

[1] *W.E.S.*, p. 13. [2] *Ibid.*, pp. 8–9.

as *The Path to Perfection*, which mirrored his absorbing and Catholic interest in spirituality and his conviction that life's supreme quest is for holiness.

Dr Sangster was a pietist, but he differed from the usual idea of that term in three respects. He knew not only that men and women needed to be reformed, but also that economic and social disabilities cramp them. He had an infectious gaiety and no one could have considered him a spoil-sport.[1] Moreover, the range of his reading and interests (hill-climbing and visiting ancient churches, abbeys, and castles) were those of a man of culture.

Sangster believed that no task in the world was more important than the preacher's. The minister was concerning himself with the central human problem—the transformation of human character by the proclamation of the grace of God. 'The cure of cancer,' he wrote, 'would be a trifle beside the cure of the cancer of the soul.'[2] He firmly believed that preaching was the Sacrament of the Word, and adopted Bernard Manning's definition of it as 'a manifestation of the Incarnate Word, from the Written Word, by the spoken word.'[3] He wished to maintain expository preaching because so much of the preaching of the day was marginal, taking its cue from the events of the day as recorded in the newspapers, not from the Word of God.

[1] See the delightful story of how he shocked two narrow pietistical landladies in a stuffy guest-house in Scotland by dressing up as a matador and was asked to leave, upon which all of the other guests also decided to pack up. *Ibid.*, pp. 4–5.

[2] Article written for *The British Weekly* late in April 1952, entitled 'My Ministry—Fragments of Autobiography.'

[3] Cited in *The Craft of the Sermon* (1954), p. 25.

He was an incomparable craftsman in the preparation, architectonic construction, illustrations, and applications of his sermons. If treated in the light of their content, he maintains there are six types of sermons: Biblical Interpretation; Ethical and Devotional (he says each needs the other); Doctrinal; Philosophic and Apologetic; Social; and Evangelistic. Each type of preaching is necessary and he preached examples of each kind, even if it is both in doctrinal sermons interpreted through experience and in devotional sermons that he specializes. And he insists that, however important instruction is, in the form of explanation or argument, the final task is persuasion to capture the will. It is for this reason that he justifies evangelistic preaching.[1] Often one of his doctrinal sermons ends with a ringing appeal for commitment; but Sangster would be the last to suggest that the preacher should *always*, like an evangelical alarm-clock, be striking for decisions.

Sangster also supplies two further classifications of sermons, the one by structure or architecture, the other by the psychological approach. Combining the two analyses, it is possible to say that for Biblical interpretation the appropriate structure is exposition and the suitable psychological manner is authoritative. Similarly, the apologetical sermon best proceeds by the method of argument and its psychological approach is persuasive.[2]

Of more immediate interest, however, is the quality of Sangster's printed sermons, from which the two

[1] *Ibid.*, p. 44, where Sangster writes: 'Unquestionably the great end of Christian preaching is to win men and women to a whole-soul committal to Christ and their spiritual up-building in him.'

[2] *Ibid.*, pp. 59, 99.

volumes of *Westminster Sermons*[1] are selected for consideration. The second volume, consisting of sermons for the Christian Year, following the general structure of the Apostles' Creed, shows Sangster at his doctrinal best. The first volume indicates his versatility and variety.

After reading other expository preachers, Sangster immediately strikes one with the note of crisp, urgent brevity.[2] No beating about the bush with either prolonged introductions (as often in James Stewart) or concluding perorations (like the Victorian orators).

Hardly less striking are the vividly fresh and apt illustrations. A New Year sermon, intriguingly titled 'Remember to Forget,' bids his congregation forget their tactlessness, their sins, and the hurtful things done against them in the past. It ends thus:

> It was Christmas time in my home. One of my guests had come a couple of days early and saw me sending off the last of my Christmas cards. He was startled to see a certain name and address. 'Surely, you're not sending a greeting to *him*,' he said.
>
> 'Why not?' I asked.
>
> 'But you remember,' he began, 'eighteen months ago.'
>
> I remembered, then, the thing the man had publicly said about me, but I remembered also resolving at the time, with God's help, that I would remember to forget. And God had 'made' me to forget!
>
> I posted the card.[3]

Or Sangster has only to announce as his text 2

[1] Volume I, 'At Morning Worship,' appeared in 1960 and volume II, 'At Fast and Festival,' a year later.

[2] See vol. II, pp. 10–11, for a vivid picture of the inadequacy of a knowledge of God apart from his revelation in Christ.

[3] *Westminster Sermons*, I, p. 10. A précis of this sermon appeared in *Reader's Digest*.

Corinthians 5.8 (RV), 'At home in the Lord,' when he immediately captures the hearer's interest with a rapid account of the homing instinct of birds, beasts, fish (and by analogy) in men. The sources of his illustrations cover biographical incident, natural science, visits to antiquities or foreign lands, and, supremely, the great saints of the Christian tradition, as well as his own wide experiences. Sometimes a very recondite source can provide an apt citation. Insisting that the State cannot make people good, he quotes Bernard Bosanquet's *The Philosophical Theory of the State*, with its conclusion that all the State can do is 'to hinder the hindrances to the good.'[1]

As John Wesley pruned all the elegant classical quotations from his oral sermons to preach plain truth to plain people, so did this twentieth-century Methodist preacher leash in his very obvious love of classical and romantic English poetry. He retained the lyrical element in his appeals by the frequent citations of hymns of Wesley and Watts, using extraordinarily apt verses as the summaries of belief or sung avowals of adoration.

This clear instructor always employs a memorable structure for his sermons, with terse sub-headings. For example, in a sermon on Christ as the Master of Time, the sub-divisions and lessons are: (1) the past is not dead; (2) the future is not ours; (3) now is the acceptable time.[2] Another admirable sermon, entitled 'Four Judgments on Jesus,' is based on evaluations of Jesus recorded in the New Testament, arranged in ascending order of importance. Jesus was said to be devil-possessed, a good man, the Christ, culminating in Thomas' confession, 'My Lord and my God.'[3]

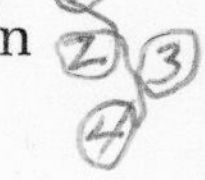

[1] *Ibid.*, I, p. 29. [2] *Ibid.*, I, p. 136. [3] *Ibid.*, II, sermon 3.

Often one discovers with delight in Sangster an inspired phrase or word-picture, or a memorable epigram. Referring to the parable of the Good Samaritan, Sangster says, 'Jesus took that term [Samaritan] from the vocabulary of the brothel and made it adjectival of the saints.'[1] He can sum up the folly of materialism in one sentence, describing the man whose skeleton was found in Pompeii's volcanic ash clutching trinkets: 'He ran back for the bangles and lost his life.'[2] Then there is his moving title for a sermon on Christ going up to Jerusalem, 'His Destination is on His Face.' Typical is his terse comment on the right response to Christ's Lordship: 'It isn't cheer; it's discipleship. It isn't admiration; it's consecration.'[3]

A final quality needs to be noticed, one that proves that those who preach the historic Christian faith can select intriguing texts and develop commonplace texts in fascinating new ways. Sangster took the rather unpromising text 'Aaron shall bear the iniquity of the holy things' (Exodus 28.38).[4] Moving from a reference to the offerings of blemished animals to God in the days of the Old Covenant, Sangster preaches on the guilt in our penitence, worship, prayers, service, and giving, and of Christ a greater High Priest than Aaron who made the perfect offering of himself on the Cross.[5] An old and central theme ingeniously treated is Sangster's sermon, 'Ambassadors for Christ.'[6] This is greatly assisted by the fact that he had recently read Lord Templewood's *Ambassador on Special Mission*, which hardly qualifies as

[1] *Ibid.*, I, sermon 5.
[2] *Ibid.*, II, p. 40.
[3] *Ibid.*, II, p. 43.
[4] *Ibid.*, II, p. 44.
[5] *Ibid.*, II, p. 137.
[6] *Ibid.*, II, sermon 3.

a diplomatic classic, least of all a spiritual one, but gave him insights into the calling of an ambassador. The Christian, like the ambassador, says Sangster, is to represent his own country in an alien land. He has direct access to the King (or President) he represents. This ambassador was on a special mission. Sooner or later every ambassador is relieved of his post, waiting to be called home. By using these analogies, Dr Sangster provided a sermon which was one long illuminating image of the Christian's duty, privileges, dignity, and destination.

After considering these qualities in his preaching, one is not surprised that he prefaces the first volume of the *Westminster Sermons* with the following tribute to his people: 'They sit without intellectual pride and their faces light up as your points register in their mind. To serve such people—and God through them—is a privilege of which no man is worthy.'[1] Magnificently did Dr Sangster serve them in his vigour, compassion, and consecration.[2] He, too, as he would in his modesty be the first to admit, was not the perfect preacher. Occasionally, one detects in him a certain peccadillo—the tendency to use impressive scientific jargon, without translating it, or even an insensitive reference.[3] Nor does he always avoid the danger of the most famous preachers—sensationalism. All such blemishes are as nothing compared with the basic integrity of the preacher of a universal gospel, of Christian spirituality and deep human compassion, who in his final illness trod the most difficult

[1] *Ibid.*, I, sermon 12. [2] *Ibid.*, I, p. xi.

[3] *Ibid.*, II, p. 94, for an unexplained reference to the fourth dimension. See also II, p. 18 referring to 'mankind crucified on a clock.'

steps on the path to perfection. He was, said his friend Dr Leslie Weatherhead, 'one of the bravest saints I have ever known.'

4 · *James S. Stewart*

The first of our evangelical trio of preachers was of Welsh stock, the second an Englishman, and the third is a Scotsman. The Reverend Professor James Stuart Stewart is the most renowned living preacher in the Church of Scotland, a communion that exalts both Christianity and culture in its ministry.

The only appropriate term for his preaching is 'heraldic' and it is taken from the title of a book of his, *Heralds of God* (1946), which clarifies the tasks and resources of the preacher of the Gospel. Since the herald's task is proclamation, the same image is implicit in Stewart's book on the message of the modern preacher, *A Faith to Proclaim* (1953).

The quiet intensity and authority with which Stewart prays, reads the lessons, and preaches, are an index of the urgency and excitement of the herald's task. He is heraldic also in the proclamation of the mighty acts of God culminating in the Incarnation, the Cross and the Resurrection of Jesus Christ, and in his stirring appeals to commitment.

In one other way his seem to be more heraldic than any other sermons being preached today. This is in their romantic, chivalric mood, which represents the Christian life as a crusade in the gallant company and communion of the saints. The musical analogy would be Sir Edward Elgar's setting to the *Froissart Overture*, where the trumpets summon to courage above the insistent drums calling to dogged marching and above dissuasive, wailing violins. The Christian faith, for Stewart, demands the daring of faith and Christ is the intrepid young Prince of Glory and his chosen bodyguard an ecumenical company from Augustine to the Covenanters, from Perpetua to Helen Keller, from D. L. Moody to G. K. Chesterton, who wear the red badge of courage on their shoulders and the gaiety of troubadours on their lips.

This gift of imagination has to be trained and controlled. C. S. Lewis makes it the servant of his philosophy; Stewart keeps his eagle in the cage of a well-structured sermon. More than this, his imagination is the servant of Scriptural exposition and it is stimulated by an astonishing command of the resources of English literature. Simply to read in full every poem, drama, novel, essay, history, and biography that he refers to in his sermons would almost constitute a Christian liberal education.

Other qualities in his topically evangelical preaching are notable, precisely because they are so rarely practised today. So much modern preaching is hesitant where Stewart is assured, so vague where Stewart is definite, moralistic where Stewart announces good news (the gift of Christ and not what *we give up* to be Christians). So much modern preaching is merely further diagnosis of the dreary political and social crisis, where Stewart proclaims the Incarnation, the Cross, the Resurrection and the Second Coming of Christ, to be the single all-important cosmic crisis, by which God judges, forgives, renews, and raises hope in men. Stewart is direct where others are devious, exhilarating where others are dull.

Moreover, if the evangelistic note is strongly sounded, it does not drown out the ecumenical, the missionary, the liturgical or prophetic. Although Stewart is a good Presbyterian, he admits a higher allegiance to the coming Great Church which will more adequately represent the Universal Christ. He is, to be sure, primarily a preacher in Scotland (even though he has been a theological lecturer, with great acceptance, in both the United States and Australia);[1] yet the place of the explorers of our faith in new continents and his understanding of the cosmic implications of the faith give his sermons an urgently missionary character. The devotional element in his sermons is strong, especially in their conclusions, and a typical insight is the insistence that Christianity is not complimenting Christ 'as genius, or artist, or teacher, or social reformer,' but, rather, 'bowing to Christ as Commander.'[2] Nor is the concern for Christian social action forgotten. Stewart is, indeed, the cultured, scholarly, ecumenical evangelical.

He was born in July 1896 in Dundee, Scotland. He was minister at North Morningside Church, Edinburgh, 1935–1946. Since 1947 he has been Professor of New Testament Language, Literature and Theology at New College in the University of Edinburgh, and since 1952 he has been a Chaplain to the Queen.

He is an unusual combination in experience and interest: the scholar-teacher-pastor-preacher. His academic

[1] The lectures given in the U.S.A. were the Lyman Beecher lectures on preaching at Yale University, published as *A Faith to Proclaim* (1953). In 1959 Dr Stewart was Turnbull Trust preacher in the Scots Church, Melbourne, Australia. His Duff Missionary Lectures of 1953 were published as *Thine is the Kingdom.*

[2] *The Gates of New Life*, p. 98.

record at the universities of St Andrews, Edinburgh and Bonn, as well as his later lectureships, were an indication of his unusual scholarly gifts. A similar clue was provided by his appointment to the joint editorship of the English translation of Schleiermacher's great work, *The Christian Faith* (trans. 1928), while his study of St Paul's theology, *A Man in Christ* (1935), showed that the researcher was also a superb expositor and teacher. The concern of the teacher-pastor was uppermost in the preparation of *The Life and Teaching of Jesus Christ* (1932) which was planned as a Bible-study course in preparation for Church membership and which has had a remarkable success.

The two volumes of Dr Stewart's collected sermons, which Messrs T. and T. Clark of Edinburgh published in the format reserved for their distinguished 'Preacher and Scholar' series, were the fruits of his 22 years in the pastoral ministry. Both volumes immediately became exceedingly popular and Stewart himself, after leaving the regular pastorate for his theological chair, was frequently to be seen in the most important pulpits in London as well as Scotland.

There are in his sermons, as composed and preached, the clarity of the teacher, the research and thought of the scholar, the practical concern of the pastor, and the authority and urgency of the preacher. Yet, true as this analysis is, it fails to elicit the particular magic of the appeal of Dr Stewart's personality. It is not a dramatic presence in the way of an unconventional approach like Dick Sheppard's or Studdert Kennedy's, nor in the daring gestures or flamboyant appearance of a Joseph Parker of the City Temple. From the opening sentences, throughout the prayers and the reading of the lessons, until the sermon is over, the final blessing said, Dr Stewart is the lightning-conductor of the God whom Gerard Manley Hopkins defined as 'Lightning and Love.' He seems as insubstantial as the auditors of Cardinal Newman report that man of God to have appeared, though Stewart seems to rush rather than to glide into the pulpit, as a boy speeding on God's errands. The parallel, of course, goes little further; for Newman's psychological penetration was as brilliant as his capacity to make orthodoxy enchanting; in the latter Stewart takes after Newman, but no one else can match the 'Augustine of our own calamitous era' as Newman tracks down the unworthy motives of the soul in the very thickets of illusion where it is hiding and drags it out into the noonday glare of Christ's holiness. Newman's style, too, produces its effects as inconspicuously as snow upon snow. In comparison, Stewart's is a richly begemmed and enamelled medieval Gospel cover, while Newman's is of white leather tooled with gold.

The important point in this comparison is not where Stewart falls short of Newman, but where he does not. Both conveyed an impression of spiritual and unworldly intensity, of having entered the pulpit from the presence-chamber of the King of Kings, and of having counted the whole world and its pretensions and pomposities as mere baubles in comparison with the riches of Christ.

For all his scholarship, James Stewart has the simplicity and integrity of Christ's true servant. It is significant that in the two volumes of his published sermons I recall only three personal experiences to which he refers.[1] One will be cited because it seems perfectly to exemplify Dr Stewart's ideal of the ministry. Apparently Stewart was visiting a little church in the Highlands where a saying of the famous Glasgow theologian and preacher, James Denney, was given pride of place on the vestry wall. It ran: 'No man can give at once the impression that he himself is clever and that Christ is mighty to save.'[2] However learned Dr Stewart's preaching is, it is *hidden* learning; if it were obtrusive learning it would draw attention to the herald, not to the Sovereign. Stewart cites Beecher's witty description that distinguishes between a God-commending and self-commending sermon: 'A sermon is not like a Chinese fire-cracker to be fired off for the noise it makes. It is the hunter's gun, and at every discharge he should look to see his game fall.'[3] Stewart, cultured as he was, was willing to be despised by the shallow coxcombs, because he struck in his sermons for a verdict for Christ. This crusader may commend his Christ most romantically, but he demands scars in Christ's service as proofs of the obedience of faith.

5 · *His Message*

Clearly, his first task is not to debate, but to declare the mighty acts of God in Jesus Christ. These are neither abstractions nor theories, but facts. Moreover, these facts of sacred history are *historical*, *unique*, and

[1] *The Strong Name*, p. 113, and *The Gates of New Life*, pp. 66 and 81. With this reserve should be contrasted the confidences of an intimate character in Weatherhead's sermons, stiff with eavesdroppings.

[2] *The Gates of New Life*, p. 81.

[3] *Heralds of God*, p. 121.

eschatological.[1] As historical, they assure us that the Incarnation of the Son of God was not a dream but a deed; as unique they are unrepeatable, 'once-for-all,' decisive facts; as eschatological facts, they were the transparent signs for men and women of faith that the Age of the Messiah had begun, the time of promise was now fulfilled, and God, who in times past had sent the prophets, had now established his new reign with the advent of his Son. The Incarnation, the Cross, the Resurrection together constitute three aspects of the one event that radically transforms the human condition and men's place before God. This, in short, is the Gospel or Good News of God's decisive intervention in history which constituted the core of what C. H. Dodd has called *The Apostolic Preaching* and which Professor Stewart believes must constitute the core of contemporary preaching.

This retelling of the mighty acts of God, which preaching essentially is, carries its own authority. As Bullinger once said: 'The preaching of the Word of God is itself a Divine word.'[2] For this reason it must be commended as the truth, and not as a means to an end. Here Stewart rightly counters the modern treachery that commends the Gospel as morale-builder, as the bulwark of democracy (whether the British or the American way of life), as a lever for social regeneration, or, one is tempted to add, as a theological aspirin guaranteeing 'peace of mind.' These may, indeed, be by-products of the preaching of the Gospel; but the Gospel should be preached not because of these advantages but because it is the truth about God and man.

[1] *A Faith to Proclaim*, pp. 18 ff.

[2] *Praedicatio divini verbi est verbum divinum* (Bullinger).

Furthermore, the claims of the Gospel must be pitched high, as high as in the New Testament itself. Like B. L. Manning and C. S. Lewis, Stewart believes that it is the reduced Christianity within the Church rather than the secularism outside which is the greater danger to the Christian faith in our times. He will have no truck with insipid religious generalities. These are the platitudes of an anaemic and pallid Christianity, or, in Kierkegaard's terms, a 'vaporized Christianity.' He maintains that Christianity cannot shrink from the ultimate alternatives: 'Either, in Christ, God the Creator and Redeemer came right into human life, or else the Gospels are the record of a lie.'[1]

Moreover, the strictly cosmic implications of the Gospel cannot be presented as casually as a butcher hands a ham to a customer across the counter, or as impersonally as an I.B.M. automaton reacts to the pressing of a button. Preaching is 'from faith to faith.' It is a holy and healthful contagion. Faith is conveyed by urgent, costly, caring enthusiasm. The energizing link between the preacher, the message and the congregation is the Holy Spirit who gives an internal testimony to the truth of the Word of God. Stewart provides his own explanation of 'from faith to faith' in the following way: 'for faith first unites to Christ and then Christ the Creative Word being thus present, arouses faith beyond and brings in His new creation.'[2] Preaching is, in effect, the self-testimony of the Risen Jesus.

The Resurrection is, indeed, for Stewart the heart of the Gospel. It is not a 'codicil to the Divine last will and testament'[1] made known on the Cross: it is, rather, a

[1] *A Faith to Proclaim*, p. 35.

[2] *Ibid.*, p. 46.

recreation by God. In the typically romantic statements of Stewart, the Resurrection 'meant that the world had died in the night and been reborn,' and 'this stupendous miracle signified the storming of history and the transforming of the world.'[2] Occasionally, in Stewart, rapture races on far beyond reason, and usually just at the point where we seek for a definition. But if we wait long enough, it is usually to be found. In plain language, the Resurrection means for Stewart that Christ is a conquering not a defeated hero, and that his liberation from the grave is a Divine vindication of Righteousness and therefore a cosmic victory for the Kingdom of God over the forces of darkness. The Resurrection means also that God's power is available for man's weakness, and that Christ is the unseen Companion of the Christian, who enables the new Israel of the Spirit (brought into being by the Cross-Resurrection-Pentecost series of events) to become convinced that death itself is defeated.[3] This new life is marked by supernatural joy, infinite horizons of hope, and a radiant confidence.

The Cross, according to Stewart, must be proclaimed within the context of the world's suffering and the world's sin. Thus viewed, it is a revelation of the hatefulness of sin and of the Divine judgment on sin, while it is also a revelation of the holy love of God seeking and saving the unworthy. Even as the words are uttered 'It is finished,' the Cross is a victory of faith over fear, of obedience over indiscipline, of sacrifice over selfishness, of inclusiveness over exclusiveness, of forgiveness over retaliation, and of holiness over sin. It is, above all, a

[1] *Ibid.*, p. 105. [2] *Ibid.*, p. 107.

[3] This analysis is fully expounded in chapter 4 of *A Faith to Proclaim*.

challenge to Christ's disciples to take up their crosses and follow him.[1]

Now Stewart does not imply that the proclamation of the Gospel is merely retelling the old, old story of Jesus and his love. In the extremely valuable concluding chapter of *A Faith to Proclaim* he acknowledges that Christendom is in a great dilemma caused by the contrast between the promise and the power of the Gospel and the relative impotence of empirical Christianity. To explain this failure of communication or failure of power (as Stewart believes it to be), it is suggested that a restatement or reconstruction of faith in the light of modern reason is required. Another diagnosis locates the trouble in the lack of social emphasis, and recalls that it was said of the early Christian revolutionaries, 'these are they that turned the world upside down.' Yet, important as the apologist's and the social reformer's tasks undoubtedly are, he judges that the preacher's is even more fundamental. It is to avoid the over-intellectualism of the apologist and the danger in the social reformer of valuing Christianity as a means for establishing social justice instead of as 'a vital relationship to a living Christ.'[2] The herald's duty is to bring uncommitted men to the allegiance of his Sovereign Lord, in whose service is perfect freedom.

Although Stewart presents claims on men's allegiance in the same way Jesus and his apostles did in the New Testament, and although these claims have been confirmed by saints who have experienced Christ's transforming power in the greatest days of the Church's

[1] These themes are developed in chapter 2 of *Heralds of God.*
[2] *A Faith to Proclaim*, p. 143.

history, yet our preacher knows that the cultured despisers will scoff at this supposed communion with Christ. The sceptic will deride it as 'romantic untheological mysticism, muddle-headed mawkish sentiment, with no relevance to the dust and blood of life's arena, sure to collapse in times of strain and trouble.'[1]

To these charges Stewart has a ringing and persuasive series of replies. Faith in Christ cannot be introverted emotionalism because again and again it has held and gripped men in the most desperate times. Even more, it has demanded the decision of heroic choice, not permitted easy evasions. And here I cannot resist the illustration which Stewart gives, not because it is apt but because it is so characteristic of his understanding of Christianity as courage:

> 'You have not made much out of all these years,' said one Devon man who had stayed ashore and grown sleek and prosperous and wealthy to another who had served in the fleet of Francis Drake.
>
> 'No,' said the other, 'I've not made much. I've been cold, hungry, shipwrecked, desperately frightened often: but I've been with the greatest Captain who ever sailed the seas!'[2]

St Paul's existential decision for Christ cost him shipwreck, stoning, imprisonment and death. Father Damien's dedication to Molokai for Christ's despised and rejected ones cost him leprosy. Such sacrificial commitments are not the consequences of gullibility, or following a mere fiction.

Moreover, far from Christian commitment being a

[1] *A Faith to Proclaim*, p. 143. [2] *Ibid.*, pp. 150–151.

soothing or comfortable experience, it is desperately heart-searching, humiliating, and unsettling experience, forcing us to cry, 'Lord, have mercy!' as our sins come before the light of his pure countenance.

Finally, says Stewart, Christ mysticism is a logical consequence of the Resurrection of Christ. This, he says, is the sequence: 'risen from the dead; therefore, alive forever; therefore, our Contemporary; therefore, able to confront us face to face.'[1]

6 · *His Method*

The fullest advice that Professor Stewart has to offer on the methods of sermon preparation and delivery is found in *Heralds of God*, whereas its sequel, *A Faith to Proclaim*, is more concerned with the content than the form or manner of preaching. It will be our concern in this section to consider his theory, and then his practice. His first concern is to insist on expository preaching.

His second plea is for the fullest possible use of the festivals of the Christian Year. This is related to a concentration on the central events in the Incarnation of Jesus, which it is the herald's duty to proclaim. It has a deep devotional value for preacher and congregation, and it links the local Church with the universal Church through celebrating these festivals. Their chief value for the preacher is that they summon him from the by-paths to the great highway of redemption.[2]

Thirdly, Stewart urges that the preacher shall always visualize his congregation as he prepares a sermon for them. This will remove the formality and artificiality

[1] *Ibid.*, p. 152. [2] *Heralds of God*, p. 111.

that can spoil sermons and provide the qualities of 'directness, liveliness, verve and immediacy, which are so essential.'[1] It is to retain the very same qualities that Stewart urges theological students to prepare a full manuscript for the pulpit, but to learn it so well that they can be independent of it. Thus they will be able to combine the advantages of order with ardour.

On the structure of sermons, he advises that introductions be kept short, that whether sermon 'divisions' or 'headings' of study be used or not they be flexible in number and that, if used, it is bad psychology to announce all the headings at the outset and leave no surprises in store. He does not reject the traditional sermon opening which started with the explaining the historical background of the text announced, but prefers the modern opening with present-day experience. As for sermon endings, Stewart believes they should clinch the entire sermon's purpose and should never hesitate to use the direct personal appeal. He prefers the quiet close to any crashing chords. He dislikes elaborate perorations.

This finely imaginative preacher is well aware of the importance of freshness and fertility of illustrations, arguing 'Truth made concrete will find a way past many a door when abstractions knock in vain.'[2] But he rightly warns against the use of the threadbare anecdote or the hackneyed quotation, and even against the tendency to use anecdotes, appeals and 'homiletical gush' as substitutes for thinking, for thinking is also Divine Service. Since Stewart's sermons are as full of illuminating illustrations as Perpendicular Gothic architecture is of windows, it is almost incredible to read that Stewart

[1] *Heralds of God*, p. 119. [2] *Ibid.*, p. 142.

advised the Divinity students of St Andrews and Edinburgh to use illustrations 'sparingly and appropriately.'[1] Stewart, a mighty quoter, advises the same rule for citations: 'be sparing.'[2] Then, as if to demonstrate that the eminent can break all the rules, Stewart brings us up with a shock by insisting on the duty of exegetical honesty, by which he chiefly means avoiding the peril of over-allegorizing! Finally, he suggests—and it is contrary to the frequently funereal pace of Scottish sermons—that too much *Andante* with never a touch of *Allegro* or even *Presto* can be fatal. His own preaching has exactly the pace and verve to excite and hold the interest of the liveliest listeners, as if they were wedding guests.

7 · *Stewart's Sermons*

It will be interesting to compare Stewart's practice with his theories, and as evidence of his practice there are the 49 printed sermons which appear in *The Gates of New Life* (1937) and *The Strong Name* (1941).

First, we must apply the heraldic test to these sermons: How many of them are, in fact, expositions of the mighty acts of God, announcements of the Gospel? Or, to put the question in a slightly different way, how many of them are doctrinal sermons suitable for the great festivals of the Christian Year? There are 8 definitely doctrinal sermons in *The Gates of New Life*[3] and 9 definitely doctrinal sermons in *The Strong Name*.[4] These doctrinal sermons are concerned with such central themes as the Sovereignty of God, the Holy Trinity, Advent,

[1] *Ibid.*, p. 143. [2] *Ibid.*, p. 145.
[3] Such as Sermons II, V, IX, X, XVII, XX, XXI, and XXV.
[4] Such as Sermons II, IV, V, VII, VIII, XVII, XIX, and XX.

the Person of Jesus (Human and Divine), the Work of Christ, the Resurrection, the Ascension, the Church, and the Sacraments.

The heraldic implications of the preacher's task are overwhelmingly present, however, in the 14 practical sermons on the nature of the Christian Life to be found in *The Gates of New Life* and in the 8 sermons of a similar character in *The Strong Name*. It is always *Christian* life. Some of the more striking titles will indicate the Christological emphases: 'The Romance of Orthodoxy,' 'The Triumphant Adequacy of Christ' and 'Our Worries and Christ's Peace.'

Furthermore, even Stewart's sermons can definitely be labelled 'Apologetical,' as in three cases in his first, and as in seven cases in his second volume of sermons, it is never philosophy of religion or theism which he contends for, but always Christianity.[1] Humanism, for example, is exposed in a sermon entitled 'A Modern Substitute for the Gospel.' A series of four sermons on God and the Fact of Suffering clearly reveals the Christological basis of confidence in two sub-titles: 'Wearing the Thorns as a Crown' and 'The Cross of Victory.' By all these tests, it appears clearly to me that Stewart's preaching is fully heraldic, evangelical and expository. In fact, if I were to describe their distinctive flavour, I would be tempted to call them 'doctrinal-lyrical' sermons, because the doctrinal illuminates the mind to compel the heart to confess its adoration.

Why does Stewart rely so much on illustration? Clearly, it is partly because he has a strongly visual

[1] The Apologetical Sermons in *The Gates of New Life* are Nos. III, XVI, and XVIII and in *The Strong Name* they are Nos. XI–XV inclusive, XXI and XXII.

imagination. It is also because he knows that the loyalty he seeks to win for Christ depends upon engaging the will, and the key to the will is the imagination. In image after image, he suggests that it is the daring, the gallant, the generous, the chivalrous, the men of action (like generals, or explorers), the martyrs (whether Perpetua in the sand of the arena, or Hugh Mackail the covenanter in the Scottish heather),[1] who are Christ's elect. The cloud of witnesses are not left in the clouds: on the contrary they are brought to earth again by his imagination to march past the preacher's reviewing stand and greet the present Church militant with a *sursum corda*!

We can already see that the value of the witnesses is that they bridge the remote Biblical world of nineteen centuries ago with the contemporary world: this is the true apostolic succession for Stewart. And he never ceases to be amazed by the true Catholicity of Christ's appeal through varied nations and changing centuries: 'Who can this be who can grip and captivate the souls of men so utterly different as Luther the Reformer and Loyola the Jesuit, as Francis the Friar and Moody the evangelist, as G. K. Chesterton and General Booth, as Cardinal Newman and David Livingstone?'[2] Many a preacher uses the same technique, but none I think is so concerned to be as chivalrous in his attitude towards women (compare John Knox for an earlier Presbyterian view!), as ecumenically representative in his selection of saints, or bases his selections and citations on more voracious reading of biographies.[3]

[1] For these two illustrations see pp. 204 and 249 of *The Strong Name*.

[2] Each sermon has, on average, 3 literary and 3 historical references or citations.

[3] *Ibid.*, p. 87.

It is also important to see how far Stewart's practice is in line with his advice about the beginnings, the subdivisions, and the ending of sermons. It cannot, alas, be said that his introductions are always brief. In the first sermon in *The Gates of New Life* it takes four and a half pages to list the variety of doubts and the sermon is four-fifths through before Christ is brought forward as the clue to the faith that can dispel doubt. Yet his opening comment on John 14.27 goes right to the point of his theme: 'This was Christ's last will and testament. This was his only legacy. . . . He had no material possessions. . . . He gave peace.'[1]

His sermon starts are almost always in the modern manner. His stirring military sermon in which God is likened to vanguard and rearguard is an admirable example of the modern, confidential approach: 'How do you regard human life? I suppose the three most frequent descriptions of life, the three most popular pictures, are these—a battle, a voyage, and a march.'[2]

His endings frequently take the form of direct evangelical appeals, moving in their sincerity and simplicity, as the following: 'Listen, young knight of Jesus Christ! You have seen the cross—blood-red on the hill of Calvary, blood-red with "love divine, all loves excelling," blood-red for your redemption, blood-red with God's great agony. The cross—its very shape like an anchor—binds, holds, grips your soul with grace and mercy. In the love of this be pure. In the grip of this stand steady. In the strength of this, come victor. The

[1] From Sermon XV in *The Gates of New Life*. The diffuse nature of the style is still in evidence, even though I have reduced the opening paragraph from 59 words to 20.

[2] *Ibid.*, Sermon IX.

cross—for ever and for ever!'[1] It is hardly fair to detach the appeal from the sermon on 'The Anchors of the Soul,' but it is sufficient to show that Stewart believes in direct, passionate, and evangelical appeals for a verdict for Christ. Other endings are quiet dedications, reiterations of the Divine promises, remembrances of the power and peace of Christ, or apt conclusions from hymns.

Stewart never tells all his plans at the beginning of a sermon, as he allows division after new division of his theme to unfold. Certainly, he is not tied to the same number of divisions in each sermon, though 3 or 4 are the commonest numbers. Some of his ingenious sermon analyses deserve to be mentioned. His recounting of the spiritual biography of Mark as 'A Drama in Four Acts'[2] and as a type of Christian's pilgrimage is admirably divided into: Recantation, Remorse, Restoration, Reparation. A less ingenious but no less thoughtful sermon on the Ascension of Christ, explains the expediency of this mighty act of God: firstly, for the spiritualizing of religion; secondly, for the universalizing of the Gospel; thirdly, for the energizing of evangelism; and, fourthly, for the fortifying of faith.[3]

8 · *Light—and Shadows*

Stewart is one of the glories of the Scottish pulpit and his reputation is international. Some of his sermons are among the most felicitous and memorable pulpit utterances of our time. 'Vanguard and Rearguard' and

[1] *Ibid.*, p. 111.
[2] *Ibid.*, Sermon XII.
[3] *The Strong Name*, Sermon V.

'The Universality of Jesus' from *The Gates of New Life*, and 'The Gospel of the Ascension' and 'The Strong Name of the Trinity' in *The Strong Name*, are four masterpieces. For artistry in construction, luminous illustrations, solid orthodox divinity kept fascinating and relevant, it would be difficult to find better preaching in our time than Stewart's.

For all their excellencies, however, it is permissible to ask some questions about them, and those of a quite fundamental nature. Granted the preacher is a herald and he must state the acts and facts of the Gospel; yet can there be facts without interpretations? Thus, is not the herald an apologist inevitably and rightly so? And does Stewart allow sufficiently for the variety and disunity of the New Testament interpretations dependent upon the different angles from which the disciples view their Lord and Master? Yet, again, has not the modern preacher in a post-Christian era to drop the romantic, chivalric and even medieval approach because he cannot count on even the memory of the Christian style in the modern adolescent? If Tennyson and Browning were a little out of date in the age of T. S. Eliot and Hemingway, where is there room for them in the age of Camus or Sartre, of Becket and Tennessee Williams and Wesker?

In any age, I think there would have been found critics to carp at the prolixity of his sermons and the repetitiousness of his style, which blunts its impact by too many words of equivalent meaning, by his occasional sentimentality, and his over-elaborated descriptions.[1] The effect is too Pre-Raphaelite in its chivalry and its

[1] *Ibid.*, p. 200.

detail: too consciously literary and artificial. There is too much 'Burne' and insufficient 'Jones.'

Others would want to criticize Stewart for falling a prey to over-allegorization, a defect which he warned theological students against. The odd thing is that some of his most original and memorable sermons were written by disregarding these rules. The sermon on 'The Universality of Jesus,' for example, is a fanciful and brilliant interpretation of a minor piece of information in the Gospel record, to the effect that the superscription of Christ's Cross was trilingual. From this Stewart launches into a claim that Christ is the King of Culture, Government and Religion. It is an admirable lesson, but based on a creaking Biblical foundation. Similarly, while there are undoubtedly four important 'Anchors of the Soul' in times of crisis to be found in Hope, Duty, Prayer and the Cross of Christ, it is surely using the text as a pretext to claim that this is the meaning of the incidental nautical reference in Acts 27.29.[1] Nor is it legitimate to extend our Lord's warning against all breakers of marriage, 'Whom God hath joined, let no man put asunder,' as a general principle on which the need for the correlation of Religion and Character, Faith and Reason, the Human Soul and Jesus may be based.[2] It is not, in the strictest sense, 'exegetical honesty.'[3]

It has been worth while to linger over the qualities and few defects of the highly literary sermons of James S. Stewart, because they mark the end of an epoch. In one sense, they are the last glow of the oratory of the Victorian age, presuming a leisurely culture, a relish for

[1] *Gates of New Life*, Sermon XI. [2] *Ibid.*, Sermon XIV.
[3] *Heralds of God*, p. 153.

history and biography, and an appreciation of style. The scholarship, of course, is good mid-twentieth-century New Testament scholarship and the mood is that of a Church on guard. Even so, Stewart may be the last of the polished literary preachers in Britain. In the fearful new world of the mid-twentieth century, radically new types of Christian witness will be called for in the post-Christian age, and, therefore, new modes of preaching. Some of them will need to be as daring and direct as the blows of the resistance movement in enemy-occupied territory; others will be combined-operations approaches with other religious groups in a world of machines and automata which depreciate both divine and human values. There will be little time for 'coddling the saints': all the concentration will have to be on 'catching the sinners.'

—— 9 ——

Apologetical and Theological Preaching

ARCHBISHOP TEMPLE & PROFESSOR FARMER

WHAT is 'apologetical' preaching? The noun 'apology' has both a weak and a strong meaning. In common speech an apology is an expression of regret. Its historic stronger meaning is an explanation or vindication. It is in the stronger sense that 'apologetical' is applied to preaching. Such preaching, therefore, explains the reasonableness of the Christian faith and vindicates or justifies the faith from every type of criticism. Apologetical preaching bears in mind those who are hostile or indifferent to the Christian revelation and whose objections have to be met with fairness and answered with conviction and relevance. Two distinguished apologetical preachers and writers in England in our period have been Archbishop William Temple, the Anglican leader, and Professor H. H. Farmer, the Presbyterian theologian.

The versatile William Temple—theologian, philosopher, social and educational reformer, ecumenical statesman, and 'the People's Archbishop'—was the greatest exponent and defender of the Christian faith in the England of his day. Alike in pulpit and on public platform, his sermons and addresses proclaimed that the

Christian revelation is the highest wisdom and that in its light economists, politicians, philosophers and artists shall see light. His moral influence penetrated through all layers of English life, and his death in 1944 was felt to be a hard blow not only to England but to the Christian cause itself.

Though not a man of the same magnitude or influence in public life, Professor Farmer of the University of Cambridge is also a Christian philosopher and a distinguished lecturer and preacher. He has particularly addressed himself to answering criticisms of Christianity advanced from the standpoint of the behavioural sciences (an area hardly touched upon by the Archbishop). Moreover, he has produced admirable books on the form and content of preaching which are classics of their kind, and his published sermons command the assent of the intellect and captivate the will and the imagination. In this respect they complement the sermons and addresses of the Archbishop. The latter succeeded in convincing the mind and in challenging the will, but he was not so successful in catching the imagination, except in his later devotional works and his broadcast sermons of 1942, where the Scripture provided a much-needed narrative basis for his meditations.

In two important respects Temple and Farmer are alike. Both were trained as philosophers and both attained the distinction of being appointed Gifford Lecturers. Certainly they both believed that reason is the candle of the Lord. Of even greater interest is the fact that each increasingly turned from a philosophical to a definitely theological approach. That is to say, their expositions of religion became less explanations of

Christianity as the highest practical wisdom than proclamations of the Gospel as the way of redemption from pride, complacency, anxiety, fear, callousness and evil. As the skyscape darkened under the threat of totalitarianism in the thirties, both men sensed that man's chief foe was not ignorance, but the paralysis or the rebellion of the will. Consequently his greatest need was for the transformation of egotism by grace. Thus, in their later work, the emphasis changes from the apologetical to the strictly theological, from the revelational to the redemptive.[1]

1 · *William Temple: the Making of an Apologist*

By upbringing, native gifts, education, and opportunities, as well as by intellectual and spiritual self-discipline, he was superbly equipped to be a defender and vindicator of the Christian faith. He was born in 1881, the second son of Frederick Temple, then Bishop of Exeter and subsequently Bishop of London and Archbishop of Canterbury. He grew up in Fulham Palace, London, and went to Rugby School where his father had been Headmaster in the great tradition of Dr Thomas Arnold. From Rugby he won an exhibition to Balliol College, Oxford, where he gained a 'double first' (class honours) in philosophy, classics and ancient history, and was elected President of the Oxford Union (the University's debating society). In 1904 he was elected a Fellow of Queen's College, Oxford, and Lecturer in Philosophy. The next year he declared his independence

[1] See Archbishop A. M. Ramsey's *An Era in Anglican Theology: From Gore to Temple* (1960), Preface, p. viii, and Chap. 10.

and showed his profound social concern in joining the Workers' Educational Association, the Presidency of which he held from 1908 to 1924. In 1909, after some doctrinal hesitations, he was ordained as priest of the Church of England. From 1910 to 1914 he was Headmaster of Repton School, and for the three following years Rector of St James', Piccadilly, London. He then resigned to take a leading part in the organization of the Life and Liberty Movement of the National Church and in the same year there appeared his first philosophical volume of importance. Its title was *Mens Creatrix* (Creative Mind).

Thereafter his career was a steady ascent to greater ecclesiastical and public responsibilities. In 1919 he was appointed Canon of Westminster and his sermons in Westminster Abbey and elsewhere were distributed to a wider public in the book, *Fellowship with God*. In 1921 he was consecrated Bishop of Manchester. Three years later his notable vindication of Christianity appeared under the title of *Christus Veritas* (Christ the Truth). Others acknowledged his deep interest in the social implications and obligations of Christianity by electing him as Chairman of the important international Conference on Politics, Economics, and Citizenship (COPEC) held in Birmingham. In 1926 he published *Personal Religion and the Life of Fellowship*.

In 1929 he was enthroned as Archbishop of York and for the thirteen years that he held this high office he was more than the Anglican leader of the Ecumenical Movement. He was both Chairman of the Continuation Committee of the Faith and Order Movement, and of the famous Edinburgh Conference in 1937. In 1931 his closely argued, pithily expressed and well-illustrated addresses given to the Mission to Oxford University were published as *The Christian Faith and Life*.

Amid an unusually busy and responsible public life he found time to prepare the Gifford Lectures at Glasgow University which were published as *Nature, Man, and God* (1934). His greatest works on spirituality, the two volumes of *Readings in St John's Gospel*, appeared in 1939 and 1940. His courageous and controversial volume, *Christianity and the Social Order*, was published in 1942 as a Penguin Special paperback. In the same year he also gave a moving series of broadcast addresses, *Palm Sunday to Easter*.

Most important of all, he was enthroned as Archbishop of Canterbury on 23rd April 1942, in the midst of the Second World War, at a time when his great gifts of mind and spirit were sorely needed. His enthronement sermon, which sounded the ecumenical note, was widely hailed. The publication in 1944 of *The Church Looks Forward*, consisting of his sermons and speeches during the first eighteen months after his enthronement in the Chair of St Augustine, were a proof of his power and the future promise of his leadership. On 26th October 1944 this apparently indefatigable servant of God and all conditions of men found his rest—in death. Tributes from all over the world made it clear that the Church of England and the Ecumenical Movement had lost, not only a philosophical theologian and social reformer of greatness, but a saint of rare humility, serenity, charity, lucidity and courage.

2 · *The Teacher and his Teaching*

Only an exceptionally gifted teacher can write highly complex philosophical and theological tomes for the experts and prepare equally lucid yet cogent addresses for the wayfaring man. William Temple could and did.

In *Mens Creatrix* Temple showed that if reality is sought by the different paths of philosophy, science, and art, these paths will never meet unless there be a God in whom these values eternally exist. In the companion volume, *Christus Veritas,* he demonstrated what Christianity had to say about the nature of God. Both were highly technical volumes. Yet their essence is distilled in the admirably written *Christian Faith and Life* which has been used in hundreds of rectories and vicarages as a basis for preparing candidates for Confirmation.[1]

This single volume of eight addresses given at the Mission to Oxford University from brief notes was prepared from a verbatim record of a *Church Times* reporter. It is thus an excellent example of Temple's addresses *as they were heard.* It exemplifies the Archbishop's teaching gifts, though one would look elsewhere for his devotional meditations and social ethical teaching. Here he stands revealed as the apologist winning a hearing for Christianity from intelligent youth. His eight themes are: the meaning of 'God'; Christ's place in History; the Moral Standard; Sin and Repentance; the Crucifixion; the Holy Spirit in Life; Prayer and the Sacraments; and the Christian Society.

[1] In a brief newspaper article, entitled 'Back to Temple,' Canon Roger Lloyd stated that he had prepared over 2,000 candidates for Confirmation on the basis of *Christian Faith and Life.*

Temple begins by arguing that the most satisfactory explanation of the universe is the hypothesis of its creation by intelligent purpose. Life is seen to have four gradations: matter, life, mind, and spirit. God, who is 'the union of absolute goodness and absolute power,' provides the clue to our understanding and the power to pursue his purposes. Man resembles God, dimly yet truly, in the capacity to understand, to make conscious moral choices, and to live in fellowship. The purpose of life is expressed most fully in the Word-made-flesh, the incarnate Christ—'the rational principle that governs the world, and also the utterance of God by which He creates the world.'[1]

He then moves on to the Crucifixion by using two related texts: 'Let there be light and there was light' and 'Nevertheless not My will, but Thine be done.' This enables him to compare the Creation and the Agony in the Garden. He continues:

> In these two quotations is depicted the difference for God between creating the universe with all its millions of stars, and the making of a selfish soul into a loving one. To create was easy; the will of God produces its own fulfilment; no effort there. . . . But to convert a heart like our hearts from the self-centredness which is natural to them into the love which is God's own nature, which they must reach if they are to be in fellowship with Him—that costs the agony and bloody sweat and the death upon the Cross.[2]

Temple's penetrating clarity enlivens the well-worn and often stale themes of prayer and the sacraments. Our Lord's teaching on prayer is summed up as confidence, perseverance, and correspondence to God's will. Quite

[1] *Op. cit.*, p. 25.

[2] *Ibid.*, p. 73.

typical is the profound simplicity of his advice: 'The proper outline of a Christian prayer is not, "Please do for me what I want." It is, "Please do with me what You want." '[1]

Christ's work must be continued through his Society, the Church, which originally 'constituted a single personality, because all governed by one spirit and purpose, and the centre of unity in any personality is its purpose.'[2] This the first Church, submitting itself to the guidance of the Holy Spirit, discovered that divisions based on religious history, race, culture, economics, and sex, were transcended so as to be negligible.

Temple's final appeal is to accept the sovereignty of Christ as King and Lord of all life. An answer is necessary 'because to give no answer is to answer "No." ' Temple confidently concluded: 'But you will answer "Yes," and so take your part in the great fellowship of worship and service, the eternal Church, the communion of saints, the army in heaven which rides in the train of the Word of God as He goes forth conquering and to conquer.'[3]

The qualities of this series of addresses are many. After the first, each subsequent address uses as its floor the ceiling of its predecessor, thus providing a logically interrelated structure. Sentences and words tend to be short. Technical terms are few and always defined. Commonplace themes appear in a new light as treated by Temple. For example, he says that 'Legislation is really the fruit of moral advance and not the cause of it.' As one ponders this, a convincing statement follows that 'you only get legislation when people feel that the evil

[1] *Ibid.*, p. 109. [2] *Ibid.*, p. 125. [3] *Ibid.*, p. 139.

cannot be tolerated at all.' He also has a gift for apt illustration. Repentance is interpreted in Roycean fashion as transvaluation—it is adopting God's viewpoint and values instead of one's own. The point is brought home by likening the world to a shop window 'in which some mischievous person has got overnight and shifted all the price-labels round so that the cheap things have the high price-labels, and the really precious things are priced low.' As a result, 'we let ourselves be taken in' and 'repentance means getting those price-labels back in the right place.'[1]

Sublime succinctness and clarity, coupled with uncommon sense, are equally to be found in *Personal Religion and the Life of Fellowship.* Always amazed by the condescension of the Incarnation, Temple finds a novel way of expressing it in the concept of the Supreme as servant. 'For Plato as for Mohammed,' he remarks, 'while all things else serve the Supreme, the Supreme is no servant. But when God became incarnate, He said, "I am among you as one that serveth." '[2] Again, on the authority of the Incarnation, Temple asserts that Christianity is far the most materialistic of religions because it can dominate the flesh without running away from it. And how simply and yet incisively he deals with the pessimist's plaint that 'you can't change human nature.' 'To this,' says Temple, 'the Christian replies, "No; I can't, but God can; to do this He was incarnate; to do this He died upon the Cross; to do this by the power of His Spirit is the task of the Church." '[3]

In almost every one of his religious writings, Temple saw that the adoration of God in worship is the highest

[1] *Ibid.*, p. 68. [2] *Op. cit.*, p. 12. [3] *Ibid.*, p. 25.

human privilege, and that its true consequence is service to humanity. The devotional and social were the two sides of his theological coin. Thus he can describe the Holy Communion as both the means of grace and the symbol of a transformed human society. Bread and wine, so he maintains, are the perfect symbols of the economic life of man. Bread is an instance of God's gifts to man made available by human co-operation with God. On God's part there is the gift of the seed, the soil, the sun, and the rain. On man's part the labour of ploughing the land, scattering the seed, the gathering of the harvest, the threshing of the flour, the baking of the bread, and its distribution for the satisfaction of men's needs. Thus:

> In the Holy Communion service we take the bread and wine —man's industrial and commercial life in symbol—and offer it to God; because we have offered it to Him, He gives it back to us as the means of nurturing us, not in our animal nature alone, but as agents of His purpose, limbs of a body responsive to His will; and as we receive it back from Him, we share it with one another in a true fellowship. If we think of the service in this way, it is a perfect picture of what secular society should be; and a Christian civilization is one where the citizens seek to make their ordered life something of which that service is the symbol.[1]

Even when the Archbishop is meditating on the words spoken from the Cross, he can provide very practical conclusions from so mystical a study. After remarking on the consideration of Christ, who wishes to spare his Mother from seeing his final agonies, Temple pierces the conscience with the quiet questions: 'Will you ask yourself, each one of you who listen, whether when you

[1] *The Hope of a New World* (1940), pp. 69–70.

are in pain or sickness you think of your closest friends chiefly in order to save them trouble and distress? Or, do you think of them chiefly as there to meet your needs and do you service?'[1]

It is *Christianity and Social Order* which spells out most clearly the Christian basis of a more just re-ordering of society. Here he claimed that the four basic Christian principles the Church must proclaim are: Freedom, Membership, Service, and Sacrifice. These are the canons by which every sensitive Christian must judge social, economic, and political issues, for they express the mind of Christ. These principles and their application were fearlessly declared on public platforms, yet they were implicit in most of his sermons as well.

His learning, courage, charity and serenity were ever more clearly manifested in his written and spoken words. As a speaker he was effortless, perhaps too effortless. Dr F. A. Iremonger, his biographer, asserts that 'to speak five times in one day cost him little more than to speak once.'[2] His versatility was almost as deep as it was wide. Social reformers counted on his support and considered him to be in the prophetic succession of F. D. Maurice, Westcott, Scott Holland and Charles Gore. Debaters and hecklers found him a formidable foe of confused thinking and impertinence of manner. Philosophers and theologians admired his comprehensiveness and acuity. Simple men and women were reassured in their faith because so intelligent a man gloried in the obedience of a Christian, and the poor felt that he fought power and affluence as their protector.

[1] *Palm Sunday to Easter* (1942), p. 24.
[2] *William Temple, Archbishop of Canterbury* (1948), p. 483.

How did he succeed in commending himself to such varied types of congregations or audiences? Certainly it was not by an exterior attractiveness, except for his great gusty laughter. He was a stocky man, without a bell-like voice. Yet his was, according to R. H. Tawney, 'the voice of first-hand experience and personal meditation,' and his sayings 'for all their delusive simplicity' were often profound. Dr Iremonger sums up by declaring that his impact was due to 'obvious authority, intense conviction, and a mastery of words which placed him among the most lucid teachers of Christendom.'[1]

It was obviously the high quality of the Archbishop's thought and character, rather than any deliberate craftsmanship in his sermons and addresses, that gained wide recognition for him. This, indeed, may account in part for the unequal impact of his sermons. D. R. Davies, a great admirer of Temple, claimed that he could reach great spiritual and prophetic heights in his Ordination charges, but that he often seemed satisfied with lower levels (which were still high by comparison with those of other Anglican dignitaries). Davies argues that his chief defect as a prophetic preacher was to mix the styles of the pulpit and the platform, so that he seemed to argue in the pulpit and to preach on the platform.[2]

Others felt that, for all his intellectual sympathy with the under-privileged and his battle in later years with ill health, he had been protected from the agonies of disappointment and bereavement. They felt that he thus proclaimed a confident order in the universe, where others had experienced the most shattering disorder. Thus his preaching seemed as if he had changed the

[1] *Ibid.*, p. 485. [2] *The London Quarterly.*

Psalmist's 'Out of the depths' to his own 'On the heights I cry unto Thee, O God.' He worked for the common man, but found it very difficult to sustain conversation with him informally.[1] Only occasionally was he a great and moving preacher, but he was a sublime doctrinal preacher, apologist, and devotional commentator.

3 · *Professor Farmer: The Philosopher as Preacher*

Although not as eminent a philosopher as Archbishop William Temple, Professor Farmer is a superior preacher precisely because he does not lecture from the pulpit. His twelve years of pastoral experience in the English Presbyterian ministry have proved an invaluable initiation into compassion. He has been both Warrack Lecturer in Preaching in the Scottish Universities (1940) and Lyman Beecher Lecturer in Preaching at Yale University (1946), as well as Gifford Lecturer in Natural Theology at Glasgow University (1950–1951).

He has held theological chairs in the United States and in England. From 1931 to 1935 he was Riley Professor of Christian Doctrine at Hartford Theological Seminary in Connecticut. For the next 25 years he was Barbour Professor of Systematic Theology in Westminster College, Cambridge, and for the last 11 of those years he concurrently held the Norris-Hulse Professorship of Divinity in the University of Cambridge, where he was also a Fellow of Peterhouse. As Norris-Hulse Professor he was the successor of the eminent New Testament

[1] Iremonger, *op. cit.*, p. 496.

scholar, Dr C. H. Dodd,[1] and therefore the second Free Church divine to hold a Cambridge University Professorship since the seventeenth century.

Both his thought and his preaching have been marked by their strong fidelity to the Bible, their honesty in facing up to mental and moral difficulties, and their deep relevance and independence of current fashions. Another distinctive characteristic, especially in so able a mind, is his modesty. Dr Farmer is never the conscious 'Pulpit Master' but always 'the Servant of the Word.' He is constantly aware that if he is not under the authority of the Word of God he would be overreaching himself.

Professor Farmer has written most acutely and engagingly of the task of the contemporary preacher in two volumes, *The Servant of the Word* (1941) and *God and Men* (1947) respectively, the fruits of his Warrack and Beecher lectureships.

He recognizes that the preacher has to face the acute competition of the radio and television and no longer has the privileged position of being the only mentor of the people as in the days when illiteracy was rampant, or in more recent times when his only serious rival was the school teacher whose power often ended when school days were over. Because these means of communication penetrate not only into every village but into every living-room, he believes that preaching is coming again into its own. Dictators in our own day as well as commercial advertisers are exemplars of the 'terrible potency of speech.' National crises have underscored the central importance of beliefs that are worth dying for as well as living for. The Christian preacher stands as the

[1] Dr C. H. Dodd is Editor-in-chief of *The New English Bible.*

'representative of the universal supra-national church,'[1] and every Ecumenical Conference from Edinburgh to New Delhi, via Oxford, Amsterdam, Evanston and Lund, bears witness to the 'great new fact of our time.' Above all, he insists that the most recent theology stresses the importance of preaching.

Since Dr Farmer is a theological preacher this must be clarified. Biblical theology today in three characteristic emphases makes the pulpit the throne of Christ. This is so, first, because of the insistence on the importance of the 'Christ-event'—the unguessable, historically given, Church-creating event of the advent of Jesus Christ with its transformation of human nature.

The re-telling of that event, accompanied by the power of the Holy Spirit, re-creates the new community the Church. It is significant that both Bultmann and Tillich, with whom this type of theology originated, are preachers of great distinction.

The second modern theological emphasis is termed 'realized eschatology' and is particularly associated with another scholar-preacher: Dr C. H. Dodd. This stresses that God's mighty saving act began in Christ's coming, but it is not yet complete. God's campaign was won in the Cross and the Resurrection but 'mopping-up operations' in the enemy-occupied territory of this world have still to be completed. In this view bearing witness to Christ's saving act is itself a part of the act of salvation. This, too, puts an essential emphasis on preaching.

The third modern theological emphasis on religion as a personal encounter between the 'I' of God and the 'Thou' of man addressed by God and most movingly

[1] *The Servant of the Word*, p. 12.

expressed by the Jewish theologian, Dr Martin Buber, has been a central concern of Dr Farmer's thought. In *The World and God* (1932), in *God and Men* (1948), in *Revelation and Religion* (1954), as also in his books of sermons and in *Towards Belief in God* (1942), Professor Farmer has insisted that God confronts men as 'absolute demand' and 'final succour.' That is, the Living God makes an absolute claim upon the lives of the men he has created and destined for eternal fellowship with himself in holy love, but also whom he claims he helps by his grace. Moreover, the claim and succour of God always come to human beings, not as isolates, but through the agency of others. True preaching is the proclamation in the name of God and by the power of God which mediates both the demand and the gift of God.[1]

It follows that poor preaching is permitting obstacles to get in the way of this Divine-human encounter. Among such obstacles Dr Farmer would include reading the sermon because it prohibits the face-to-face relationship of preacher to congregation. Equally destructive of a radical personalism is rhetoric, for 'all suggestion of literary preciosity should be suspect.'[2] Similarly, superfluous adjectives should be pruned ruthlessly, and quotations should be sparingly used. Both are distracting, the former because they do not go directly to the point, and the latter because they suggest the second-hand. Above all such impersonal usages as 'one is . . .' must be excised in favour of the use of the personal pronoun 'you.'

Similarly, if the example of the Bible recommends personal pronouns, then verbs also are to have the pre-

[1] *Ibid.*, pp. 13–38.

[2] *Ibid.*, p. 60.

eminence because the Bible does not deal with abstractions or arguments, since it always prefers to describe the *activity* of God. No one in our time has stressed more frequently than Dr Farmer the need for concrete speech about God, since God's supreme Word was the *Word-made-flesh,* who went about doing good. In a delightful passage, he comments on the admirable concreteness of American speech contrasted with the more abstract tendencies of English talk:

> That is why American speech, and Americans are all active people, is so strangely refreshing and sometimes disconcerting. We in Britain like things draped, and we call it refinement and politeness. We put over a stall or shop 'refreshments'; the American puts up 'eats,' and when you read the word, instantly you can see men inside munching their steak. We put up 'no admittance'; the American puts up 'keep out,' and instantly your whole sensory motor system jumps and quivers in response. We put up at a railway crossing, 'the public is warned that it is dangerous to cross the line'; the American puts up 'stop, look listen!'[1]

In the process of preaching there must be, besides the presentation of God's claim and succour, an element of shared meaning. If the sharing is to be real participation, then not only is all arrogant dogmatism, frivolity, and triviality excluded, but so is spellbinding and hypnotic preaching, since this is a *manipulation* of personality. The preacher must, therefore, appeal to truth verified in experience.

Moreover, while he appeals to reason, experience and the feelings, in a word to the whole man in the whole community, he must beware of playing fast and loose

[1] *Ibid.*, p. 101.

with the feelings. There is an astringent Calvinism in Dr Farmer which warns against the mere aestheticism of music and art. 'I suspect,' he says, 'that in church many a man has mistaken the oscillation of his diaphragm in harmony with a ten-foot organ pipe or the quivering of his heart-strings to the melting sweetness of a boy's voice, for a visitation of the Holy Spirit.'[1] While the warning is necessary, it seems to me to neglect the complementary truth that beauty can be a handmaid of God as well as a distraction. He rightly insists that the main safeguard against all these dangers is that preaching 'should be governed by the spirit of worship,'[2] a concern for the objectivity of Divine Revelation and a candid determination that the sermon shall convey personal truth.

A most important facet of Dr Farmer's teaching and preaching has been the demand that theological truth be related to the basic needs of twentieth-century man. This theologian is always the apologist stressing the relevance of the Christian faith and life to the demands of the present, yet never diluting doctrine to make it appear contemporary.

The fifth chapter of *The Servant of the Word* contains a most perceptive analysis of the modern spirit and of the way the Christian Gospel meets its deepest needs. First, men today are like prisoners in the world suffering from 'barbed-wire sickness.' They have a sense of the sheer futility of human existence. This is met constructively by Christianity's 'affirmation of a divine purpose in history which a man is called to serve here and now and yet which transcends history in its final consummation.'

[1] *Ibid.*, p. 76. [2] *Ibid.*, p. 77

Secondly, man feels himself to be a cipher or even a nonentity in the mass organization of modern society and the depersonalization of industry. This need is met by the assurance of Christ that the eternal purpose is a design of love giving the fullest personal significance to every individual. Thirdly, modern man has a yearning for security, for even a life of adventure requires a stable background—a concrete airstrip for the take-off. This is supplied by the Christian doctrine of providence, with its assurance of an overshadowing Divine Presence and purpose in history. Fourthly, our contemporaries are fearfully aware of the tremendous forces of wickedness and unreason. Here, again, the Christian message declares that there is a Cross at its heart and yet the Divine love wins its victory through the horrors of sin and suffering. Fifthly and finally, men need an absolute in conduct and 'in the call to loyal discipleship to Christ there is satisfaction for the deep, ineradicable need for a fixed point, an absolute in the realm of conduct.' Farmer rightly concludes: 'Our preaching has got to be strongly doctrinal . . . in such wise that doctrine and life are seen to be inseparably bound up together.'[1] But equally 'the strongest apologetic, so far as teaching and preaching are concerned, is always a sound dogmatic.'[2]

4 · *Attempting to Win the Sceptic*

Dr Farmer, like John Oman, his former teacher at Westminster College, Cambridge, has always advocated *Honest Religion*.[3] Following the Divine injunction, his

[1] *Ibid.*, p. 143. [2] *God and Men*, p. 14.
[3] The title of a notable book by Principal John Oman.

invitation is always, 'Come, let us reason together.' He insists, however, that in speaking to the sceptic both parties to the debate shall give the matter a prolonged and serious consideration. He has little time for the critic of Christianity who only brings with him a 'casual, flippant, feet-on-the-mantelpiece attitude.' The latter attitude, he declares, is as irresponsible as if a man should set up 'as a judge of dramatic art on the basis of once having seen in his youth a Punch and Judy show.'[1] It follows equally that the churchgoer in search of Christian revelation must fulfil the same conditions of the enterprise as the sceptic. That is, he must be serious-minded, practically alert, sincere, imbued with a spirit of adventure, and willing to accept a wide context for truth.[2]

Dr Farmer never forgets that the impersonal scientific method tends to foster suspicion of the deep personalism of Christianity. The scientist in the laboratory studying the digestive processes of earthworms behaves in a completely different way at home in the family. In the laboratory he is rightly only interested in the most general characteristics of earthworms; at home he is interested in the 'uniquely personal wife and family.' Earthworms he must manipulate; persons he has no right to manipulate. The trust that lies at the foundations of science derives from a belief that objects are mechanically necessitated to act as they do and that their behaviour is entirely predictable, but the basis of his confidence at home is that his family is not at the mercy of the environmental stimuli.

He rightly claims that the Christian and personalistic view of man does far greater justice to his essential

[1] *God and Men*, p. 17. [2] *Ibid.*, p. 14.

nature than the naturalistic, cultural, vitalist and collective views of human nature, though he recognizes the partial truth for which each view stands amongst the alternatives to Christianity.[1]

The sign of a good defender of the Christian faith is his fairness to opponents. He admits the strength of the case for unbelief and declares that it lies in the fact that God's love is *not* apparent in nature or history. He holds that, apart from faith, Nature can do little more than persuade man of his own utter insignificance in the vast universe, of the destructive intentions of deluge, tornado, earthquake and volcano, and the 'dark inscrutabilities of nature' as seen in the wart-hog, the tarantula, the cholera microbe, and the hookworm. Her competitive and fierce fecundity argue the neutrality rather than the goodwill of the Creator. He quotes Blake's 'Tiger':

> Did He smile His work to see?
> Did He who made the lamb make thee?

The argument from human history is not more conducive to faith's explanation than the argument from Nature. Farmer catalogues 'the endless, endless procession of the generations of mankind being born, suffering bitterly so many of them, living at most a few short years and then dying century after century' and the rise and fall of civilizations, including the latest civilization 'with its atomic bombs dropped on teeming cities, its slaughter of young lives, its massacre of Jews, and all the horrors of this time.'[2]

[1] These views, considered in *God and Men*, are treated more fully, along with other competing interpretations of life, in *Towards Belief in God*.

[2] *God and Men*, pp. 182–183.

It is this capacity to present the opponent's argument with fairness and even force, that produces confidence in Farmer's own arguments for faith's partial solution to the riddles of existence. He insists, however, that it is precisely because the existence of God cannot be read out of the facts of nature and history that God's holy love *had to be revealed*. The Christian faith is that in Jesus Christ the light has shined out of darkness. It is darkness out of which it has shone and will continue to remain black in many ways, but there is sufficient light for those who elect to walk in it. Moreover, this light shines precisely where the darkness is deepest black: from the Son of God impaled on an instrument of torture, the Cross. The victory of Christ's faith was won *on the Cross* before it was vindicated in the Resurrection. It was a victory of faith won through brutal flogging and agonizing execution as the result of the conjoint chicanery of the political and ecclesiastical powers and the victim whose faith held was one who had lived his life in the confidence that God's love was wholly trustworthy. Clearly this faith, which having endured such a tragic miscarriage of human justice could cry, 'Father, into Thy hands I commend my spirit,' is a *tested* faith adequate to all the bitter exigencies and ordeals of life. Finally, God's saving action in Christ is to be consummated in a Kingdom beyond space and time, which gives importance and urgency to this life in the service of God and men, but ultimacy only to the life to come. By such considerations, here only too baldly summarized, Farmer counters with faith the scepticism of the agnostic.

5 · *Farmer's Developing Thought*

The fullest expression of Professor Farmer's thought shows two marked characteristics: at once the development of a more radical and perceptive criticism of Christianity's competitors and the deeper recognition of the distinctness of the Christian faith.

In his fullest defence and exposition of Christian truth, *Towards Belief in God*, Professor Farmer insists that a *demonstrative* proof of God's existence is impossible, because God is in a class by himself as 'infinite, transcendent, ultimate reality which is the source and ground of all being.' Furthermore, since we cannot prove the existence of a personal friend as a personal entity, how much less can we prove the existence of a Divine person! God is always 'Eternal Thou' and thus he is at all times and in all places 'subject' and never an 'object'. Moreover, since he has no localized body, being infinite Spirit, demonstrative proof of him is even more out of the question than in the case of finite persons. Yet again, God is a purpose wholly directed towards good; his will is the source of the final values of the universe and this cannot be grasped by a spectator attitude. He is disclosed not in abstract argument but in action and decision.[1] God is therefore known both as absolute demand or claim and as final succour.[2]

Professor Farmer then proceeds to show how modern bias may all too easily influence men not to accept the Christian interpretation. The modern interest in the comparative study of religions may well make a man suspicious of accepting Christianity's claims just because

[1] *Towards Belief in God*, pp. 31–38. [2] *Ibid.*, p. 49.

he is so well aware of the superstition, bigotry and cruelty in so much of religion, as well as of the widely divergent ideas of God in different religions. Furthermore, the obsessive primacy of the physical in human experience and in human science makes it difficult for men to accept as real the 'values'—truth, goodness, beauty—which form the content of value judgments, but which cannot be seen or touched or exactly measured.

The situation is, however, made much more difficult by new theories of religion, sociological and psychological. Durkheim, the sociologist, argued that the religious experience of mankind can be explained in terms of the interplay between the forces of society and the individual. Thus religion becomes a way of being related to the larger group. Thus the voice of God is no more than the voice of Society. But Dr Farmer points out that prophetic souls have often condemned whole societies not in their own individual interests, but in the interests of a better, diviner society in which every individual is to be treated as an end in himself. He further points out that the deepest ethics, such as those of Jesus, have a creativeness and inwardness that go far beyond the 'oughts' of society. The existence of spiritual nonconformity is itself proof that conscience is not entirely controlled by society. The unanswerable question is: 'How should a pressure of society become a pressure against society?'[1] The sociological analysis of religion is utterly confuted by Christ on his Cross, for he was repudiated by Jewish society, misunderstood and deserted by his own disciples and sustained only by the conviction of the providential power of God.

[1] *Ibid.*, p. 155.

In equally trenchant fashion Professor Farmer deals with the psychological theory of religion that the idea of God is a projection in adult life of a Father in heaven to console man for his frustration and failure. He admits that men may and do turn to God under the pressure of need, but denies that the same factor alone creates God. He finds the theory untenable on three grounds. First, there is the element of absolute demand in religion which *condemns* rather than consoles. Secondly, how can this supposed phantasy (if it be such) produce permanently beneficial effects on human character, since the psychologist's aim is to explode phantasies in order to rebuild character on firmer foundations? Thirdly, even if Freud's idea of religion accounts for its origin (which is denied), even so this is to say nothing about the ultimate truth of it.[1]

As might be expected, Professor Farmer looks into the menacing face of evil, directly and frankly. He insists that Christianity has 'never claimed to take the sting out of evil by explaining it, but rather by giving victory over it.'[2] He wittily points out that the failure of atheism to solve all mysteries actually becomes a part of theism's case! A theoretical solution for the problem of evil is not possible because theism asserts the reality of a transcendent Divine purpose which cannot be understood fully by a finite world and even unillumined darkness gives a place for the exercise of faith and trust, as might be expected if the world is a training-ground for personalities. Nor should it be forgotten that if the Christian has a problem in explaining evil in the universe created by a good God, the atheist has an equal

[1] *Ibid.*, pp. 171 ff. [2] *Ibid.*, p. 231.

problem in explaining the presence of goodness, love and sacrifice in a merely neutral or fundamentally evil world. As suggested earlier, one of the most interesting factors which Dr Farmer takes account of is the presence of beauty as an argument for theism, or belief in God. Beauty, whether of the sunset, of the kingfisher, or of the rose, is a superfluity in the universe: it is a sheerly gratuitous extra. It fulfils no useful function, but how it gladdens life! It seems to be man alone who appreciates this superfluous quality of beauty which appears to be characteristic of all creation as we know it. Moreover, it has influenced man to produce his own drawing, painting, sculpture, which form a significant part of our human experience.

If apologetics enables Dr Farmer to rid the ground of obstacles to faith, his positive convictions as to the meaning of Christianity, the content and mode of faith, are expressed with the utmost vigour and clarity in his two important volumes of sermons. He is never in danger of thinking that reason can replace faith; but he will not make the opposite mistake of making faith irrational. He is too good a philosopher to fall into the latter error and too good a Christian and theologian to risk the former peril. He believes and reasons in order that he may understand, as Paul, Augustine, Anselm, Luther and Calvin before him.

8 · *As 'Servant of the Word'*

The clarity, candidness, conviction and relevance of Professor Farmer's two volumes of sermons, *Things Not Seen* (1927) and *The Healing Cross* (1941), are the fruits of a deep and devout mind working for twelve years in the context of a parish ministry and later with innumerable brief contacts with many congregations both large and small. With characteristic insight, Dr Farmer disallows the significance of the isolated sermons which the circumstances of his tenure of a theological chair compel him to preach, dubbing himself only a 'mendicant friar.'[1] Despite the disclaimer, he is no pundit descending from a tower in the clouds into the pulpit, nor an irresponsible 'free-lance' preacher. He is at all times God's ordained minister, or, in his own book title, ever 'The Servant of the Word.'

These two books are alike and yet different. Alike in that both are sub-titled 'Studies in the Christian Interpretation of Life,' both also are studies in Christian doctrine and Christian ethics as arising out of doctrine, and both reveal not only a structuring of correlated themes but a clear plan in each sermon. They are different, however, in three other respects. While the Cross is important in the first volume it is absolutely central in the second, or to put it another way, the first volume is Theo-centric and the second is Christo-centric. In the second place, the earlier volume tends to consider religion in terms of integration and adjustment, in the conviction that Christianity 'can make men more poised, more harmonious, more strong, more dignified, more hopeful, more at peace with themselves, even in the present restricted and inadequate world.'[2] In the later volume Christianity is defended not in pragmatic-psychological terms but in theologically pragmatic terms. As the Preface indicates, the Christian message consists in setting

[1] *The Servant of the Word*, p. 95. [2] *Things Not Seen*, p. 23.

forth the Christian way 'in the life of individual discipleship, in the faith and hope that those who are thus given a new, or renewed understanding of that way may be moved by the Spirit of God to make, or remake, their choice to walk therein come what may.'[1] And, thirdly, there is a new astringent note of severity, as a 'call to adventure, to danger, to heroic and costing enterprise.'[2]

Each volume is full of incisive judgments and definitions. The power of God, for example, is defined, not as force, but as effectiveness in achieving ends. Revelation is distinguished as God seeking to give us himself in contrast with discovery as leaving us to develop our own powers. The Old and New Testament conceptions of holiness are distinguished thus: 'Uzzah touched the ark and was slain; there was one who touched the hem of the garment of the Holy One and was healed.'[3] The foregoing examples are all taken from the first volume of sermons.

The second volume abounds in similar spiritual discernment. In teaching us that we owe God gratitude for disappointments, he observes, 'If we had gained Canaan, we might have lost Heaven.'[4] Christ in his loneliness needs not our pity but accepts our adoration. Forgiveness is more often an experience of the mature than of the beginner in the Christian life. The Christian affirmation about Christ becomes a conviction only after experiment.

In addition to perceptiveness (indeed, rather as a mark of perceptiveness) the reader will note the many epigrams which condense Dr Farmer's wisdom. Here

[1] *The Healing Cross*, p. x. [2] *Ibid.*, p. ix.
[3] *Ibid.*, p. 70. [4] *The Healing Cross*, p. 75.

are some liberally sprinkled through *Things Not Seen*. 'A dumb God spells a dead faith.' 'Without religion morals easily become mere manners.' 'A good character is just as likely to get crucified as to get a peerage.' 'The Cross was . . . a parable in flesh and blood.'[1]

The Healing Cross provides epigrams that are often as brilliant as they are true. Among them are the following examples: 'Christ's work is not merely to satisfy need, but to show us what our needs are.' 'Suffering must be a vocation before it can be a victory.' 'The Kingdom of God is love, but it is not gush.' 'He, and above all, His Cross, is assuredly Light, for Light is . . . the principle of Exposure and the principle of Life.' 'The temple of faith . . . is only well-built when it is built on the very edge of the pit of self-distrust.' 'The long littleness of the self-enclosed life' deserves comparison with T. S. Eliot's 'I have measured out my life with coffee spoons.' Finally, there is the admirable comparison of the Incarnation and the Cross: 'The Babe symbolizes the weakness of divine love as it were in repose; the Cross is the weakness of divine love in action, in fiercest possible wrestling with the evil of men's hearts.'[2]

It will be readily observed also that this philosopher is true to his own advice to keep language in the pulpit concrete. The proof is that his sermons abound in imagery. There are 17 metaphors or similes in *Things Not Seen* and 26 in *The Healing Cross*. Some are strikingly original; all are apt. The highly creative images include one which conceives of God like some transcendent

[1] The citations in this paragraph are to be found, respectively, on pp. 36, 67, 102, 161 of *Things Not Seen*.

[2] The citations in this paragraph are to be found, respectively, on pp. 117, 140, 146, 159, 9 (twice), and 100 of *The Healing Cross*.

customs officer bidding the soul for the common good declare everything and keep nothing back, and another which likens sin to leprosy in the sphere of the spirit because it anaesthetizes the skin. The decadent Roman culture is finely described as 'little better than a bunch of flowers on a grave giving pleasure to the eye, but doing nothing to stop the corruption and despair within.'[1] Immortality as a continuation of life beyond the grave is distinguished from the radical re-creation of Resurrection by being described as a 'roof-garden' idea and the Kingdom of God is said to be misconceived as a garden city.

Far from being decoration for Dr Farmer's thought, many of the metaphors are memorably repugnant like a scar that forces our attention reluctantly, and sometimes they are scientifically clinical. Frequently Dr Farmer refers to the disorderly explosion of the passions in such terms. Christian 'niceness' is blown away like mist before ancestral passions. Powerful emotion can corrupt the conscience and drag judgment at its own smoking chariot-wheels or, like the torrid sun, produce a crop of plausible excuses. Two examples of scientific images are the description of a true vow as condensing 'out of the vapour of feeling a solid mass and momentum of directed will,'[2] or the likening of the Cross to a penetrating X-ray. The simpler images also have a quality of inevitability. Futility is like a spider putting forth filaments into the void[3] and settling into a crevice, or a moth fluttering in the flame, or like running a race in

[1] *Things Not Seen*, p. 129. [2] *The Healing Cross*, p. 26.

[3] This image, evidently a favourite of Farmer's, appears in both *Things Not Seen*, p. 18, and in *The Healing Cross*, pp. 1–2.

which the track is a moving ribbon for ever slipping back. Passivity is a straw on the stream of events.

Dr Farmer in *The Servant of the Word* warned ministers to be very sparing of quotations, it may be recalled, because they are either distracting or suggest that the approach to the congregation is second-hand. For this reason it is usually very difficult to track his literary borrowings, even though Shakespearian echoes may be detected here and there. Where they are declared, however, their variety and appropriateness are impressive. *Things Not Seen* contains 29 references and citations. These include Tagore, Olive Schreiner, Emerson, Carlyle, Coleridge, Browning, Keats, Whitman, Hawthorne, Ibsen, Newman, George Macdonald, a few saints and several theologians. *The Healing Cross* has 27 equally wide-ranging citations and references. These include Santayana, Lincoln, Holmes, Hugo, Milton, Shaw, Chesterton, Jerome K. Jerome, Kreisler, Beethoven, Cobden, Bright, Kagawa, Schweitzer, St Francis, Grenfell, Joad, F. W. Robertson (a great favourite), McLeod Campbell, John Oman and Skinner (his theological teachers), Stephen Graham, Shakespeare and Luther. This motley and magnificent company proves the essential compatibility of Christianity and culture in this preacher.

In all our attempt to analyse Dr Farmer's great gifts as a preacher and teacher (he is both at the same time) one thing is lacking. That is the analysis of a single sermon. This can be made good by a brief consideration of the eleventh sermon in *The Healing Cross* which is entitled 'Justice and the Gospel.'[1] The text is Isaiah

[1] pp. 105–112.

45.21, 'A just God and a Saviour.' The theme is a comparison of the functions, the moods, the directions and the agents of justice and love, and their need of each other. In other words, this is a most significant topic, but a highly abstract one.

It begins with a concrete image or pair of images on the London skyscape: the great cross on the dome of St Paul's Cathedral and the figure of Justice, eyes bandaged and scales in her hands, which surmounts the Central Criminal Court in Ludgate Hill. The concern of cathedral and court is with sin. Then follows the first section which traces the aloofness and distance between the two institutions in history and this is symbolized by the rights of sanctuary in Jewish and Roman temples and in medieval Christian churches for the fleeing criminal. The distance is seen in different functions: detection and punishment is the aim of justice and absolution and forgiveness the aim of the Gospel. In mood, too, there is this difference: justice is coldly impartial and almost pitiless, while the Gospel is warmly personal. The difference persists in the direction in which each looks: justice looks to the criminal's past and Gospel to the sinner's future. The agents used by each act in contrary fashion: justice compels while Gospel persuades.

The second section of the sermon argues that the cleavage between law and Gospel is too deep. It is, in the first place, bad for justice. Justice, aloof from the spirit of the Gospel, isolates the sinner too much from his fellows, from the solidarity of society, and the criminal knows that justice is not done. Justice also falsely isolates the guilty man's act from himself, his struggles, hopes, aspirations and his inner bent. So again the defendant knows that justice is not done to his individuality.

The third section argues that the separation is bad for the Gospel. Apart from justice the Gospel is apt to speak of love both divine and human as ignoring and overlooking sin. This is to forget that Divine forgiveness 'searches and pursues and tears out and exposes all the evil in us every bit as ruthlessly as the detectives and prosecuting counsel of the Central Criminal Court.'[1] Then follows an admirable illustration from G. K. Chesterton's criticism of Jerome's *The Passing of the Third Floor Back* as presenting the Redeemer not as a divine detective, but as a divine dupe. The conclusion is that while the Gospel is always the declaration of the utterly gracious and undeserved goodness of God to us, equally it is a declaration of the severity of God, eradicating evil from men, 'severe because it is good' and 'good because it is severe.'

This sermon has been selected because it demonstrates so many of Professor Farmer's qualities as a preacher. It is a model of clarity in profundity: the thought speaks for itself, and therefore disdains any rhetorical tricks or flowery decking out. Yet because it is profound it could easily become abstract: therefore the theme is announced in terms of two architectural images that are well-known features of London, and the positive, active and holy quality of redemptive love is illustrated from a Chesterton citation. The divisions are clear and logical and the conclusion is firm. The whole is an illumination of the function of justice and the Christian Gospel and of the incompleteness of each without the

[1] *The Healing Cross*, p. 111.

other. The final reference is rightly and inevitably to the Cross which is both judgment and mercy.

7 · *Summing-up*

Dr Farmer's gifts and characteristics as a preacher are easier to define than to emulate. Chief among them is the combination of reverence before Divine revelation with an equal concern for candidness in religion. The professor is himself always a pupil. The apologist is ever scrupulously fair to his opponents. He states the counter-considerations with force. But he always acknowledges that the revelation of God is the primary datum of Christian experience: the priority, ultimacy, mystery and majesty of God demanding in his holiness and succouring in his mercy manifest in Jesus Christ is his perennial theme.

His second dominant gift is a passionate concern for relevance. This has been superbly expressed in the Preface to *The Healing Cross* (though it is the constant concern of every theological book and sermon he has ever produced). There he says that the Message presented to mankind today must be a cosmic Christianity commensurate with the great forces sweeping through the modern world, or it will seem 'too small to be true.' The Message must also be proclaimed with a strongly agnostic note running through it to emphasize the mystery of God, otherwise it will be 'too confident to be true.' The Message must also be presented so that the note of austerity is heard in challenge and demand, otherwise it will seem 'too easy to be true.' Finally, although it is a Message presented in the context of social solidarity and as the Gospel of the universal Church it must inevitably be a Gospel to persons, who are to be God's agents to the world. Dr Farmer's own preaching is marked by the same notes.

In criticizing him, I am able to fault him on two relatively minor points. The first is in his suppression of his own gift for the appreciation of beauty in nature and in style. In this he is exceedingly ambiguous. For while, on the one hand, in typically Calvinist fashion, he regards aestheticism (visual or musical) as the snare of the senses, on the other he argues that the sense of beauty as a superfluous and non-functional value in the universe is a testimony to God. His often strikingly original images are proof that the philosopher also has the mind of a poet. His reluctant use of them, his dislike of fine writing in sermons (which happily had not developed by the time he wrote *Things Not Seen*), and his evident distrust of the feelings, mean that he is also a frustrated poet in his preaching. While sharing his dislike of a merely pretty or falsely artificial style which covers the nudity of thought with an ornate costume of fussy imagery, others may feel that he has sacrificed too much of his imaginative gifts. Certainly in this century which has seen the impact of the liturgical movement and the extraordinary increase in the public appreciation of art, he seems to be hiding a very relevant gift under a bushel. How vividly, for example, he writes of the sense of beauty being a human perception denied to the animal creation: 'When the horse stops browsing to admire the view; when the frog grows ecstatic over the colour of the water-lilies; when the bee gives up collecting honey and lies on its back in a rose admiring the sky, we will overhaul the argument.'[1] Yes, but this was in his aesthetically unregenerate days!

The other criticism is also allied to his increasing concern for austerity, and may be connected with his removal from a preaching to a teaching appointment in the Church. It is that his later sermons have a telegrammatic concision more suitable to the lecture room than the pulpit. Unwilling to repeat himself and fearful of inducing boredom, he does not allow sufficient time for the frequently paradoxical statements of religious truth to be grasped by the congregation. His later thought is, indeed, notably paradoxical in character as is appropriate to the communication of Divine revelation, as Paul, Kierkegaard and Barth have shown; but this is all the more reason for allowing a congregation the leisure to apprehend these difficult statements of truth.

All in all, however, Dr Farmer, who has resisted every temptation to become a pulpit personality, though a man of marked character, is an excellent example of the scholar as preacher and of the renewal of Biblical and theological preaching in our own day, which is radically personal, resolutely relevant and brings mind, will and culture to the captivity of Christ.

[1] *Things Not Seen*, p. 53.

Select Index

Select Index

Figures in bold type after a name indicate biographical details